GETTING OVER OURSELVES

GETTING
OVER
OURSELVES

GETTING OVER OURSELVES

Moving Beyond a Culture of
Burnout, Loneliness, and Narcissism

CHRISTINA CONGLETON

WILEY

Library of Congress Cataloging-in-Publication Data

Names: Congleton, Christina, author.
Title: Getting over ourselves : moving beyond a culture of burnout, loneliness, and narcissism / Christina Congleton.
Description: Hoboken, New Jersey : Wiley, [2024] | Includes bibliographical references and index.
Identifiers: LCCN 2023027945 (print) | LCCN 2023027946 (ebook) | ISBN 9781394169856 (cloth) | ISBN 9781394169870 (adobe pdf) | ISBN 9781394169863 (epub)
Subjects: LCSH: Self-actualization (Psychology) | Burn out (Psychology)
Classification: LCC BF637.S4 C6553 2024 (print) | LCC BF637.S4 (ebook) | DDC 158.1—dc23/eng/20230707
LC record available at https://lccn.loc.gov/2023027945
LC ebook record available at https://lccn.loc.gov/2023027946

Cover Design: PAUL MCCARTHY
Cover Images: GETTY IMAGES: © FRANKRAMSPOTT

SKY10057784_101923

This book is dedicated to those who will inherit tomorrow the outcomes of our choices and imaginings today—Ana, George, Lennox, Lola, Olivia, Oscar, Preston, Sebastian, Trey, Tycho, Xavier, and Zuri, to name a few.

Contents

Acknowledgments

I'm so grateful to have had the opportunity to write this book. While I am the only author on the cover, I know this book's existence is really a confluence of influences and efforts. There are a great number of people I could acknowledge. Here's an attempt.

I would like to thank Sally Baker for impeccable timing and for helping me begin to turn a vision into reality. Big thanks to everyone at Wiley—especially Tom Dinse, Deborah Schindlar, Susan Geraghty, and Victoria Savanh—for reading, editing, answering questions, and helping keep everything on track. Thanks also to Lauren Sharp and Chelsey Heller for early correspondence and help with my book ideas, and to Dave Ratner for helping me understand contracts. All of the images you see inside this book were adapted and drawn by the talented artist and designer Yvonne Blanco, with whom I'm very grateful to partner.

I'd like to thank every scientist who contributed to the information contained in this book. I know a single scientific study often takes years of work by a whole team of people. Thank you for the work you do. Thanks especially to Drs. David Gow, Sara Lazar, and Pilyoung Kim for giving me opportunities to understand science firsthand. Deep bows of gratitude to all the brilliant scholars of human development, particularly Robert Kegan for your inspiring teaching at the Harvard Graduate School of Education. I am grateful to Katie Heikkinen, EdD, for reviewing the material on psychological development with her keen expertise. Thank you also Professor

Ronald Heifetz for your impactful experiential course at the Harvard Kennedy School of Government, and for teaching me to use *The American Heritage Dictionary of Indo-European Roots* to understand deep meaning in language, a practice that stayed with me and that permeates this book.

I'm fortunate to have been a student of the Diamond Approach (DA) for a number of years—thank you to every teacher I have worked with—particularly Gina Crago, Anne Laney, and Andreas Mouskos for your commitment to teaching. I have benefited greatly from it. Big thanks to my "small group" led by Chris Krueger, as well as the training group that was led by Marilyn Giglio, and really all the DA groups I've been part of—it's a gift to be in the company of real truth-seekers. And thanks, of course, to Hameed Ali, Karen Johnson, and your fellow early explorers for bringing a pioneering path of realization into the world.

I am indebted to colleagues Janice Muñiz, Heather Andersen, Rebecca Ghanadan, Susan David, and Sandra Ellison for opening important doors in my career. Sandra, I think it was from you that I first heard the term *toxic achiever*. Deep appreciation to the team at Cascade Leadership Partners—Jack Jefferies, Gisele Garcia Shelley, Mark Smith, and also Liz Lewis, Dana Feehan, and Shannon Pilcher—your belief in me has enabled me to author and reauthor myself in amazing ways. Thanks also to the outstanding organization that is the Center for Creative Leadership and every individual I get to work with there—I am so fortunate to be part of it. And to every client I have the opportunity work with—thank you for allowing me to do what I love—and for teaching me so much and helping me grow.

Thank you to Hope Robertson, Farooq Malik, and Kate Azrak, as well as Julia Dengel and Michael Jaro—heart friends in difficult times. Thanks, Hope, for teaching me about biodiversity and telling me about honeybees and almond trees. Thanks also to the many leadership coaching colleagues who help me learn and enrich my world: Jackie Kindall, Zitty Nxumalo, Minji Wong, Elise Foster, all of Poyee Dorrian's supervision group, and so many more.

Thank you to Rania Khan for being an incredible person and friend. Thanks Johanna Congleton, for being my sister and looking over some of the information in the book that falls within your expertise, and to our late parents for their love and commitment to us. Thank you to my mother-in-law, Lori Artiomow, for helping out while I was writing. Thank you Ms. Ashley and Ms. Ash, and everyone at school, for creating a loving and magical holding environment for my son during the year I was working on this book. Finally, thank you to my son for being the light of my life, and my husband, Alex, for bringing his own brilliance to the ideas in this book and also doing some of the grunt work; for being my first sounding board, reader, editor, and supporter; for all the large and small ways you made the creation of this book possible—belonging to our family means the world to me.

Introduction

Welcome.

Let me begin with some strange invitations to our journey: I hope this book makes you uncomfortable. I hope it disappoints you at times. I hope this book helps you give up.

But more than this, I hope this book helps you fully remember, or maybe experience for the first time, the "you" that can be with that discomfort and disappointment; a "you" who gives up on what you know isn't needed; a "you" with wide, generous arms who knows how to embrace what is before you, including your failures to embrace. Not a new you. Not an improved you. An available you—available to the beauty life is offering and the difficulty it is presenting, available to exuberant play, and laughter, and disagreement, and heated debate, and relaxation, and celebration, and perhaps quite a bit of hard work.

Most of all, I hope this book helps you be available to friendship. I think that's what is most needed at this time. I don't know whether we need friends for the end of the world or for the beginning, or both at the same time. There is so much uncertainty and complexity right now, it's impossible to tell how things will go. But whatever happens, wouldn't it be nice to have a friend, or many, at your side? Or, if you are more inclined toward solitude, to know there is a friend somewhere, holding you close at heart?

In that spirit, my intention in writing this book is not to be an expert or authority, but rather a companion. It's called *Getting Over Ourselves* and not *Getting Over Yourself*, for a reason. I am in this with you. I wrote this book because I wanted to get over my self, and I knew that putting it in my own words would help me find the pathways I was looking for. Now I invite you along with me.

This book is presented in three parts and nine chapters. Part I considers the urgency of our times, and presents the idea that human beings may be on the edge of new psychological and cultural potentials. Chapter 1 looks at connections between environmental precariousness and human stress in Western culture, and describes how shifts toward hyper-individualization that began in the late 1970s and early 1980s are dominating the state of our world today. Chapter 2 takes the millennial generation as a case study in how these shifts have shaped the experience of self, and specifically looks at millennial stereotypes including selfie generation, lonely, burnout, and lost. Chapter 3 goes into the deeper history of our hyper-individualized Western society, and connects this history to established models of psychological development. Chapter 4 takes us to the cutting edge of Western psychological development, and considers what it means in the context of a postmodern, "post-truth" world.

Part II explores how the challenges we face might also contain the medicine we need, cracking open millennial stereotypes and understanding these pain points as doorways to deeper truths. We explore selfies and self-realization, loneliness and oneness, burnout and wholeheartedness, and being lost and liberated, in Chapters 5, 6, 7 and 8, respectively. I present practices you can try for yourself, and potentially anchor into, to help navigate novel forms of meaning-making and unfamiliar ways of relating.

Finally, in a brief Part III, I consider how we can be good friends between worlds—the world we know today and a world we might live into. We look not at the what but the how of reimagining our world, by coming together with slowness, deep listening, and fierce love.

Overall, this book looks at the ways we Westerners are often constrained by our small, isolated, stressed, "neoliberal" selves. Getting over our selves does not entail losing our selves, but rather expanding into a more relaxed, connected sense of who we are. In fact, getting over our selves doesn't mean losing much of anything. And we have so much to gain—including finding ways to preserve our sensitive, highly interconnected planet for the generations to come.

One of the things this journey invites us into is being with paradox. When our mind needs room for contradiction, poetry is often a better entryway than prose. Rainer Maria Rilke was a poet who handled paradox well, probably because he himself lived through strong polarities. Born in Prague in 1875 to a mother who was grief-stricken by the prior loss of a baby daughter, Rilke was initially raised as a girl. Then at age 10 he was sent by his emotionally distant father to military school. After finding his calling as a poet, Rilke composed *The Book of Hours* as arguably improper love letters to an older married woman and transcendent "Love Poems to God."

"You, sent out beyond your recall, / go to the limits of your longing. / Embody me," Rilke wrote in poem I 59. "Flare up like a flame / and make big shadows I can move in. / Let everything happen to you: beauty and terror. / Just keep going. No feeling is final."[1]

These times on earth seem to be calling us to venture beyond our recall—to the limits of our knowing and our longing. It's a time when we must be willing to flare like flames and make big shadows; and we need to keep going.

Rilke died almost exactly 100 years ago, in 1926 at the age of 51. He completed *The Book of Hours* before he was 28 years old. Thus, in keeping with the theme of paradox, this poem simultaneously invokes the wisdom of an ancestor offering some guidance, and the energy of a young adult raising the sails as we set out.

Rilke ended I 59 with the words, "Nearby is the country they call life. / You will know it by its seriousness. / Give me your hand." (See the Notes section at the end of the book for the original German.) Here, I extend my hand to you. Let's see what we find out together.

Part I

The Urgency to Get Over Our Selves

"The real problem is in the minds and hearts of men. We will not change the hearts of other men by mechanisms, but by changing our hearts and speaking bravely."

Albert Einstein, *New York Times*, 1946,
on the threat of nuclear war

"Let us stand up. Let us be a concerned generation. Let us remain awake through a great revolution."

Martin Luther King Jr., Oberlin College, June 1965,
on racial injustice and social change

"The top environmental problems are selfishness, greed and apathy . . . and to deal with these we need a spiritual and cultural transformation."

James Gustave Speth on the environmental crisis

The Urgency to Get Over Our Selves

Chapter 1

A World on Edge

We know it is time to wake up. The planet is growing feverish, with scientists predicting disastrous consequences if we cannot curb the increase in global temperature. Poisoned air kills millions of people every year. Extinction rates are accelerating. Our oceans are rising, acidifying and swirling with garbage, their fish so overrun with plastic it ends up on our dinner tables and in our bloodstreams.

In 2019 Greta Thunberg addressed world leaders at the UN Climate Action Summit. There were amused murmurings from the crowd as the petite 16-year-old began to speak, but the tone in the room quickly grew sober. "We are in the beginning of a mass extinction, and all you can talk about is money and fairy tales of eternal economic growth. How dare you!" Thunberg accused. "You say you hear us and that you understand the urgency . . . How dare you pretend that this can be solved with just 'business as usual' and some technical solutions? . . . The world is waking up. And change is coming, whether you like it or not."[1]

Yet change is slow to arrive. People are increasingly conscious of the existential threats Thunberg described, but we can't seem to get a handle on it. For example, roughly 70% of those surveyed by Yale and George Mason Universities in 2019 agreed that global warming was happening, were worried about it, and described it as personally important, with the youngest respondents reporting the greatest concern. A far smaller number of people, however, were willing to donate money, volunteer, or contact government officials about the issue. Only about 10% said they had taken action.[2]

From time to time the world's attention is captured by a clarion call to "wake up," as in Thunberg's address, and we're shaken from the trance of the status quo. But the sense of urgency always dissipates. There is a familiar wave of alarm and excitement that crests into entertainment, meme-making, then dips toward banality and boredom. The wake-up call recedes from consciousness. It's like the alarm goes off, we rouse a little, and hit snooze once again.

I use the term *we* broadly, for all of human beings—but especially Western human beings from industrialized areas—because I believe the environmental crisis is demanding a widespread, more fundamental examination of our human condition. It's clear that some groups of people are profiting from environmental destruction while others are exploited, and we need to face this and make corrections. Still, I don't think it helps for some of us to claim we are "awake" and point at others as "asleep." The story of "us" and "them" is a story of separation and competition, driven by the same kind of thinking that contributes to the destruction we must reduce. Our task now is to tell a story of mutual awakening and togetherness. If there's one thing that has become clear to me through my years of research and work with people, it's that we need each other.

Paradise Burning

Poet Robert Frost pondered whether the world would end in fire or ice. From what we know of melting glaciers and recent observations of earth's hottest years on record, the odds are clearly in fire's favor.

A 2022 UN report shows changing patterns in wildfire activity, including record-breaking fire seasons in previously low-risk areas like the Arctic and the Amazon rainforest. The report predicts a 30% to almost 60% increase in wildfire events by the end of the century due to climate, land-use, and population change. Disastrously, scientists anticipate that as wildfires destroy critical carbon sinks such as peatlands and rainforests, they will "accelerate the positive feedback loop in the carbon cycle, making it more difficult to halt rising temperatures."[3] Each fire tilts us further toward a steep hill, while simultaneously rendering our brakes less and less effective.

The reality of increasing fire activity hit home in the United States in recent years with particularly brutal wildfire seasons in the West and Southwest. In late 2018 the deadly Camp Fire burned through Butte County in Northern California, violently erasing the towns of Concow and Paradise.

Three years later, between Christmas and New Year's day of 2021, my husband and I watched the orange glow of the Marshall Fire out on the horizon, burning 30 miles north of our home. The fire consumed over 1,000 structures in Boulder County in a matter of hours, making it the most disastrous in Colorado history in terms of lost property. It ravaged houses and business centers in its suburban path of destruction. It burned the spiritual center we frequented to the ground. It killed two people. Although the links between this winter grassland fire and climate change are less clear than California's Camp Fire or even Colorado's 2020 Cameron Peak Fire that burned a record 208,663 acres, Colorado's climate-related drought conditions likely played a factor in the blaze.[4]

Symbolically, fire has many positive connotations. It can represent the beauty of purification and transformation, a sense of eternity, hope, or spiritual passion. But it can also point to destructive desire (as in Frost's "Fire and Ice"), obsession, madness, and the infernos of hell.

In recent years, intellectuals and activists have increasingly pointed to connections between the warming climate and the flames of human desire that sustain today's capitalist systems. Harvard Business School professor Rebecca Henderson begins her 2020 book *Reimagining Capitalism in a World on Fire* by personalizing the decline of the world's forests for which she has a "deep and abiding love." Referring to her early career as a consultant who helped businesses profit, Henderson states, "my comfortable life was one of the reasons the forests were in danger. . . . I came to believe that our singular focus on profit at any price was putting the future of the planet and everyone on it at risk."[5]

In *Overheated: How Capitalism Broke the Planet—and How We Fight Back*, Kate Aronoff takes a different approach, guiding our gaze to the top of the trickle-down economy and squarely on the fossil fuel industry. She writes:

> Capitalism hasn't tended to be a popular protagonist in stories about the climate crisis . . . it's tempting to turn inward . . . seeking personal absolution by lowering your carbon footprint: have fewer kids, take fewer flights, and turn off the lights when you leave the room. Yet, not long after Watt first fine-tuned his steam engine, just ninety corporations—almost all of them fossil fuel producers—have been responsible for two-thirds of all greenhouse gas emissions. Since 1965, just twenty shareholder and state-owned fossil fuel producers have spewed out 35 percent of the world's energy-related carbon dioxide and methane emissions. The richest 5 percent of the world's population, by and large those most insulated from the effects of the climate crisis, consume more energy than the poorest 50 percent.[6]

In reading Henderson and Aronoff, we might see two competing approaches to our current crisis: individual responsibility versus systemic change. I propose it's most helpful to see this as a both-and scenario, where these views are equally important and completely intertwined. Henderson starts with the personal and goes on to examine the systemic, reimagining approaches to finance, industry self-regulation, and governance. Aronoff maintains a systemic focus but inevitably includes the personal, noting connections between climate change and individual overwork in capitalist systems.

On the one hand, most all of us who live in industrialized countries are party to a capitalist system. We support and participate in capitalism with our money, time, and attention, thus collectively generating the system we inhabit.

At the same time the system shapes, limits, and propels us, giving rise to our behaviors, our feelings, our thoughts, and our very identities. Therefore, although we create the system, it also creates us. We might even say it traps us in an endless feedback loop, a feedback loop that has become the fuel, the fire, and the wreckage of our current situation (see Figure 1.1).

That's what this book is about—how the system creates us while we create the system. This closed cycle will continue until something changes, until we step back to see the whole dynamic for what it is, until we face head-on the fires that burn in our environment and in our own psyches, that grow increasingly hot and devilish. Until we wake up and together create something new.

Figure 1.1 Feedback loop

Stressed to Death

For many of us, our current capitalist system brings material comforts and health-related luxuries that were unimaginable in ages past. It's so easy to take for granted the small and large wonders of modernity—the space heater in my office, the digital thermometer that has been helping me monitor my ill toddler's temperature, the child-palatable bubble-gum flavored amoxicillin we use to treat his ear infection, the computer that allows me to connect with clients and colleagues from the comfort of my home and that allows me to type these words. If I stop and reflect, the list of gratitudes goes on and on. In his 2018 book *Enlightenment Now*,[7] Steven Pinker presents one graph after another of improvements in the human condition we have observed over the past centuries that have occurred in tandem with the rise of science and capitalism: increased life expectancy and global wealth; decreased famine, improved nutrition; declines in battle deaths and homicides. In so many ways, our modern world is looking bright.

Still, capitalism as we know it today brings unique forms of human suffering that, similar to the climate crisis, seem to be reaching a toxic crescendo. Some types of suffering are borne by those with less material wealth and access to formal power, a truth that often goes unacknowledged by the people the system favors. Yet even those of us who enjoy some of capitalism's excesses are essentially unsettled. In the United States and other industrialized countries, it is as if the turbulence in our natural world is mirrored by an epidemic of busyness, the average person's day a frantic hurry from one activity to the next.

When the 2020 pandemic first hit, many of the millions of Americans sheltering at home felt compelled to take on additional projects and activities in their supposed extra time. Aspirational bread making caused General Mills' flour sales to surge by 75%.[8] Celebrities tweeted to remind us that Shakespeare wrote one of his masterpieces during a quarantine. Even as commuting was suspended and all-day pajamas became a reality for those who had the ability to telecommute, people struggled to sink in and relax. In fact, many professionals felt *pressure* in the face of a more spacious schedule. "Stop trying to be productive," urged Taylor Lorenz in the July 2020 *New York Times*, her article illustrated with a tense, wide-eyed shut-in, surrounded on his bed by books, art projects, and dumbbells. "The urge to overachieve," Lorenz wrote, "even in times of global crisis, is reflective of America's always-on work culture."[9]

Rates of anxiety nearly tripled during the COVID-19 pandemic,[10] but American stress was not a new phenomenon. Journalist and think tank director Brigid Schulte described in her 2014 book *Overwhelmed*, "[T]his is how it feels to live my life: scattered, fragmented, and exhausting. I am always doing more than one thing at a time and feel I never do any one particularly well. I am always behind and always late, with one more thing and one more thing and one more thing to do before rushing out the door."[11] Many of us can relate. Modern busyness keeps us at the edge of our seat, with no time to look up from the next task on the to-do list and no time to consider the bigger picture of our lives.

Critics point out that this busyness is often self-imposed. Overscheduling and workaholism are now worn as badges of honor among those with relative privilege. In his 2012 *New York Times* article "The 'Busy' Trap," Tim Kreider alleged, "Busyness serves as a kind of existential reassurance, a hedge against emptiness; obviously your life cannot possibly be silly or trivial or meaningless if you are so busy, completely booked, in demand every hour of the day. . . . I can't help but wonder whether all this histrionic exhaustion isn't a way of covering up the fact that most of what we do doesn't matter."[12] Further explorations led to coinage of the term *busy-bragging*, an idea that was scientifically validated by a team of business school researchers whose experiments supported the conclusion, "The busy person is perceived as high status."[13] As *Inc. Magazine* put it,"' I'm busy' really means 'I'm important.'"[14]

However, status signaling does not entirely explain the busyness epidemic. In 2021 the Brookings Institute described a "middle class time squeeze," with average workers struggling to balance the demands of paid work and family care in a culture where work has become central. The researchers state:

> While many participants expressed anger and resentment about their workplaces controlling and demanding more and more of their time, their solutions to the time squeeze they experienced centered on personal strategies such as self-discipline, making endless to-do lists, and emphasizing "time management." Although our participants framed time management as an individual responsibility, they also shared the perception that living their lives at a frantic pace, rigidly scheduled down to the minute, did not allow them to authentically connect with their families, learn and grow as people, fulfill their own physical and emotional needs, or contribute to their communities. These themes suggest that middle-class Americans may be mistakenly blaming themselves for struggles that are pervasive and systematic, and that women tend to bear a disproportionate burden of stress and self-blame when policies are not developed to address the time squeeze.[15]

In other words, individuals tend to pin the busyness epidemic squarely on themselves, and that's a mistake. Writing about busybragging in *The Guardian*, Oliver Burkeman says, "The real culprit is a socioeconomic system that relentlessly instrumentalizes everyone, forcing us to become productivity machines, valued by our output alone. (We're complicit, obviously, since we are that system.)"[16] He points to the same cycle I illustrated in the previous section: a closed loop where we find ourselves running in circles.

It's a cycle that is killing us. *Karoshi*, a Japanese term for "death by overwork" that was once reserved for that culture, is now recognized as a global phenomenon. The World Health Organization and International Labour Organization found that in 2016, nearly 500 million people worldwide had been exposed to overwork, resulting in close to 750,000 deaths and millions of additional years of life lost due to heart disease and stroke.[17]

The United States is relatively low on the list of countries where overwork leads to death, yet statistics show we are an incredibly frazzled population. Gallup's 2022 State of the Workplace Report identified US and Canadian workers as among the most stressed in the world, with half of respondents experiencing stress for much of the day.[18] In 2020 The American Psychological Association (APA) declared a "National Mental Health Crisis,"[19] and in 2022 it found that more than a quarter of US adults are so stressed they can't function, with the highest rates of incapacitating stress reported by the youngest respondents. Eighty-three percent of professionals report work-related stress each year, often to a level that is "paralyzing."[20] This stress is estimated to cost almost $200 billion in health care costs each year and to cause 120,000 deaths via intertwining health-related routes including smoking, excessive drinking, depression, and cardiovascular disease.[21]

All things considered, it makes sense that most people are not actively combatting climate change, even if they can see the existential threat looming on the horizon. Stress is going to kill them first.

A Failed Prediction

It wasn't supposed to be this way. Today's portrait of stress and overwork stands in stark contrast to where some imagined we would be, including one of the world's most famous economists, John Maynard

Keynes. In 1930 Keynes wrote the essay "Economic Possibilities for Our Grandchildren," predicting that within 100 years the "struggle for subsistence" would be a thing of the past. Keynes envisioned a world of advanced technology and economic growth, where the average person would not wrestle with work-life balance, but rather with questions of how to best use their leisure time; how to live, as he put it, "wisely and agreeably well." Keynes foresaw a work week of just 15 hours.[22]

As we near 2030, the endpoint of Keynes's prediction, his vision seems a bit ridiculous. Keynes was not entirely wrong. Working hours have declined significantly in the wake of the Industrial Revolution. Available data shows that annual average working hours in the US have dropped from 2,316 in 1929 to 1,757 in 2017, for a reduction of about 25%, although the decline has leveled off in recent decades.[23]

Yet these numbers contradict the way many Americans experience their working hours. Leisure time seems to have dwindled with economic growth and technological development. Innovations such as the smart phone as well as tele-working arrangements have blurred the boundaries of work, bringing the office to our dinner tables and night stands. According to a 2019 LinkedIn study, the majority of US employees—almost 60%—check in with their boss or coworkers *daily* during vacation,[24] and a third report feeling guilty for taking off any time at all.[25] In 2018, US professionals forfeited 768 million vacation days, essentially leaving billions of dollars in benefits on the table.[26]

The average person does not enjoy abundant free time, nor has Keynes's vision of widespread financial security materialized in the United States. In 2021, 38 million people—11% of the population—were living in poverty.[27] More than 10% of households were food insecure.[28] In 2022 the number of Americans without health insurance hit an all-time low, yet 26 million people still lacked that safety net.[29]

Even the time-strapped US middle class is now struggling to afford the three Hs: housing, health care, and higher education. In April 2022 *Time Magazine* wrote, "The costs of all three H's have soared over the past few decades," and many who identify as middle class have been left "reaching" for these basic elements of the American dream.[30]

We'll never know whether Keynes's world of material security and abundant leisure would have materialized. A sharp pivot in the 1980s launched us into a different type of economic experiment, toward a set of policies and practices most often associated with scholars and politicians like Friedrich Hayek, Margaret Thatcher, and Ronald Reagan. The pivot was toward what some call *neoliberalism*, and although its impacts have in many ways remained under the radar, it continues to have profound implications for the way we live today.

Keynes Versus Hayek

The turbulent years of the Great Depression and World War II were marked not only by physical battlegrounds but also intellectual wars over how the world should operate. When it came to economic policy the main figures in capitalism were Keynes, a Brit who was born, educated, and spent his career in Cambridge, England; and Friedrich Hayek, an Austrian educated in Vienna, who would go on to teach and influence at schools of economics in London, Chicago, and Freiburg.

The differences between Keynes's and Hayek's approaches are nuanced, and I leave it to economists to describe them in detail. But the heart of their disagreement was over government intervention in capitalist markets. Keynes advocated for more intervention, particularly during recessions and depressions, and Hayek advocated for less. Keynes believed in a kind hand of government, and Hayek put his faith in the invisible hand of the market.

After World War II, Keynes's ideas won over much of the world. Although Keynes himself died in 1946, Keynesianism was already shaping economic policy in his home country of Great Britain, in Australia, and in the United States, where it would reign triumphant for decades. In *Keynes Hayek: The Clash That Defined Modern Economics*,[31] Nicholas Wapshott calls the years of 1946 to 1980 "the Age of Keynes." The United States' 1946 Employment Act followed Keynesian logic in naming the federal government as responsible for full employment, and Presidents Truman, Eisenhower, Kennedy, Johnson, Nixon, and Carter all employed Keynesian messaging and strategies to the approval of the public.

Meanwhile, Hayek and his supporters waited in the wings. A year before the end of World War II, Hayek had published an oblique challenge to Keynesianism called *The Road to Serfdom*,[32] in which he rejected government intervention as a cure for unemployment and other economic ills. As Wapshott describes, "The principal targets of *The Road to Serfdom* are what Hayek deemed the twin evils of socialism and fascism. . . . He reiterated his belief that as economic planners cannot know the will of others, they end up acting like despots." Hayek was convinced that free markets, not governmental planning, most reliably represented individual needs and desires, and therefore best translated into individual freedoms. His approach was also called *liberalism*.

The Road to Serfdom was controversial but successful, and although the ideas it laid out were not in vogue at the time, Hayek attracted ardent fans and collaborators, among them young economist Milton Friedman. Starting with the first meeting of the Mont Pèlerin Society in 1947, these like-minded scholars quietly strengthened their network and influence. They bided their time, anticipating chinks in the Keynesian armor.

As Hayek predicted, it took decades for these vulnerabilities to appear, but when they did liberal economists and politicians were ready. In the 1970s Britain struggled with a weak economy, eventually entering a "Winter of Discontent" characterized by widespread worker strikes. Following the 1973 oil crisis, the US entered a period of "stagflation," meaning rising prices (a.k.a inflation) accompanied by high unemployment. This was a nightmare scenario that Keynesian economists had hardly believed possible. With the dominant economic paradigm unable to offer good answers, stagflation as Friedman says "discredited essentially the Keynesian vision."[33]

Margaret Thatcher, an avowed Hayekian, was elected British prime minister in 1979. She was famous for pulling one of Hayek's books from her purse, slamming it on a table and declaring, "This is what we believe!" A year later, Ronald Reagan defeated Jimmy Carter in the US presidential election, having campaigned on lower taxes and smaller government. "Government is not the solution to our problem, government is the problem," he declared at his 1981 inaugural address.[34] With Milton Friedman as his economic advisor, he would put into action many of the ideas that had been cultivated over the decades since that first meeting of the Mont Pèlerin Society. With Thatcher and Reagan's ideals and policies taking over both sides of the Atlantic, Hayek's time had come.

Just as Keynes's 100-year experiment did not run to completion, we cannot say that Hayek's vision was ever truly realized. The past 40-odd years have been characterized by hybrid influences from Keynes and Hayek. Still, Hayekian emphasis on individual freedom and responsibility captured the cultural imagination in ways that remain prevalent today. Wapshott describes, "The freewheeling Reagan years had altered the mood in America. Private enterprise replaced communal action as the preferred way to change society. The free-loving flower children of the 1960s 'Love Generation' had given way to the self-centered 'Me Generation' of the 80s and 90s. Bob Dylan's 'The Times They Are a-Changin'' had been superseded by Gordon Gekko's mantra 'Greed is Good.'"[35]

What came to be called *neoliberalism* affected across party lines and around the world from the 1980s onward. As economic anthropologist Jason Hickel writes, "After Reagan and Thatcher, these policies were carried forward even by putatively progressive administrations such as Clinton's in the USA and Blair's in Britain, thus sealing the new economic consensus across party lines."[36] Historian Gary Gerstle[37] calls Bill Clinton the "facilitator" of neoliberalism, with political moves including support of the North American Free Trade Agreement (NAFTA), loosening regulation of the banking industry through repeal of the Glass-Steagall Act, and passage of the Personal Responsibility and Work Opportunity Act, a bill that sounds like a line out of a Hayekian playbook.

The neoliberal agenda that swept in during the early 1980s promised freedom and prosperity, but just as flaws in Keynesian economics were exposed in the 1970s, free market capitalism eventually came under fire. In 2016 research economists from the International Monetary Fund published a paper called "Neoliberalism: Oversold?" in which they acknowledged that "instead of delivering growth, some neoliberal policies have increased inequality."[38] Others launched more severe critiques, with journalist and activist George Monbiot calling neoliberalism "the ideology at the root of all our problems."[39]

But whether you gently poke or aggressively prod at neoliberalism's 40-year experiment, the results look troubling. "Income inequality in the US has increased since 1980 and is greater than in peer countries," Pew Research wrote in 2020,[40] with charts showing widening gaps between the top 10% and bottom 10% of wage earners from 1980 to 2018. French economist Thomas Piketty has traced similar trends, his graph of income inequality in the United States showing a steep drop after World War II that held steady in the age of Keynes, followed by rising inequality from the beginning of the neoliberal era in 1980.[41]

Then there is the matter of wage stagnation. In 1930 Keynes predicted increasing productivity over time, and indeed his vision has been realized in the United States. But average income, at least for average workers, has not kept up. Although there are a variety of ways to calculate the relationship between productivity and wages,[42] reputable models show a dissociation between the two starting right around—you guessed it—1980. In sum, policies of the neoliberal era appear to have divorced productivity from prosperity and widened the gap between the haves and have-nots in this country (see Figure 1.2).

Eight years after the 2008 financial crash, economic scholars Michael Jacobs and Mariana Mazzucato questioned capitalism on the whole:

> On the one hand the capitalist economies of the developed world, which for two hundred years transformed human society through an unparalleled dynamism, have over the past decade looked profoundly dysfunctional. Not only did the financial crash lead to the deepest and longest recession in modern history; nearly a decade later, few advanced economies have returned to anything like a normal or stable condition, and growth prospects remain deeply uncertain. Even during the pre-crash period when economic growth was strong, living standards for the majority of households in developed countries barely rose. Inequality between the richest groups and the rest of society has now grown to levels not seen since the nineteenth century. Meanwhile continued environmental pressures, especially those of climate change, have raised profound risks for global prosperity.[43]

It's tempting to nostalgically turn back toward Keynesianism, or fish around for other past models that might serve us better. At the

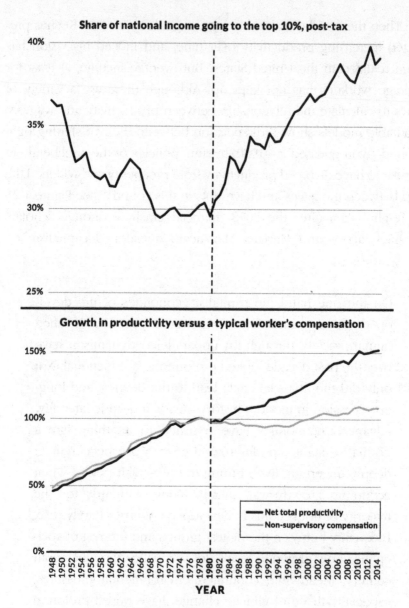

Figure 1.2 The neoliberal turn

Sources: Gabriel Zucman, https://gabriel-zucman.eu/usdina/ and https://www.epi. org/blog/growing-inequalities-reflecting-growing-employer-power-have-generated-a-productivity-pay-gap-since-1979-productivity-has-grown-3-5-times-as-much-as-pay-for-the-typical-worker/#:~:text=In%20contrast%2C%20productivity%20grew %2085.1,prices%20rather%20than%20consumer%20prices.

very least, recent titles like *Rethinking Capitalism* and *Reimagining Capitalism* point to the need for some robust tinkering. But mustn't there also be possibilities we have not yet explored, realities not bound by capitalism? Is there really, as Thatcher proclaimed at a women's conference in 1980, "no alternative"?[44]

In *Capitalist Realism: Is There No Alternative?* Mark Fisher writes, "it is easier to imagine the end of the world than it is to imagine the end of capitalism. That slogan captures precisely what I mean by 'capitalist realism': the widespread sense that not only is capitalism the only viable political and economic system, but also that it is now impossible even to *imagine* a coherent alternative to it." Fisher points out that capitalism has slippery ways of absorbing even anti-capitalism, of commodifying and selling back to us our own distaste for inequality and consumerism. He uses the example of Disney's *Wall-E*, a film that "shows an earth so despoiled that human beings are no longer capable of inhabiting it. We're left in no doubt that consumer capitalism and corporations . . . [are] responsible for this depredation; and when we eventually see the human beings in offworld exile, they are infantile and obese, interacting via screen interfaces . . . supping indeterminate slop from cups." Fisher goes on to say, "A film like *Wall-E* exemplifies what Robert Pfaller has called 'interpassivity': the film performs our anti-capitalism for us, allowing us to continue to consume with impunity."[45] In this way, the system remains closed. We consume our own anti-consumerism, and the cycle keeps spinning.

The book you are reading now is not intended to be anti-capitalism, pro-communism, pro- or anti-socialism, or really an argument for or against any -ism at all. It is an invitation to conversation, creativity, and above all a deep exploration of who and what we take ourselves to be, and what we might create together. After all, new systems of organization seem not to emerge from limited rejiggerings of the old. They emerge from leaps forward in the ways human beings experience themselves and the world. Where do we think capitalism came from in the first place? As R. J. Holton writes in *The Transition from Feudalism to Capitalism*, "The concept of 'capitalism' emerged in the mid-nineteenth century as one of a number of key concepts designed to characterize the changing nature of Western European society . . . all such notions entailed a sense of qualitative change in the character of entire social systems (or wholes) not simply in some particular sphere of social activity."[46] If we can remain awake to this potential for qualitative change, we might be able to step back, recognize more fully the crash course we seem to be on, and have the chance to discover viable and surprising alternate pathways.

The Heart and Soul of Neoliberalism

Deep in the human psyche is a tension between oneness and separateness[47]; between unity and individuality, between human being as wave and human being as particle. We begin in the womb, in complete union and symbiosis, then separate at birth only to attach again, emotionally and psychologically, to caregivers and community. As we grow, we launch further into the world, continuing a dance of individuality and mutuality that develops over a lifetime.

We can see this dance of oneness and separateness in the ways human beings experiment and struggle with modes of organization. On the one hand, there are arrangements where the collective comes before the individual, or the individual may not be considered to exist at all. This is expressed, for example, in the Japanese saying, "the nail that stands out gets pounded down," and in the common American sports idiom, "There is no 'I' in team." This saying was amended and propelled toward the other extreme by basketball stars Michael Jordan, who said, "There is an I in 'win,'" and Kobe Bryant who added, "There's no 'I' in team. But there's an m-e in that motherfucker."[48] Arrangements on the opposite end of the spectrum prioritize the individual above the group, and in the same fashion may not acknowledge the existence of the collective.

Neoliberalism is an approach that, like any economic system, reaches into human experience and touches these fundamental issues of identity. Margaret Thatcher knew as much. In a 1981 interview she explained, "it isn't that I set out on economic policies; it's that I set out really to change the approach, and changing the economics is the means of changing that approach. If you change the approach you really are after the heart and soul of the nation. Economics are the method; the object is to change the heart and soul."[49]

In a wide swing toward one end of the individual-collective spectrum, neoliberalism stands for human-as-particle, an expression that burst forth and has been building since the Enlightenment in the 1600s and 1700s, which we will discuss further in Chapter 3. Neoliberalism assumes, even depends on, the existence of an independent, rational, self-interested individual. That individual's task is to progress toward their chosen goals in a complex and competitive world. As Thatcher famously declared, "who is society? There is no such thing! There are individual men and women and there are families and no government can do anything except through people and people look to themselves first."[50] Similarly, Reagan advisor Milton Friedman stated, "Every individual should be regarded as an end in himself."[51]

I want to highlight two drawbacks to this perspective. First, by emphasizing individual responsibility above all else, neoliberalism fails to recognize that the playing field is not level for everyone who must compete. Such a worldview is unconscious to historical and current-day inequalities that perpetuate injustice. It creates a system that keeps the have-nots in their place and holds them responsible for it. As author and dissident of neoliberalism George Monbiot describes, "We internalise and reproduce its creeds. The rich persuade themselves that they acquired their wealth through merit, ignoring the advantages—such as education, inheritance and class—that may have helped to secure it. The poor begin to blame themselves for their failures, even when they can do little to change their circumstances."[52] I can't help but think of pop icon Kim Kardashian's response during a 2022 *Variety* interview, when asked for her best business advice for women. "Get your fucking ass up and work. It seems like nobody wants to work these days," she replied. Faced with backlash, Kardashian claimed the comment was taken out of context. But many pointed to Kardashian as the one missing context—of the advantages she was born into and the connections she was able to capitalize on in her pursuit of success.[53]

The second problem with our current neoliberal tack is that, as we have been exploring in this chapter, even those who enjoy relative privileges are trapped in a limited orbit. Hayek's approach to economics was built on values of freedom and liberty. He aimed to do away with despots and emancipate the individual to pursue their own interests and dreams. This is an admirable vision at face value, and one that resonates deeply with American ideals. What I am proposing in this book, however, is that rather than eliminating tyrants, neoliberalism caused them to proliferate. For better and for worse, neoliberalism has made each of us the king of our own castle, responsible for building, defending and fighting in service of an empire of "self."

Today, the head that wears the neoliberal crown is growing heavy. We are realizing that even with all that freedom to choose, we are not truly free. Rather, we are trapped, isolated within fortresses of "self," separated from the earth, from each other, and our own deeper longings. We are told we have the power and also the responsibility to generate our own "brand," our own "well-being," and even our own "destiny." But this is a Herculean and some might say a Sisyphean task, where the boulder never quite steadies at the top of the hill. We are tired, anxious, lonely, and depressed. We are resigning, disengaging, or just "quiet quitting." Externally and internally, we see physical and psychological landscapes ravaged by endless battles of self-interest that swirl into sinkholes of destruction and emptiness. The whole thing is collapsing; we are faltering. And nowhere do we see the urgency of this moment expressed more clearly than in the generation whose birth coincided with the rise of neoliberalism, the largest generation in the United States, the millennial generation.

Chapter 2

Lost Heroes

In 2000, as the oldest members of the millennial generation were entering adulthood and the youngest were emerging from infancy, historians Neil Howe and William Strauss published *Millennials Rising: The Next Great Generation*. They wrote in prophetic tones, describing millennials as a cohort that would follow deep rhythms of Western history to become archetypal heroes, the likes of which had not been seen since the "Greatest" Generation fought World War II. Strauss and Howe predicted that millennials would push the United States "into a new era." The country would be, they envisioned, "on the brink of becoming someplace very new, very 'millennial' in the fullest sense of the word. That's when the 'end of history' stops, and the beginning of a new history, their *Millennial* history, starts."[1]

As someone born at the end of 1980, right on the cusp between Generation X and the millennials (as well as the beginning of the neoliberal era), I read Strauss and Howe's account with fascination and visions of grandeur. Hearing echoes of Roosevelt's words to the Greatest Generation in 1936, I wondered what our millennial "rendezvous with destiny" might be.

About the same time, however, other titles were emerging that painted a much grimmer portrait of me and my peers, such as psychologist Jean Twenge's 2006 *Generation Me: Why Today's Young*

Americans Are More Confident, Assertive, Entitled—and More Miserable Than Ever Before.[2] Rather than rising heroes, Twenge saw millennials as self-focused and fragile. Their individualism created "unprecedented freedom to pursue what makes them happy," but their "high expectations, combined with an increasingly competitive world, have led to a darker flip side, in which they blame other people for their problems and sink into anxiety and depression." Twenge was clear about her disagreement with Strauss and Howe's grand predictions for the millennial generation. "Even the subtitle, *The Next Great Generation*," she wrote, "displays the hubris fed to the young by their adoring elders."

This bleaker narrative gained traction. Over the years the millennial wings on which we might have risen turned to wax and melted in the sun. *Millennial* grew to be synonymous with *entitled*, and *Time* magazine ran a 2013 cover story declaring millennials the "Me, me, me Generation," a negatively exaggerated version of our "Me Generation" boomer elders.[3] Suddenly millennials were being blamed for "killing" everything from department stores to the sport of golf to napkins.[4] During the global pandemic, COVID-19 was hinted at as a "millennial bug,"[5] and in 2022 after the Federal Reserve (which is not run by millennials) printed enough money to nearly double the United States' money supply within two years,[6] CNBC nonetheless suggested, "The size of the millennial generation is to blame for sky-high inflation."[7] It seems the generation that dwells in parents' basements and loves avocado toast is truly "fun to hate,"[8] and convenient to scapegoat. Author and English professor Mark Bauerlein has gone so far as to write two books that label millennials "the dumbest generation."[9]

Yet, despite the bad press, the blame and the name-calling, vestiges of the millennial "Greatest Generation" narrative still exist. Josh Tickell's 2018 book *The Revolution Generation: How Millennials Can Save America and the World (Before It's Too Late)*[10] explores whisperings of a "great millennial awakening," and follows millennials to Standing Rock and inside state houses. Tickell believes millennials can make good on Strauss and Howe's predictions by enacting significant civic and economic shifts including ranked-choice voting, a $15/hour minimum wage, and an embrace of blockchain currencies. Charlotte Alter's 2020 title *The Ones We've Been Waiting For: How a New Generation of Leaders Will Transform America*[11] sounds like the fruition of Strauss and Howe's vision, and profiles millennial political wave–makers such as Pete Buttigieg, Alexandria Ocasio-Cortez, and Elise Stefanik.

Even *Time's* "Me, me, me Generation" cover story back in 2013 ran a paradoxical subtitle: "Millennials are lazy, entitled narcissists who still live with their parents. Why they'll save us all." At the close of his article, Joel Stein wrote, "a generation's greatness isn't determined by data; it's determined by how they react to the challenges that befall them. . . . Whether you think millennials are the new greatest generation of optimistic entrepreneurs or a group of 80 million people about to implode in a dwarf star of tears when their expectations are unmet depends largely on how you view change."[12]

It also depends on what you believe needs changing. As millennials like myself enter midlife, we are taking hold of our narrative and acknowledging our less-than-desirable attributes. Further, we are identifying the societal and systemic forces that have shaped us to the core. And many of us are not happy about it. In *Kids These Days: Human Capital and the Making of Millennials*,[13] journalist Malcolm Harris writes, "Over the past forty years, we have witnessed an accelerated and historically unprecedented pace of change as capitalism emerged as the single dominant mode of organizing society. . . . The profiteers call this process 'disruption,' while commentators on the left generally call it 'neoliberalism' or 'late capitalism.' Millennials know it better as 'the world,' or 'America,' or 'Everything.' And Everything sucks." Harris goes on to describe a neoliberal system that has treated millennials like "productive machinery": high-pressure schooling that primed children for overwork, universities functioning like corporations, a precarious and disempowering employment landscape, and declining mental health that is increasingly treated with medication. Likewise, in her recent book *Can't Even: How Millennials Became the Burnout Generation*,[14] Anne Helen Petersen laments, "America is broken, and we, too, along with it."

This brokenness is reflected in millennial stereotypes: we are called the selfie generation, a lonely generation, the burnout generation, and a lost generation. In this chapter we'll explore these epithets one by one, and trace clear lines between each stereotype and the neoliberal landscape that, along with its freedoms and upsides, is causing suffering. Although specific to millennials, these stereotypes comprise a case study within an era of hyper-individualism and unchecked growth, that members of any age group may find relatable.

The following passages are not optimistic, but they are only the beginning of the story. Later we will explore how our brokenness may be a secret key; the cracks in our armor could be openings into new possibilities that will help us heal, and help heal our world. But first, we turn to the darker side of the millennial tale.

Selfie Generation

Just a few months after *Time* ran its "Me, me, me Generation" cover story, Oxford Dictionaries declared its 2013 word of the year: *selfie*. First used online in 2002, *selfie* pervaded the English lexicon from 2012 to 2013, its use soaring by 17,000%.[15] The following year, Charles M. Blow wrote an op-ed in the *New York Times* drawing on the Pew Research Center's findings on "Millennials in Adulthood."[16] Pew characterized millennials as "unmoored" from political parties, religious organizations, and even the institution of marriage, and identified us as the first "digital natives" who lived into, rather than had to adapt to, the rise of tech innovations like Facebook. "All in all, we seem to be experiencing a wave of liberal-minded detach-ees, a generation in which institutions are subordinate to the individual and social networks are digitally generated rather than interpersonally accrued," Blow concluded. "This is not only the generation of the self; it's the generation of the selfie."[17]

By the time Blow wrote his op-ed, millennials had already been linked to the psychological construct that selfies invoke—narcissism. Narcissism is defined as excessive interest in or admiration of oneself and one's physical appearance, and narcissistic personality disorder is characterized by "need for admiration, entitlement, and lack of empathy."[18] It was Professor Jean Twenge, author of *Generation Me* who demonstrated millennial narcissism with data. Using archives of research that employed a measure called the Narcissistic Personality Inventory, Twenge studied changes in typical college students' scores over the past few decades and found a clear upward trend. Compared to a college student in 1982, a student in 2009 was significantly more likely to endorse a statement such as, "I think I am a special person" or "I can live my life any way I want to." Twenge and colleagues published a paper with the title "Egos Inflating over Time," writing, "These data are consistent with theories positing an increase in individualism in American society and with previous studies finding generational increases in other individualistic traits such as self-esteem and agency."[19]

Twenge and others have focused on the self-esteem movement of the 1980s and 1990s as a potential root cause of millennial self-focus. Incorporating self-esteem into the public school curriculum was championed in particular between 1986 and 1990 by the California Task Force to Promote Self-esteem and Personal and Social Responsibility, led by assemblyman John Vasconcellos. "Self-esteem is the likeliest candidate for a *social vaccine*, something that empowers us to live responsibly and that inoculates us against the lures of crime, violence, substance abuse, teen pregnancy, child abuse, chronic welfare dependency, and educational failure," the task force wrote in its final report. "The lack of self-esteem is central to most personal and social ills plaguing our state and nation as we approach the end of the twentieth century."[20]

Considering the task force's words in context, self-esteem seems like a natural companion to the neoliberal zeitgeist of the time. If there was no such thing as society, as Margaret Thatcher had declared, then what other source could widespread problems be traced back to, if not the individual? And what could be more important than building up, shoring up, and inoculating that individual, so that as adults, millennial children would contribute productively, and successfully promote their own self-interests in a competitive culture and economy? If an individual was an end in itself, as Milton Friedman said, then surely nothing could be more important than ensuring the hardiness of that individual.

As it turned out, science did not actually back up the task force's assertions. Associations between self-esteem and positive outcomes were found to be "mixed, insignificant or absent," but Vasconcellos exaggerated them to the public as "positive and compelling." Will Storr, author of *Selfie: How We Became So Self-Obsessed and What It's Doing to Us*, calls this "the great self-esteem con."[21] Based on the task force's misrepresentations, self-esteem captivated the nation's attention and many schools adopted its advice. As a result, millennials were told "You are special," learned to recite "I am lovable," and in some cases were handed those now-infamous participation trophies.

As millennials matured, it didn't take much to move from the "self" to the "selfie" generation Blow described in his op-ed. We were digital natives, reared on a steady diet of self-esteem, who inevitably translated our self-focus into our rapidly evolving technological landscape. We turned the cameras back on ourselves to create, then dominate Facebook and other platforms with curated content streams[22]; we became the world's first YouTube stars; and, yes, we popularized the selfie. Here I must invoke Kim Kardashian once again, the "selfie queen" and fellow millennial cusper. In 2015 she published *Selfish*, an art book of 300 of her own selfies.[23]

Alicia Eler, author of *The Selfie Generation: How Our Self Images Are Changing Our Notions of Privacy, Sex, Consent, and Culture*[24] calls Kardashian the "embodiment of the selfie." She writes, "Even though Internet celebrity has become a normalized aspiration for many Americans—to become famous is a desired accomplishment—the process to get there, which includes successfully capitalizing on your own image, is considered a narcissistic impulse. To be a culture that celebrates individualism yet also casually labels that individual narcissistic is awkward." She points to the strange dance that we as millennials find ourselves in: we must have a strong sense of self but not admire it too narcissistically; we must capitalize on our image without being too captivated by it. Professor L. Ayu Saraswati sees something more sinister than awkwardness, tying the selfie explicitly to neoliberalism in her book *Pain Generation: Social Media, Feminist Activism, and the Neoliberal Selfie*.[25] She writes, "The neoliberal self(ie) gaze is a mode of seeing and storifying the self on social media as a good neoliberal subject who is appealing, inspiring, and entertaining. . . . It is thus a propped-up, prosthetic extension and performance of the self."

This performance of the self on social media can have negative impacts, even fatal consequences, for those who create and consume its content. The quest for the perfect selfie has resulted in hundreds of deaths in recent years, as people (most often in their 20s) have fallen from cliffs, drowned in dangerous waters, or been struck by trains while pursuing extreme selfie backgrounds.[26]

It is the photo foreground, however, that most often preoccupies selfie-takers. Along with the ascent of riskier selfie backgrounds, people seem to be taking more extreme measures to ensure a perfect face. The American Academy of Facial Plastic and Reconstructive Surgery (AAFPRS) reported, "2019 was a stand-out year for the selfie with a full 72% of AAFPRS members reporting patients seeking cosmetic procedures to look better for their selfies—up 15% from 2018!" The AAFPRS president attributed the "dramatic rise in facial plastic surgery interest to the increasing age and purchasing power of Millennials."[27]

Selfie-takers want to look better *for* their photos, and sometimes they want to look *more similar to* those photos. Dr. Tijion Esho coined the term *Snapchat dysmorphia* after patients began presenting their own filtered and airbrushed photos as templates for plastic surgery.[28] Although this kind of surgery isn't necessarily dangerous, it can be related to body dysmorphic disorder, a clinical condition characterized by obsessive thoughts about slight or imagined physical defects that interfere with a person's everyday life.

Millennial Danny Bowman has been profiled by multiple media outlets as a former "selfie addict." (The term *selfitis*, the obsessive taking of selfies, began as a hoax but was later taken up by researchers who created a real "selfitis behavior scale."[29]) As a slim, blonde, conventionally attractive teenager, Bowman nonetheless found endless flaws in his appearance and could spend upwards of 10 hours taking 200 self-shots a day. He eventually withdrew from his social life, dropped out of school, and attempted suicide before receiving treatment for his mental health. "I was constantly in search of taking the perfect selfie and when I realised I couldn't I wanted to die," Bowman told the *Mirror*. "I lost my friends, my education, my health, and almost my life."[30]

If creating selfies has its hazards, scrolling through the selfies and status updates of others may be equally or even more dangerous for mental health. In a clever quasi-experimental study, researchers from Tel Aviv University and MIT were able to use the staggered

2004 to 2006 rollout of Facebook on US college campuses to test the relationship between access to social media and records of mental health services. "Our main finding," the authors wrote, "is that the introduction of Facebook at a college had a negative effect on student mental health." Further, the researchers estimated that the introduction of Facebook could account for approximately 24% of the increase in severe depression among college students since the new millennium.[31]

Of course, not all social media use is the same, and the relationship between social media and mental health is nuanced. Although researchers have found certain benefits to *actively* participating in social media through creating posts, sending direct messages, and the like, they have found particularly negative effects when it comes to passively scrolling through other people's (often highly curated) lives. Passive Facebook use has been linked to social comparison and feelings of envy, which are in turn associated with declines in well-being.[32] And although Facebook may not be responsible for making us lonely, studies show it could be reinforcing or exacerbating the loneliness that is already there. A study at the University of Pennsylvania found that limiting social media use to 30 minutes a day led to significant decreases in anxiety, fear of missing out, depression, and loneliness.[33]

In his *Atlantic* essay "Is Facebook Making Us Lonely?"[34] Stephen Marche speaks to American individualism, writing, "Today, the one common feature in American secular culture is its celebration of the self that breaks away from the constrictions of the family and the state, and, in its greatest expressions, from all limits entirely." He explores the contradictions and interrelations among social media, isolation, narcissism, and health. "Our omnipresent new technologies lure us toward increasingly superficial connections at exactly the same moment that they make avoiding the mess of human interaction easy," he writes. "Narcissism is the flip side of loneliness, and either condition is a fighting retreat from the messy reality of other people." Although Marche doesn't speak about the selfie generation explicitly, the coin he is turning in his hand is one millennials are familiar with—we are a selfie generation, a digitally networked generation, and also a lonely generation in the midst of a health crisis.

Lonely Generation

"The social media generation is the one that feels most alone," the international research and analytics group YouGov wrote in 2019.[35] Their research revealed that almost a third of millennials had no best friend, 27% had no close friends, and 22% had *no friends at all*. Thirty percent of millennials reported feeling lonely often or always, compared to 20% of Gen Xers and only 15% of baby boomers. Similarly, Cigna's 2020 report on loneliness in the workplace found that over 70% of millennials were lonely, their loneliness levels surpassed only by their younger Gen Z colleagues.[36]

Loneliness is not unique to millennials nor is it a simple by-product of social media—experts have been talking about a loneliness "epidemic" since at least the late 1990s.[37] In 2023 the US Surgeon General Vivek Murthy released the first-ever advisory on "our epidemic of loneliness and isolation."[38] This epidemic is believed to affect half of US adults and involves a number of physical and psychological health implications, with scientists suggesting that loneliness is as bad for your health as lack of exercise or smoking.[39] Lonely people have been found to be at greater risk for infections, heart disease, and depression, and they don't live as long—one meta-study estimated a 26% increase in the chance of early death.[40]

Loneliness was once thought to plague the elderly, but we now know it is taking a particular toll on younger generations. "Never finding love" and "dying alone" have been cited as top millennial fears,[41] and in one survey 42% of millennial women indicated they were more afraid of loneliness than a cancer diagnosis (only 29% of Gen X and 27% of boomer women reported the same).[42] During the COVID-19 pandemic, Professor Richard Weissbourd's research team at Harvard found that 43% of young adults (younger millennials and older Gen Zers) experienced an increase in loneliness. "Our data also suggest that lonely young adults are even more likely than lonely people generally to lack basic forms of human attention and emotional sustenance," they wrote. "About half of lonely young adults in our survey, for example, reported that no one in the past few weeks had 'taken more than just a few minutes' to ask how they are doing in a way that made them feel like the person 'genuinely cared.'"[43]

Blue Cross Blue Shield found that 92% of millennials experienced a negative impact of the pandemic on their mental health, accompanied by increases in alcohol consumption, smoking, and recreational drug use.[44]

They also found continued increases in a number of behavioral health conditions for millennials including major depression, ADHD, and psychotic disorders. Rates of major depression rose a troubling 43% in millennials even before the pandemic, from 2014 to 2018.

Perhaps most alarming, in 2019 Blue Cross Blue Shield described a "millennial health shock" projected to replicate mortality rates associated with the Vietnam War and the HIV/AIDS crisis. "Millennials are seeing their health decline faster than the previous generation as they age," the report stated. "This extends to both physical health conditions, such as hypertension and high cholesterol, and behavioral health conditions, such as major depression and hyperactivity. Without intervention, millennials could feasibly see mortality rates climb more than 40% compared to Gen-Xers at the same age."[45]

Although precise causes of the health shock are not yet clear, we know millennials are exhibiting an unusually high rate of "deaths of despair." A 2019 report from the Trust for America's Health identified the "devastating impact" of increasing young adult deaths from drugs (up 108%), alcohol (up 69%), and suicide (up 35%) between 2007 and 2017. The Trust notes that the opioid epidemic has been devastating for millennials, with young adult deaths from synthetic opioids rising a "staggering" 6,000% between 1999 and 2017.[46]

Some have begun to trace explicit ties among loneliness, well-being, and modern culture. Nursing scholar Colin Killeen, one of the first to call loneliness an epidemic, wrote in 1998, "A materialistic culture with its selfish ideals, causes more individuals to be lonely, which in turn can result in making people both physically and psychologically ill. . . . In today's self-obsessed climate, I am not sure that loneliness will ever go away; it is an unfortunate side effect."[47] Professor Fay Bound Alberti, author of *A Biography of Loneliness*, calls loneliness a specifically "modern epidemic" that might be assuaged if we examine it as such. She writes, "Twentieth-century philosophy, with its narratives of social alienation and fragmentation, presumes that loneliness is both a natural and inevitable part of the human condition. . . . Loneliness merely becomes part of the evolutionary 'survival of the fittest' rhetoric that is at the heart of much 21st-century rhetoric. But if loneliness is a historical phenomenon that can be rooted in specific times and places, then it is a theme societies *can* tackle, perhaps by reevaluating the relationship between rampant individualism and social responsibility."[48]

Others call out neoliberalism specifically. In her 2023 article "The Loneliness Epidemic," Professor Olivia Sagan writes, "the very word *loneliness* only picked up currency post-1800 as industrial society began dispersing us, capitalism fragmenting us and consumerism isolating us, leaving us, famously, to bowl alone, live alone, age alone and die alone . . . we are bombarded with the message that our prosperity is based on competitive self-interest, individualism and consumption, messages of core use to neoliberal economics . . . an increase in materialism has also been associated with loneliness and tragically, in this logic, we buy stuff that makes us feel lonelier so we buy more stuff."[49]

The connections Sagan draws between neoliberalism and loneliness are supported by a 2021 study in which, simply by exposing research participants to neoliberal ideology, social psychology researchers increased people's experiences of social disconnection and competition, which in turn increased their loneliness and reduced well-being. The researchers concluded,

> Despite suggestions that this political philosophy might promote individual well-being because it encourages people to strive for personal growth, we found that it actually appears to be harmful to health because it can create a sense of being disconnected from others, as well as being in competition with them, in ways that feed feelings of loneliness and social isolation . . . in a world where people are becoming increasingly aware of the health-related costs of a mounting "loneliness epidemic," it may be time to broaden our critical gaze and reflect on the extent to which this too is a consequence of neoliberalism.[50]

In a May 2023 *Newsweek* op-ed, Ian Corbin and Joe Waters of the think tank Capita noted a "missed opportunity" in the surgeon general's loneliness advisory: "to point out the volatile mix of economic precarity, status anxiety, and disconnection from meaningful work that afflicts Americans in the age of neoliberalism, where the maximization of shareholder returns is the central, and often the only, guiding value of our commercial enterprises." Although the surgeon general recommends simple actions individuals can take to combat loneliness, such as calling a friend or sharing a meal, Corbin and Waters point out the systemic forces that can "make these simple life hacks seem pointless, painful or downright impossible to a growing number of Americans."[51]

Although loneliness and despair appear to be taking a significant health toll on millennials, even those who do not find themselves in the dangerous territory of depression and substance abuse can identify with a more everyday malaise. Along with an epidemic of loneliness there is, as described in Chapter 1, a crisis of stress[52] in the United States and other parts of the world, and millennials are deep in its throes. This is why we are the "burnout generation."

Burnout Generation

In 2019, millennial journalist Anne Helen Petersen could not find time to get her knives sharpened or vacuum her car. "Why can't I get this mundane stuff done?" she asked, writing in *Buzzfeed News*. "Because I'm burned out. Why am I burned out? Because I've internalized the idea that I should be working all the time. Why have I internalized that idea? Because everything and everyone in my life has reinforced it—explicitly and implicitly—since I was young. Life has always been hard, but many millennials are unequipped to deal with the particular ways in which it's become hard for us."[53]

Petersen's article struck a nerve, going viral with over seven million readers and leading to her 2020 book *Can't Even* in which she wrote, "There's a pervasive feeling that despite some of the legitimate wonders of modern society, our potential has been capped. And yet we strive, because we know nothing else. For millennials, burnout is foundational. . . . It's our base temperature."

In 2018 Gallup presaged Petersen's work, identifying millennials as more burned out than other generations, with close to 30% of millennials very often or always burned out at work, and about 70% feeling burned out at least some of the time.[54] In contrast to the image of the lazy, entitled millennial waiting around for the participation trophies of youth, in 2020 Manpower found that 73% of millennials work more than 40 hours a week, and 26% work two or more paid jobs. And although a full third of millennials expect to retire between age 65 and 69, over a quarter of respondents did not see themselves retiring before 70, with 12% expecting to "work until I die."[55]

Millennials have been called *workaholics* and *work martyrs*. We are more likely than older generations to agree with statements like "No one else at my company can do the work while I'm away" and "I want to show complete dedication to my company and job." Millennials also exhibit more "vacation shame," making it difficult for us to take off the time that might recharge our depleted batteries.[56]

At first glance, millennial burnout seems perplexing. Erin Griffith asked in the title of her 2019 *New York Times* article "Why are Young People Pretending to Love Work?" The subtitle continues "I saw the greatest minds of my generation log 18-hour days—and then boast about #hustle on Instagram. When did performative workaholism become a lifestyle?"[57] Her article points at answers, considering how "'owning one's moment' is a clever way to rebrand 'surviving the rat race,'" and how venerating work has been employed "at least since the rise of mercantilism in 16th-century Europe" as a means to keep workers motivated, productive, and distracted from "unappealing features" of the job.

Taking this a few steps further, we can see how workaholism makes perfect sense in the context of neoliberalism. Professor Thomas Teo explains in his paper "*Homo Neoliberalus*: From Personality to Forms of Subjectivity"[58] that neoliberalism has given rise to a unique way of experiencing the world, a "new form of life" that "has been emergent from the earliest development of a capitalist mode of economy." This way of life (which Teo calls the "neoliberal form of subjectivity" or NLFS for short, which we might think of as a "neoliberal self") has a number of characteristics that millennials, and anyone else living in a neoliberal context, will recognize.

First, the neoliberal self according to Teo is an "entrepreneurial entity" that requires the individual to become the "CFO, CEO, or COO of a brand called 'self' that needs to be built, marketed, distributed, and sold, as are any other goods and services." This aspect of the neoliberal self synchs perfectly with the selfie generation and the performance of the self described by Saraswati in *Pain Generation*. Similarly, in their paper, "The Psychology of Neoliberalism and the Neoliberalism of Psychology,"[59] psychology researchers Adams, Estrada-Villalta, Sullivan, and Markus describe neoliberalism as supporting "an entrepreneurial understanding of self as an ongoing development project" and "an imperative for personal growth and fulfillment." They discuss "responsibilization," a psychological construct that infuses and bolsters the entrepreneurial self. "Psychological science renders people responsible for their outcomes," the researchers write. "They not only bear the onus for making good things happen, but also must shoulder the blame when bad things happen."

Through this lens, the undercurrents of responsibilization in countless modern works of motivation and self-help become obvious: Napoleon Hill's 1937 *Think and Grow Rich*,[60] in which he wrote, "Whatever the mind of man can conceive and believe it can achieve"; Robert Schuller's 1997 book *If It's Going to Be, It's Up to Me*,[61] which includes quotes like "You never suffer from a money problem, you always suffer from an idea problem"; as well as in Rhonda Byrne's blockbuster *The Secret*,[62] where she said, "Remember that your thoughts are the primary cause of everything"; and perhaps most blatantly from millennial Rachel Hollis who in *Girl, Wash Your Face*[63] declared, "You, and only you, are ultimately responsible for who you become and how happy you are." Although these messages are meant to be empowering and in some cases can be, they also encourage us to blame ourselves when things go wrong, and to regard others who are struggling as having brought difficulty onto themselves. In this way, responsibilization creates a smokescreen for overarching systemic and structural factors that cause disadvantage and harm. Responsibilization also seems to be why those experiencing the middle class time squeeze described in Chapter 1 try to improve their situation through personal strategies such as time management, and blame themselves when they continue to struggle.

Messages of responsibilization also strike deep chords with many millennials who were told, in the spirit of self-esteem, "you can be anything you want to be" and "believe it and you can achieve it." The message was a double-edged sword, that on the one hand offered encouragement and motivation, and on the other hand created tremendous pressure. If we *could* do it, but did *not* do it, then the logic of responsibilization told us it had to be a personal failing—a shortcoming in terms of effort, intelligence, or resilience. It had to be some deficiency in the self, in who we *are*. With our very identities on the line, no wonder millennials have become burned out workaholics.

What is even more astonishing to consider is that stress and burnout are not by-products of the neoliberal self. Rather, they are essential to its preservation of identity. There *is* no escape. Teo writes, "Stress is probably at the core of the emotional NLFS. . . . Neoliberalism requires a state of constant stress, a feeling of being stressed all the time as a form of existence, which is then balanced with a search for happiness."[64] In other words, the neoliberal self depends on stress for its very existence; an end to stress would mean an end to the self. Consciously, we may think we want rest and relaxation, but with the neoliberal self running subconsciously in the background, we will actually avoid it at all costs. This is supported by what we saw during the COVID-19 pandemic, when we filled our free time with more activities, more goals, more pressure and stress.

The neoliberal self may very well be at the heart of the *arrival fallacy*, psychology professor Tal Ben-Shahar's term for the experience of reaching a goal expecting to experience happiness, but finding emptiness and sadness instead.[65] The neoliberal self runs on the *pursuit* and *promise* of success, not success itself. In this sense, it really is like a hamster on a wheel—and if that hamster stops, it disappears. Therefore, it must keep running.

The neoliberal condition fuels constant, endless striving in work, and also in life in the form of "self-improvement." Neoliberalism surrounds us and is most often imperceptible; we're like fish that can't recognize the water in which we swim. However, in recent years we have seen inklings of awakening to this condition. "You Don't Have to Work on Yourself Forever," Shayla Love wrote in 2020 in Vice,[66] an article that included interviews with André Spicer, author of *The Wellness Syndrome*, and Svend Brinkmann, who wrote *Stand Firm: Resisting the Self-Improvement Craze*. Love wrote, "Paradoxically, too much personal development may distract us from tackling larger problems that contribute to our feelings of being out of control. As the global political, social, and environmental climates become more hectic, and injustices and abuses are brought to light in new ways, retreating to focus on the individual may bring about a sense of calm and autonomy—while ignoring the bigger picture."

In early 2022, Noreen Malone wrote about "The Age of Anti-Ambition."[67] "A job feels like just one more incursion, demanding attention and sapping mental energy," she said. "The act of working has been stripped bare . . . and a lot of people don't like what they see." A few months later everyone was talking about "quiet quitting," the act of *not* going above and beyond at work, of doing what is required and calling it good.

As millennials have been burning out, there seems to be a natural growth in awareness of the neoliberal self and an accompanying conscious turn toward structural problems that need to be addressed. Petersen writes in *Can't Even*, "We were raised to believe that if we worked hard enough, we could win the system—of American capitalism and meritocracy—or at least live comfortably within it.

But something happened in the late 2010s. We looked up from our work and realized, there's no winning the system when the system itself is broken."[68] As millennials have begun scrutinizing this system, we have recognized that we are not just burned out, but completely lost.

Lost Generation

"Hello, Lost Generation," Annie Lowrey began her 2020 *Atlantic* article, "Millennials Don't Stand a Chance."[69] She described a bleak economic outlook for a generation that entered the workforce during the Great Recession and hit what should have been peak earning years amidst a second, pandemic-related downturn. "There's no good news in a recession, and no good news in a pandemic. For millennials, it feels like there is never any good news at all," Lowrey ended her article.

Surprisingly, US millennials *did* receive good news following the pandemic: between 2019 and 2021 our wealth doubled, based on data from the Federal Reserve. But our slice of the pie was so skinny in the first place, it didn't take much to double. Even with recent increases, millennials are estimated to hold less than 7% of all US wealth, while baby boomers hold over 50%.[70] This disparity is not simply a matter of accrual over the lifespan. The National Bureau of Economic Research found that in 2016, median millennial wealth was "lower than the wealth of any similarly aged cohort between 1989 and 2007."[71] Boomers already held 22% of US wealth—three times that of millennials—when they were the same age.[72] In 2022, researchers from the University of Bonn found "a substantial widening of the age-related wealth gap since the 1980s" and concluded, "Wealth in the U.S. is aging."[73] (See Figure 2.1.)

It seems the neoliberal experiment has not gone well for the first generation to grow up entirely within its bounds. Ironically, the policies purported to be most closely aligned with the "American Dream"

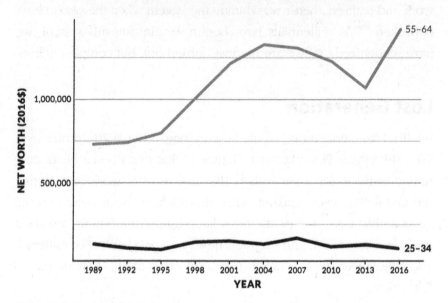

Average age-wealth profiles by constant age group

(Y-axis: NET WORTH (2016$); values 500,000 and 1,000,000. X-axis: YEAR; 1989, 1992, 1995, 1998, 2001, 2004, 2007, 2010, 2013, 2016. Upper line labeled 55–64; lower line labeled 25–34.)

Figure 2.1 Wealth age gap

of prosperity resulting from hard work in a capitalist society have had the opposite result: for the first time, a generation in the United States is characterized by downward mobility. As older generations have enjoyed soaring valuation of assets they already own, including stocks and housing, millennials have found themselves straining to enter or shut out entirely from those same markets. The median cost of buying a home, adjusted for inflation, doubled between 1970 and 2017,[74] reaching over $450,000 in 2022.[75] Long-criticized for failing to lift off and remaining at home with our parents, millennials have had to fight back against responsibilization to say it's not that homeownership isn't desirable, it just hasn't been possible.

Millennials face steeper prices than predecessors and we also carry heavy debt. We are the most educated generation, with 39% having attained a bachelor's degree, compared to 15% of silents, 25% of boomers, and 29% of Gen Xers.[76] However, that distinction

Getting Over Ourselves

has come with a price. Compared to less than $2,400 inflation-adjusted dollars in 1981, average tuition for a public four-year institution has nearly quadrupled, surging to over $9,600 by 2016. Private tuition more than tripled, rising from $10,810 in 1981 to $33,480 in 2016.[77] These high prices have translated into millennial debt. In 2016 the Federal Reserve found that millennials held a level of debt only slightly higher than Generation X held in 2001, but the composition of that debt was markedly different. Although millennials had lower credit card and mortgage debt, the average inflation-adjusted student loan debt level more than tripled compared to Gen Xers.[78]

In *Kids These Days*, Malcolm Harris points to unofficial corporatization in the neoliberal era as a source of surging education expenses. "As faculty jobs have become increasingly contingent and precarious, administration has become less so," he writes. "Formerly, administrators were more or less teachers with added responsibilities; nowadays they function more like standard corporate managers or nonprofit fundraisers—and they're paid like them too. . . . When you hire corporate managers, you get managed like a corporation, and the race for tuition dollars and grants from government and private partnerships has become the driving objective of the contemporary university administration."[79]

In this competitive, money-hungry landscape, millennials pursued college degrees based on the assumption that all that hard work would pay off once we entered the workforce. But chapters like "Work (Sucks)" from Malcom Harris and "How Work Got So Shitty" from Anne Helen Petersen tell a different story. Petersen refers to the contemporary worker as the "precariat," modeled after temporary employment arrangements that have "enabled companies to decrease their costs, while excusing themselves from any contract of responsibility between employer and employee—and in so doing, shifted the risks of everyday life back onto the individual employee."

For the precariat, "economic and class status is *precarious*," Petersen writes, "which renders them ever vigilant for even the smallest piece of bad luck that could sink them into poverty."

In her 2023 book *Generations*,[80] Jean Twenge challenged the idea of the "broke Millennial" as a "myth,"[81] citing statistics that millennial median household income as well as individual income recovered after the Great Recession. "By these measures, online carping about 'stagnant wages' should have stopped after 2015," writes Twenge. However, she also explains that "every single penny in the rise in younger adults' incomes is due to women's incomes." This means that millennial couples (that include a woman) who want to have children face the dilemma of either losing a woman's valuable earnings, or paying for childcare at a price that has "far outpaced inflation." Twenge also writes, "the average amount of student loans has doubled since the 1990s even after correcting for inflation," and she describes this as a source of financial strain. Still, Twenge sticks to the narrative that millennials are "feeling poor instead of being poor." She suggests that social media and reality television have overexposed millennials to lifestyles of the rich and famous, causing us to experience "relative deprivation" of not keeping up with the Kardashians. But if a dual college-educated, dual-income couple struggles to afford having a child in this day and age, is it really fair to say that "feeling poor" is all in their heads?

In 2017 millennial journalist and podcaster Michael Hobbes published an article called "FML" as in "Fuck my life."[82] He wrote, "What is different about us as individuals compared to previous generations is minor. What is different about the world around us is profound. Salaries have stagnated and entire sectors have cratered. At the same time, the cost of every prerequisite of a secure existence—education, housing and health care—has inflated into the stratosphere. From job security to the social safety net, all the structures that insulate us from ruin are eroding. . . . This is why the touchstone experience of millennials, the thing that truly defines us, is not helicopter parenting or unpaid internships or Pokémon Go. It is *uncertainty*."

Millennial precariousness is accompanied by a sense of disorientation—we are not only financially, but also psychologically, lost. "While it's become commonplace for other generations to call millennials 'entitled' and 'lazy,'" wrote Alicia Elliott in *Maclean's*,[83] "it seems to me that it's more accurate to say we're directionless and lost. We've become a generation of Cinderellas, told to wait for a glass slipper that no longer exists."

Another Failed Prediction?

The original "lost" generation was born almost exactly 100 years before millennials, from the early 1880s to 1900. Some parts of their story sound familiar. They grew up amidst an opioid epidemic, faced a global pandemic in early to middle adulthood, and they were more suicide-prone than other generations. In 1911, almost exactly 100 years before *Time's* "Me, me, me generation" cover story, Cornelia A. P. Comer's "letter to the rising generation" in the *Atlantic* accused the lost generation of being "'soft' and incompetent," focused on a "narrowly personal" cult of the self.[84] Losts were hit hard by the Great Depression during their mid-life earning years, and failed to attain many of the comforts of subsequent generations.[85]

Interestingly, the comparison of millennials to the lost generation does not play nicely with Strauss and Howe's prediction of our generation's heroic destiny. (See the Notes at the end of the book for more about Strauss and Howe's model of generations.) Strauss and Howe describe historical cycles they call *turnings*. Turnings progress through eras with different characteristics, from a spiritual awakening, to a social unraveling, a secular crisis, then a civic high. Strauss and Howe claim that in accordance with those rhythms, each generation comes to embody one of four archetypes—prophet, nomad, hero, or artist. Prophets are said to "burst forth" as they come of age in a spiritual awakening, issuing "angry challenges to their elders' public and private behavior" and launching "the entire society into a fever of renewal." Baby boomers are seen as having fulfilled the "prophet" archetype with their spiritually rousing "consciousness revolution" of the 1960s, similar to the "third great awakening" of the missionary generation in the mid- to late 1800s. Next, nomads "come of age with little collective self-esteem" amidst the social unraveling that follows an awakening, and define themselves in "cynical opposition" to prophets. Generation X fulfilled the "nomad" archetype, growing up amidst the heightened individualism and unraveling social fabric of the 1980s and declaring in Kurt Cobain's dispassionate words, "Oh, well, whatever, nevermind." Gen X movie stars Winona Ryder and Ethan Hawke starred in the film that captured the zeitgeist of their young adulthood, *Reality Bites*. It is Generation X, not millennials, that Strauss and Howe compare to the losts of the early 1900s. According to their model, millennials should have moved on to the next archetype, to band together and "successfully shoulder a secular crisis" in the fashion of World War II's Greatest Generation. Yet here we are, being compared to and even comparing ourselves to the losts. Are millennials stuck in nomadic disorientation, unable to move on and fulfill our role? And what would it mean to be a "hero" in today's world, anyway?

This would not be the first time a hero failed to rise. Interestingly, Strauss and Howe describe a "Civil War anomaly," writing that following the crisis of the American Civil War, "no successor generation filled the usual Hero role of building public institutions." As we've considered in this chapter, so many millennials are languishing and even dying early. At this time of ecological and social precarity, when we are needed most, it seems we're faltering. But maybe it's not too late.

Toward the end of her essay on millennial directionlessness, Alicia Elliott writes, ". . . as we watch the planet that sustains us burn, the divide between rich and poor become larger, and our consumer-driven way of life slowly collapse, we must ask ourselves: what do we want to build in its place? More importantly, what do we—the most educated generation, a generation that cares deeply about social change, and is more accepting of diversity than our parents and grandparents—want to leave behind? What do we want our legacy to be?"[86]

These are questions millennials need to face together, within and also across generations, in inter-generational solidarity. And we'll need the right orientation and approach. But before we go there, let's look at ourselves in an even more complete context. What is the deeper history of our neoliberal landscape? And where can we go from here?

Chapter 3

Spirals of Change

Imagine peering through the lens of a newly invented technology and seeing strange creatures that, until that moment, had been invisible to the human eye.

Consider how it might feel walking through the doors of a business unlike anywhere you've visited before. The air hums with conversation and is rich with the aroma of a beverage, recently imported from a foreign country, that is said to increase intelligence and wit when ingested. Around the room diverse customers gather at tables, engaging in lively debate over the very foundations of human society. Who is a potential new collaborator, and who might be a police spy?

Imagine opening the cover of an illegal text that has been smuggled into your area, a book full of secret information that will teach you how to perform tasks you never dreamed of mastering, a book that presents a mind-bending, new organization of knowledge, that challenges everything you've been taught about the world.

The creatures I'm referring to in the first case are bacteria, seen by Dutch microbiologist Antione van Leeuwenhoek through his microscope in 1683. The beverage is coffee, introduced into English and French cafés in the mid-1600s. And the book is the encyclopedia, published by French philosopher Denis Diderot in the 1750s. The period of history was the Enlightenment.[1]

Today the Age of Enlightenment is the topic of dusty history books and high-brow documentary films with soundtracks played on the harpsichord. Bacteria, coffee, and encyclopedias are typically considered mundane subjects of conversation. But this obscures the fact that within the past 400 years, the ways many of us human beings think, behave, approach our lives, and even experience our identities, have completely transformed. And these transformations remain critical to who we are today.

What Was Enlightenment?

The Enlightenment spanned many decades of the 1600s and 1700s, spreading through countries primarily in what we call the Western world. You can spend a lifetime studying and debating the Enlightenment's origins and expressions. Yet certain themes, such as authority, reason, and progress, are clear.

One of the main transformations Western humans experienced during the Enlightenment had to do with power. According to the BBC documentary *Heroes of the Enlightenment*, "At the beginning of this period, most people's lives were based on obedience and belief. They obeyed the church, which told them to obey the king, who, it said, had been chosen by God."[2] This authority structure created stability and predictability, a pyramid with a monarch and his church at the top, and peasants at the bottom. People generally expected to stay in one place and one social class their whole lives, with sons following in their father's footsteps and most women looking to marry an appropriate match. Life followed the slow turn of the seasons, cycling through time in a familiar rhythm.

The Enlightenment sparked new questions about the beliefs and duties people had historically taken for granted, and it began to shake the structure of that pyramid. Enlightenment thinkers encouraged a turn away from traditional, external sources of knowledge, toward one's own mind and observations. "I think, therefore I am," wrote French philosopher René Descartes in 1637, declaring that the only thing to withstand the test of his skepticism was the skeptic himself.

The Enlightenment has been called "a breakthrough in critical consciousness." It was a widespread appeal to use one's own reasoning in search of truth, and it forever changed the balances of power. As Professor Louis Dupré puts it, the Enlightenment "permanently inured us against one thing: the willingness to accept authority uncritically."[3]

In the decades that followed, people would continue turning toward their own reasoning, which meant asking their own questions, making their own discoveries, and proposing their own philosophies in ways that would shake up life as people knew it in much of the Western world. Isaac Newton's experiments and mathematical calculations laid new foundations for understanding the physical world, John Locke's theories revolutionized ideas of selfhood and society, and Adam Smith's inquiries paved the way for free market economics. From an era of tradition and stability burst forth an age of discovery, possibility, mobility, and change.

The ability to think for oneself was not only a *different* way of approaching life, it was, in the eyes of Enlightenment thinkers, a *better*, more *mature* way than what had come before. German philosopher Immanuel Kant began his famous 1784 essay "An Answer to the Question: What Is Enlightenment?" with the following: "Enlightenment is man's emergence from his self-imposed immaturity. Immaturity is the inability to use one's understanding without guidance from another . . . *Sapere Aude!* 'Have courage to use your own understanding!'—that is the motto of enlightenment."[4]

Following Kant's description, we see that the Enlightenment wasn't only about a new and different way of thinking. It insisted on a new standard of maturity, a standard that was an ideal toward which to strive and a moral imperative. "Laziness and cowardice are the reasons why so great a proportion of men . . . gladly remain in lifelong immaturity, and why it is so easy for others to establish themselves as their guardians," Kant wrote, expressing his distaste for pre-Enlightenment conventions. "It is so easy to be immature. If I have a book to serve as my understanding, a pastor to serve as my conscience, a physician to determine my diet for me, and so on, I need not exert myself at all."

Indeed, many Enlightenment thinkers seemed to have an allergy to the attitudes of duty and obedience that had come before. In his book *The Crisis of the European Mind 1680–1715*, intellectual historian Paul Hazard put it this way: "Never was there a greater contrast, never a more sudden transition than this! An hierarchical system ensured by authority; life firmly based on dogmatic principle—such were the things held dear by the people of the seventeenth century; but these—controls, authority, dogmas and the like—were the very things their immediate successors of the eighteenth held in cordial detestation."[5]

Therefore, the Enlightenment wasn't only a movement that offered new freedoms and possibilities. It was a movement that made demands. It raised the bar. It changed what it meant to be an adult.

From Enlightenment to the Dog Whisperer

We don't often stop and think about what constitutes an "adult" in today's US society, yet we live against a backdrop of implicit expectations. Psychologist Robert Kegan, whom we'll talk about more in the coming pages, has called these expectations the "hidden curriculum" of modern life.[6] For example, many professional job listings call for "self-starters" who are able to take initiative and work autonomously. We tend to think of a "leader" as someone who can stand alone, think for themself, and give orders rather than only follow. An adult is more or less someone who meets Kant's standards of maturity that emerged during the Enlightenment.

When we look at the landscape of contemporary self-help, we see many speakers, books, television shows, and other resources that point in a similar direction. They tell people to throw off the yoke of others' assumptions and demands, to think independently, to take responsibility and control. And they emphasize the importance of the individual. For example, one of Tony Robbins's top self-help quotes is "The power of positive thinking is the ability to generate a feeling of certainty in yourself when nothing in the environment supports you."[7] When *nothing* in the environment supports you. Robbins implies that you are on your own, or at least you *should* be able to be on your own, and you can find certainty in your aloneness. It's another way of saying, "If it's going to be, it's up to me."

Some self-help books point toward self-reliance by providing intentionally trite instructions such as "make your bed," "wash your face," or in Jordan Peterson's case by outlining *12 Rules for Life* that include "Stand up straight with your shoulders back" and "Set your house in perfect order before you criticize the world." Peterson writes, "Strengthen the individual. Start with yourself. Take care with yourself. Define who you are. Refine your personality. Choose your destination and articulate your Being" and "You can use your own standards of judgment. You can rely on yourself for guidance. You don't have to adhere to some external, arbitrary code of behaviour."[8]

We don't often associate Peterson, a baby boomer psychologist who has been called a "right-wing celebrity,"[9] with Kelly Williams Brown, the comedic red-haired millennial journalist who in 2013 turned *adulting* into a millennial term. Yet elements of their basic message sound similar. "You are the captain of your own destiny, even if it isn't all that glamorous or fabulous at the moment," Brown says. In defining "adulting" she points to responsibility and choice, writing "there are lots of things you can control, and lots of decisions are up to you. . . . *Adult* isn't a noun; it's a verb. It's the act of making correctly those decisions that fill our day."[10]

Then there is the slew of irreverent titles that told us to "unfuck" ourselves, to "get our shit together," and to be a "badass." In *The Subtle Art of Not Giving a F*ck*, Mark Manson challenges "victim mentality," telling people to think for themselves and actively steer their own life direction. Using words very different from Immanuel Kant, but echoing his advocacy for critical thinking and conscious choice, Manson writes, "Maturity is what happens when one learns to only give a fuck about what's truly fuckworthy."[11] In other words, don't become a casualty of circumstance or lazy thinking. Examine your options carefully, choose your destiny, take charge, define *yourself*, and stop giving a fuck about everything extraneous. And "love *yourself*"—Jen Sincero ends most chapters of *You Are a Badass* with these exact words.[12]

Similar undercurrents ran through a wave of reality TV shows in the 2000s, from *The Dog Whisperer*, to *Supernanny*, to *Kitchen Nightmares*. Onto the scene of a struggling dog owner, family, or restauranteur, walked Cesar Millan, Jo Frost, or Gordon Ramsey, ready to model a take-charge attitude and challenge others to do the same. "I rehabilitate dogs; I train people" is Millan's famous line.[13] He showed dog owners how to be a "pack leader," meaning a person who among other qualities is calm and assertive and knows how to set boundaries, a person who can actively create circumstances rather than simply react to them. Jo Frost, the Supernanny, taught parents how to set *behavioral* boundaries for their children and also *psychological* boundaries for themselves. For example, a mother, exasperated with her son's homework battles laments, "He just doesn't stop." Frost explains, "It's about *your* behavior changing. One of you needs to be able to say, 'I'm feeling really angry right now; let's come back to this in half an hour.' And it's not going to be [your son]. So you have to learn to step back."[14] Frost instructs parents, "It's important to step up with that authority."[15]

All of this advice and training on stepping back, stepping up, standing up straight, and consciously choosing what to give a fuck about is, from a certain perspective, very good and much-needed. Learning to think critically, to captain one's own ship, and take responsibility for oneself are all undoubtedly important elements of mature adulthood. In fact, they map directly not only onto Enlightenment principles but also known models of psychological development. Another term for what Enlightenment thinkers, and now contemporary motivational speakers, authors, and television shows often advocate for, is *self-determination* or *self-authorship* (Jordan Peterson has in fact created an online "Self-Authoring Suite"[16]). These are terms I will describe more fully in the following pages.

But first I want to plainly state a critical thesis of this book. I'm suggesting that the psychology of the Enlightenment presented a new level of adult maturity for the Western world and created an attractor, or beacon, for the human developmental journey. It has been magnetizing us ever since. However, considering what we know about human development today, and given the state of our world today, I believe we need to reconsider our guideposts. We need to appreciate but also look beyond Enlightenment principles to see what might be calling us from the further fields of our potential. As you will see, this presents a very challenging reorientation, one that runs counter to many deeply held habits and patterns of belief in the Western world. And it will require that we begin to get over our "selves," our neoliberal selves, in any case, without knowing exactly what we'll find on the other side. To help explain, let me take you on a brief tour of the known developmental terrain.

Tracing the Path of Human Development

Along with new orientations that promoted reason, science, and progress, the Enlightenment introduced new understandings of human development. John Locke saw the baby as a *tabula rasa*, or "blank slate," that required careful nurturance. Swiss philosopher Jean-Jacques Rousseau outlined stages of child development, with children first guided by their impulses and emotions, then developing a capacity to reason, and finally becoming adults capable of critical thinking. These Enlightenment thinkers laid the groundwork for modern developmental psychologists such as Jean Piaget, who in the mid-1900s observed and outlined specific stages of child development, beginning with the expression of infantile reflexes and culminating in abstract reasoning, also called *formal operations*, in adolescence and early adulthood.

It's obvious that children develop. Anyone who has raised a child from birth knows firsthand the whirlwind of physical and mental growth that takes place in the first year of life. The pace of change seems to slow with age, and until recently, a person was seen as pretty much cooked and done by the time they hit age 25. Development was over. Recent insights into neuroplasticity have challenged this view, showing us that experience continues to change the brain throughout the lifespan, and that we generate new neurons even as we die.[17] But even before this explosion of discoveries in neuroscience, research psychologists were looking more closely at life beyond the third decade, and extending Piaget's developmental framework further into adulthood.

A first of these psychologists was Jane Loevinger, a self-described "iconoclast"[18] who secured funding from the National Institute of Mental Health in the 1960s to study motherhood and personality, which was not exactly a popular topic at that time.[19] Her research and careful statistical analyses of mothers' attitudes revealed something unexpected. She stumbled on a measure of development. Based on her research findings, Loevinger turned to ideas from psychiatrist Henry Stack Sullivan as well as Piaget, whose work she was previously unfamiliar with. She began testing a model of progressive stages of a person's "self-system" or "frame of reference," which was found to develop from impulsive, to conformist, to conscientious, to integrated. Loevinger called this *ego development*.[20] In other streams of research and practice, Erik Erikson built on Sigmund Freud's psychology to describe development of the ego throughout the lifespan, and Lawrence Kohlberg followed the work of Piaget to delineate stages of moral development.

Following these and other scholars, developmental psychologists continued to expound on and extend discoveries in adult development. These include Robert Kegan, emeritus professor at Harvard, who has been describing levels of complexity in adult meaning-making since his 1982 book *The Evolving Self*[21]; scholar Susanne Cook-Greuter, whose doctoral work extended Loevinger's research to explore the further reaches of stage development[22]; William Torbert, emeritus professor at Boston College, who in collaboration with Cook-Greuter articulated developmental stages as a series of "action logics" that create a path for "seven transformations of leadership"[23] in organizational life; and Jennifer Garvey Berger, a former student of Robert Kegan who has further integrated adult developmental psychology into coaching and organizational development.

One of the main tenets of adult developmental psychology is what Kegan calls the *subject-object move*, meaning that the *subject* of one stage of development becomes the *object* of the next. In other words, a fish doesn't know it is in water unless it grows legs and lungs and walks onto land. Now this further-developed fish can see the water and recognize it as one possible experience of reality, rather than as reality itself. And this further-developed fish has more freedom and capacity, with an ability to choose between walking on land or swimming in water. It is no longer entirely *subject* to the water but can hold the water as a distinct phenomenon, as *object*.

A second tenet is that when we move from one developmental stage to the next, we do not leave behind prior stages. As independent scholar and philosopher Ken Wilber is known to say, we "transcend and include" each stage of development.[24] The fish that has grown legs can still get back into the water. Or perhaps a better way to describe it is that once a child can walk, they still have the ability to get down on their knees and crawl, sometimes they do, and there are in fact times that crawling is the most appropriate way to move through space. We can think of developmental mindsets that same way—early mindsets are not "bad." They have their own logics and usefulness.

In this book I have tried to point out how Enlightenment principles, or self-authorship, or more specifically, an exaggerated expression of self-authorship in the form of hyper-individualized neoliberal ideology, have become like the water in which we swim. I am attempting to give us a toehold onto land, so we can consider life in the water more consciously and explore some different possibilities. The map of developmental psychology is one tool that helps us find our feet. So here are descriptions of the developmental stages, from the beginning of life through the further potentials of Western adulthood.

The Opportunist (Self-Sovereign Mind)

As human beings we are born a bundle of reflexes and impulses. A brand-new baby is not hungry, it is *hunger* (and usually also *anger*). The baby is not joyful, it is joy itself. It is not relaxed in its sleep, it is the embodiment of relaxation. As adults we often find ourselves captivated and lovestruck in the presence of such simplicity and un-self-conscious expression. We are also sometimes overwhelmed by the purity of rage and distress that babies transparently display.

Gradually, a child develops to the extent that they are not completely fused with basic impulses, either physically or psychologically. For example, they can consider and make choices about whether to put an object in their mouth. They can control their bathroom urges long enough to go sit in the appropriate spot. This is the subject-object move—the child goes from being completely *subject* to, identified with, and run by their impulsive mind, to being able to hold those impulses as *object* and make a choice about them. This development is called the self-sovereign mind, or the opportunist stage, because the child can now control impulses in service of a short-term goal, such as avoiding suffering from eating something unpleasant, staying comfortable in dry pants, or receiving praise for a successful trip to the bathroom.

If you want to see the self-sovereign mind in action you can watch adorable videos of children undergoing the famous "marshmallow experiment," in which they are given a marshmallow and told they can either eat one now, or wait and have two when the experimenter returns. This creates a circumstance where the opportunistic, self-sovereign mind must remain strong, controlling or ignoring the impulse to pop the sugary treat into one's mouth, in service of earning the greater reward. Children squirm with tension, hum to distract themselves, and sometimes lose to their impulses, eating the marshmallow as if in a trance. The impulsive mind might continue trying to wiggle its way into receiving the reward, for example, by leaving one pitiful fleck of marshmallow on the napkin. But to the self-sovereign mind, the rules are clear. "You're eating, not waiting," a boy tells his impatient younger sister who insists she's passing the test, even as she tastes the marshmallow. "You still ate some of it, so [the experimenter] is still not going to give you two," her brother declares.[25]

This is another characteristic of the opportunist stage—the self-sovereign mind tends to orient in terms of externally provided rules and roles, which are taken to be black and white, right and wrong. There is no gray area. During the marshmallow test the experimenter is in charge, and she has made clear the parameters of receiving a second marshmallow. At the same time, the self-sovereign mind thinks, it's not illegal unless you get caught. "Don't show her, okay?" the older brother encourages his marshmallow-tasting sister, although his support dwindles with the size of her treat, as her transgression becomes increasingly obvious and evasion less and less of a possibility.

From our self-sovereign mind, we are keenly tuned into maximizing outcomes in our favor. What we are not particularly tuned into is other people's minds or even our own inner workings. As Jennifer Garvey Berger describes in *Changing on the Job: Developing Leaders for a Complex World*, from the self-sovereign mind, a person who is asked to describe themselves "is likely to offer a list of things she likes or does not like, or things she is good at or not. She does not orient toward thinking in abstractions about herself. Looking out from a self-sovereign mind, the world seems teeming with confusion that needs to be cut through with black-and-white decisions."[26]

The self-sovereign mind tends to develop by middle childhood, and most people will transition to the following stage by adolescence or early adulthood. This is the development toward the socialized form of mind, also called the *diplomat* in its earlier form and *expert* in its later one.

The Diplomat and Expert (Socialized Mind)

The self-sovereign mind is capable of holding impulses as object, but it is subject to and identified with short-term needs and preferences. It can self-interestedly wait a few minutes for that second marshmallow, but some of its other choices may appear brash. As Kegan says, "Most sensitive parents recognize that their 10-year-old kids love them, but would still sell them for a cold drink on a hot day. They might later regret the deal, but at the time it kind of made sense . . . when you're 10 you're orienting toward your own needs and interests."[27]

At some point we stop following the rules simply to avoid punishment and start following them because we have taken them in and called them our own. We no longer stand in line only to avoid the principal's office, but rather because that's what *people like us* do, because we are part of a social group, and deviance from the norms of that social group has consequences, including threats to our very identity. We have finally reached the stage of socialization where we no longer need prodding from carrots and sticks; we have internalized and become regulated by the rules and standards of our society. We have achieved the socialized mind.

From this mind, we are no longer completely *subject* to our individual needs and preferences, but rather can hold them as *object* in order to fit into our given social context. Our identity has extended outward and is now based on more than those individual needs; it is based on the customs of the group to which we belong. In adolescence the socialized mind is often expressed in "cliques" with strong group identity. This is why we have stereotypical "jocks," "theater kids," and intellectuals (also known as "nerds"), who tend to share certain codes of conduct and styles of dress. Even "anarchists," with their rejection of convention, may very well be operating from a socialized form of mind, donning a particular type of anarchist uniform and following largely unspoken rules of conduct—including an unquestioned, unwavering stance of rebellion. When rebellion is one's only choice, it is its own style of conformity.

The socialized mind finds its source of authority in the external environment in the form of a figurehead, an institution, a code, or a body of expertise. The earlier form of the socialized mind is called the *diplomat* because from this mind we are particularly oriented toward our group. As Cook-Greuter explains in "Nine Levels of Increasing Embrace in Ego Development: A Full-Spectrum Theory of Vertical Growth and Meaning Making, "On the one hand, there is total acceptance of the family and in-group (such as peer groups in adolescence), on the other hand, we see blind rejection of deviance and out-groups. It's 'them' against 'us' . . . you are either ally and friend and approve of us and what we do, or you are the enemy."

A later form of the socialized mind is called the *expert*. At this stage we begin to be able to take a third-person perspective on ourselves, which allows for greater self-understanding and a beginning sense of separate personhood. Cook-Greuter calls this a *conceptual watershed*. She writes, "Experts may reject their family of origin or their childhood beliefs, yet they still need a reference group that accepts and respects them. Only now they want to be accepted by others because of how they are different and special. Expertise and knowledge are ways to distinguish oneself. Professional peer groups and organizations thus supply the need for approval and belonging. Degrees, authorities, and reference books in the field also provide the needed support for defending one's approach."[28]

The socialized mind is a great achievement of adulthood. It enables us to truly enter and function well within a given society. In leadership, the diplomatic form of mind provides "social glue" to the team or organization, and the expert mind, geared toward "continuous improvement, efficiency, and perfection," brings precision and standards of excellence. But the socialized mind also has its limitations. It is the mind that Kant rather unempathetically scorned as "immature," remaining dependent on books or other people as sources of authority.

A light-hearted depiction of the socialized mind is seen in Michael Scott's character from NBC's *The Office*. We quickly learn that Michael is a boss that above all needs to be liked or at least, in his own words, "praised."[29] Gaining external approval is not just something Michael values, but something he seems to be *made up by* and *subject to*. Although he is an expert salesman who knows exactly how to charm his customers, he's not a very good manager. It's hard for him to take any type of stand based on his own authority. When Michael is told by upper management that he must fire an employee, he goes about the task by interviewing people around the office, outsourcing his power and trying to find an answer in his social surround. When Michael attempts to fire the person he has reluctantly selected, the employee convinces Michael to terminate someone else, essentially making his decision for him.[30] In another episode, Michael's GPS tells him to turn right and he drives his car straight into a lake, even as his employee, Dwight, protests. "The machine knows!" Michael yells as water hits the dash.[31] I love this scene as a metaphor for our socialized mind, the part of us that has no choice but to orient externally. Although this form of mind is great at taking directions, as well as taking in the needs and preferences of other people, it's also vulnerable to making bad decisions based on poor sources of authority.

The socialized mind can also be observed in the very-unfunny and quite-uncomfortable videos of Yale University psychologist Stanley Milgram's experiments on obedience from the early 1960s.[32] Milgram created a scenario in which an unsuspecting volunteer was told they were part of an experiment on learning, and their role would be to administer progressively stronger electric shocks to another volunteer, sitting out of sight on the other side of a partition, in the event of that person's wrong answer. In reality there would be no shocks, and the second volunteer was in fact an actor, but the participant would not know this until after the experiment was complete. Once the participant began administering the supposed electric shocks, they would hear prerecorded reactions from the actor, which included cries of pain, protests, and pleas to be released. As the volunteer gradually moved to the highest levels of voltage, the actor, who at the start of the experiment disclosed that he had a heart condition, would fall silent behind the partition. He was ostensibly incapacitated, maybe dead.

Volunteers were, not surprisingly, visibly uncomfortable with their role in the experiment. They fidgeted, grimaced, and displayed nervous laughter. But most participants, about 65%, went to the high-est voltage marked "danger: severe shock." Over the course of the experiment the self-protective, self-sovereign mind would sometimes show itself. "I refuse to take the responsibility for him getting hurt in there," says one obviously distressed participant, expressing fear of consequences for injuring the other person. "Who's going to take responsibility if something happens to that gentleman?" When the authoritative, white-coated experimenter assures the participant, "I'm responsible for anything that happens to him. Continue please," the participant goes on administering shocks. He remains distressed, his socialized mind seeming to wrestle with tensions between social norms about harming people and the authority of the man in the white coat, who tells the participant it is "absolutely essential" to con-tinue. "You have no other choice," the experimenter declares.

Sometimes, however, another form of mind would be revealed during Milgram's experiment. One participant, after he hears the actor protest and is told to continue, replies, "The experiment might require that we continue, but I still think we should find out what the condition of the gentleman is." A little later the participant states, "Look, I don't know anything about electricity; I don't profess any knowledge, nor will I go any further until I find out whether the guy is okay." His expert mind seems to be aware that it does not have the answer here. But this particular participant isn't willing to put his trust in the experimenter's expertise, either. He begins to balk at the man in the white coat's assertions. "No, it isn't essential [to continue], not one bit," he challenges. When instructed that he has no choice, he pushes back, "I have a lot of choices. My number one choice is that I wouldn't go on if I thought he was being harmed."

Here we glimpse a mind that handles pressures from the external environment in a different way from the diplomat or expert mind, seeming to hold them as object and examine them consciously, rather than reflexively succumbing to them. It's a mind that sees "a lot of choices," one that has begun to set its own rules and find its own voice of authority. It's a mind that has begun to author itself.

The Achiever (Self-Authoring Mind)

Cook-Greuter describes the next form of mind, sometimes called the *achiever stage*, as the first stage where people "have gained a measure of independence and self-authorship that makes them feel they are masters of their ships." At last we have arrived at Immanuel Kant's imperative to "use one's understanding without guidance from another"; Jordan Peterson's call to "define who you are"; Cesar Millan's instruction to step up as a calm and assertive "pack leader."

As we have seen with the many examples thus far, modern Western society values and rewards the achiever stage of functioning. In fact, Cook-Greuter describes self-authorship as "the target stage for much of Western culture," indicating that our democratic form of government and our entrepreneurial economic system revolve around this stage of development. She writes, "Our institutions of education, jurisprudence and much of business are based on the premise of independent adults pursuing their self-chosen interests within the given contours of the social environment."

Reaching the achiever stage of development is indeed a great feat. From this form of mind, a person can hold their childhood socialization, as well as competing relationships and pressures from their current surround, as *object*. They can weigh these pressures against an internal, self-chosen ideology guided by personal values, which creates the bedrock for a solid sense of self. This is the self that the self-esteem movement of the 1990s so earnestly wanted to support, that Enlightenment thinkers so passionately advocated for. The critical thinking skills of the achiever mind are particularly important today as we wade through what some call a "post-truth" world, a point we'll discuss further in the next chapter.

From the achiever mind we can be truly conscientious, planful, goal-driven, open to feedback, and scientific. A person can balance the short with the longer term, delegate responsibly, and tends to be skilled when it comes to leading a team. "Here is a vision," the achiever says, confident in the view of the world they have created. "Now let's get from point A to point B."

The achiever archetype is the basis of countless modern stories, from the unassuming Frodo Baggins in *The Lord of the Rings*, to Luke Skywalker and later Rey in *Star Wars*, to recent Disney princesses like Moana. These heroes begin by having the weight of their people, or their world, or their galaxy placed on their shoulders, then must set out independently (assisted by friends, wise or powerful guides, and funny sidekicks) to face numerous trials and tribulations and eventually save the day. These heroes, although often complex and imperfect, nonetheless express admirable characteristics, such as courage, perseverance, and willingness to sacrifice for the greater good. They shrug off assumptions about who they are or what they've been told they're capable of in order to pursue their destiny. The hero's journey is always one of development, growth, maturity. These stories tend to leave us with a sense of satisfaction and accomplishment.

The achiever mind can demonstrate great heroism in the form of out-of-the-box thinking and innovation, a willingness to question the way things are done with an independent vision or the bravery to lead rather than be led. Yet, like all stages prior, this form of mind swims in waters it cannot distance itself from and hold as object, but rather is *subject to*. And here we observe some of the suffering we've been discussing thus far.

Toxic Achieverism

On the one hand the achiever stage represents a significant attainment. On the other hand, self-authorship creates a closed, independent and thus isolated entity. Although the achiever mind can relate to and appreciate a wide range of other minds, its achievement and responsibility is fundamentally based on a sense of separateness. It is a self-generating, self-sustaining, self-perpetuating tiger chasing its tail. It is, as Milton Friedman said, an "end in itself."

The achiever stage is sometimes referred to as *strive-drive*, because from here, self-esteem and its accompanying sense of identity depend on the pursuit of chosen goals. At best, this results in getting a lot of useful things done. At worst, this can result in burnout, as well as lack of time and energy to contemplate bigger issues. Cook-Greuter writes, "the drive to succeed and achieve can readily lead to over-extension and exhaustion. Achievers find it difficult to acknowledge their limits of time and energy. Engaged in their projects, they hardly slow down to look at the present moment, to reflect upon life as a whole, or give themselves a break."[33]

Together the expert and achiever minds find value in performance, speed, and efficiency. From this perspective, a day is something to conquer and a life is something to hack. Here we find the land of hustle culture and what Erin Griffith called *performative workaholism* in her *New York Times* article on young people pretending to love work. It's what Anne Helen Petersen is talking about when she describes how millennials gravitate toward "personal cures because they seem tenable, and promise that our lives can be recentered, and regrounded, with just a bit more discipline, a new app, a better email organization strategy, or a new approach to meal planning." But as Petersen describes, these approaches turn societal problems into personal ones that no matter how hard we try, cannot be solved by "productivity apps, or a bullet journal, or face mask skin treatments, or overnight fucking oats." These solutions are "Band-Aids on an open wound,"[34] and can end up exacerbating our problems. We are hearing more these days about "toxic achievement"[35] and its links to stress and poor mental health. Achievement can also be a distraction; a way we

73

keep our heads down, keep producing, keep earning, keep consuming, and fail to address overarching social and environmental issues.

Cook-Greuter also notes that the achiever form of mind brings an "exaggerated sense of being responsible for how things turn out," which can lead to "feelings of guilt and inadequacy." This sounds much like the responsibilization of Teo's "neoliberal form of subjectivity."

Neoliberalism seems to reflect the achiever stage on overdrive. It has brought us into a developmental eddy that has turned dangerous, and now threatens us all with toxic levels of stress and the collapse of economies and ecosystems. In its most problematic forms, the achiever appears to coincide with the worst aspects of neoliberalism—unchecked production and consumption, empty efficiency, and businesses of "self" swirling down solipsistic sinkholes.

As we begin to touch the limits of the achiever mind, we see the shadowy edges of what has long been the modern Western world's brightest developmental beacon. Cook-Greuter writes, "What is not yet visible to Achievers is a more systemic view of reality. They see themselves as independent wholes rather than also interdependent parts of multiple, overarching systems."

In this tale of human development, the self-authoring achiever is not the end of the story, not even close. In fact, from a certain perspective, it is only the beginning.

Spiral to Arc

The progression of Western human development has been depicted in many different ways. I have seen it listed as a table of definitions or drawn as a ladder to climb. It can appear as nesting dolls or as the concentric rings of a tree.[36] Those concentric circles can also be stretched out vertically into the shape of a cyclone-like spiral, as shown in Figure 3.1.

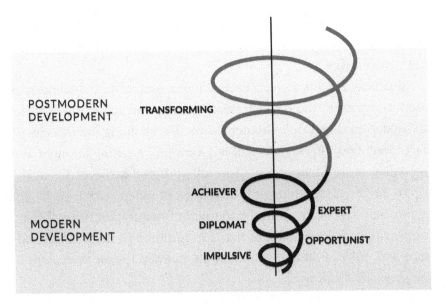

POSTMODERN DEVELOPMENT

TRANSFORMING

MODERN DEVELOPMENT

ACHIEVER

EXPERT

DIPLOMAT

OPPORTUNIST

IMPULSIVE

Figure 3.1 Spiral of human development
Source: Adapted from Susanne R. Cook-Greuter. (2004). "Making the case for a developmental perspective." *Industrial and Commercial Training, 36*(7), 275–281. https://doi.org/10.1108/00197850410563902

I like that the spiral includes the shape of a circle, like a nod to the cyclical patterns we experience in the form of seasons, days, and circadian rhythms, as well as the sense of time that people were more fully governed by in earlier times. This is the traditional model of time employed by Strauss and Howe in their theory of generational cycles. Neil Howe writes, "we adopt the insight of nearly all traditional societies: that social time is a recurring cycle in which events become meaningful only to the extent that they are what philosopher Mircea Eliade calls 'reenactments.'"[37]

However, the spiral further introduces a linear element, like the forward motion and spirit of progress that burst forth in Western culture's Enlightenment. It combines circularity and linearity, depicting a cycle that is going somewhere. The spiral is often used in the models of human development I've been describing. A whole system related to individual and cultural development called *spiral dynamics* has been built on the work of another developmental psychologist Clare Graves.

But now I want to turn to a different shape that is sometimes used to represent the developmental journey, which is the arc. The arc as depicted by Cook-Greuter shows that all along the trajectory I have described thus far, the self is ascending, growing stronger and becoming more independent. The self-authored achiever sits at the top of the arc of development, at an apex of independence, a height of the "self." From there, in the journey of maturation the self is on the way down, descending further and further into the interdependence and unity of all that is. This is the journey I want to explore in the pages that follow.

Chapter 4

Wandering at an Apex

For the first part of the developmental journey, as we grow toward achiever, individuality and independence are on the rise. In the Euro-American context, the movement toward achiever can be considered an adaptive, healthy trajectory. I have heard it said that the culture will "pull you up" the curve, to the expert-achiever space. Our self-help bookshelves, displaying all the titles we considered in the previous chapter, our preoccupation with "life hacks," and our $11.6 billion self-improvement market,[1] seem to be testaments to that.

When I look at the arc of development (Figure 4.1), I think of Euro-American society as sitting at the apex, swinging our legs, looking down from a height of individualism. In some ways it feels good up there, like we're on top of the world. But as we've been talking about all along in this book, that seat feels increasingly wobbly. Our individualism is not on stable ground, and we're hurting the planet, one another, ourselves. I think we need to keep going and begin sliding, however awkwardly, down the arc's other side. We need to come back down to earth.

The Self-Questioning Transformer

The entire right-hand side of the developmental arc is sometimes referred to as *self-transforming* or simply *transforming*. (See the

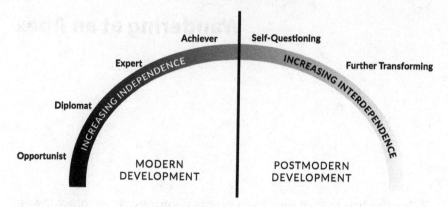

Figure 4.1 Development in western meaning-making
Source: Adapted from Cook-Greuter, Susanne. "Ego Development: A Full-Spectrum Theory Of Vertical Growth And Meaning Making." *ResearchGate*, November 18, 2021.

Notes at the end of the book for a further discussion of developmental models.) Cook-Greuter calls this the "postconventional" space, meaning, that as we move further along the arc, we move out of the conventional, modern paradigm. This also means moving out of our "selves." She writes, "The transition from conventional to postconventional meaning making signifies an overall, large-scale shift from increasing differentiation and the creation of an independent self-identity towards increasing integration and deconstruction of the separation developed in the first half of the growth trajectory."[2] In other words, in the space beyond the achiever mind, individuation begins giving way to interdependence. The sense of separate self that has all along been increasing begins decreasing. What goes up must come down.

The developmental stage that reflects the first steps into this post-conventional space is sometimes called *pluralist* or *self-questioning*, because from this mind we see that reality is constantly interpreted and constructed. It appears that everything is simply perspective, and there are a million different ways to see and interpret any given thing. Even with science, we see that knowledge is constrained and shaped by the hypotheses and measurements of the scientist. As Cook-Greuter writes, "We cannot help but filter our observations through our personal subjective lenses." She continues, "We have far less control over being 'molded' than we previously understood. Socialization, it turns out, is relentless and ongoing from the day we enter the world. It begins with the earliest inculcation of what are considered desirable thoughts, feelings, values, and behavior and what is not. It continues through schooling and is reinforced at every moment via the media, commerce, and, most subtly, by the very nature of one's native language and communication patterns."

As we enter the postconventional space, we begin to hold self-authorship as object. The control and certainty we thought we had, the narrative we believed we were in charge of, becomes exposed as a subjective and limited lens onto reality. In *Changing on the Job*, Jennifer Garvey-Berger describes an organizational leader who "had begun to notice what seemed to him to be his own inability to believe in his single-minded goals any longer. He found instead of advocating strongly for a single position, he began to see the validity in all positions around the table. . . . He found himself questioning his assumptions about the way the world worked, noticing what assumptions others were making, and understanding the ways those assumptions shaped their ideas about right and wrong. As he noticed these connections, he began reshaping—and believing less in—his own assumptions."[3] This points to the self-questioning nature of moving out of the achiever mind. And to the self-authoring achiever in us, it sure doesn't sound very appealing. It sounds like a disorienting loss of clarity and control.

But although the postconventional space is disconcerting, it is also a place where new forms of creativity and dynamism are possible. The space is called *transforming* for a reason. We have the possibility to be free not only of limitations imposed from the outside but also the limitations of our own assumptions and false idols. This is where we have hope of finding some space around the neoliberal identity, and even divesting of our perceived power and responsibility to endlessly pursue our goals, improve ourselves, and generate our own destiny. We have the possibility to be free of our *selves*.

The transforming space is marked by recognition of limitation, and at the same time, an opening into vast interconnection. Garvey-Berger writes about those who begin peeking out from the transforming mind,

> the beginning of this path is marked by some sense that the self-authored system will actually never be sufficient to handle the complexities of life. . . . As they come to understand that their current path is a tiny part of what the fullness of life offers—and that they will never develop a self-authored system large enough to grasp the fullness of life—they begin to reevaluate the direction of their lives, stop working on the self-improvement plan that has them perfecting their self-authored system, and begin to look across systems at what unites us as human, or as members of a fragile planet.

Documentary filmmaker Craig Foster offers us a beautiful glimpse of the transforming mind in *My Octopus Teacher*.[4] Foster describes entering a phase of burnout, when what sounds from his description like his achiever self began losing steam and questioning its own endless striving. Foster found himself drawn back to the ocean setting he had loved exploring in his youth. There he began diving beneath the waves without wetsuit or oxygen, to be as close as possible to the natural surround. Amidst his underwater wanderings and

Getting Over Ourselves

close observations he encountered a common octopus, with whom he gradually formed a relationship. Foster's tale is not one of heroism or triumph, but rather one of relationship and subtle transformation through vulnerability. "She was teaching me to become sensitized to the other," Foster says, and later, "What she taught me was to feel . . . that you're part of this place, not a visitor. That's a huge difference."

Where we once felt independence and separation, from the transforming mind we can experience connection, permeability, and the falling away of boundaries. We recognize that the island our "self" seemed to be is in fact constantly shaped and reshaped by the waves and the rain, and that the base of the island disappears indistinguishably into the vastness of the ocean floor.

The vulnerability and permeability that becomes possible in our self-questioning and further transforming mind is different from that of our socialized mind. Where our socialized mind has not yet found its independence and sense of authority and therefore must rely on something external, our self-questioning mind sees its own authority as inherently limited, continuously conditioned by circumstances, and relative to an infinite array of other positions of authority. Authority does not exist in a vacuum. It arises out of context, and is therefore interdependent and connected with everything else in that context.

This is where we can have true plurality and a kind of "flattening" of authority structures. We may see, for instance, that a toddler is earlier in development than an adult, and it is up to the adult to set good boundaries and lead the way—we don't want to get the direction of care and responsibility mixed up. But that doesn't mean the toddler's perspective is less valid than that of the adult. There are advantages to a perspective that is close to the ground. Anyone who has raised or worked with kids knows that young people sometimes see things most accurately, most creatively, or have the best ideas in the room. It's a child, after all, who points out that the emperor has no clothes. So, from the self-questioning mind we can listen more deeply, aware of the limits of our own filter, knowing that powerful ideas and insights can and do come from perspectives very different from our own.

At the same time, that vast expanse of perspective can be overwhelming and disorienting. Which brings me to another word from the transforming space. Although sometimes called *postconventional*, the first steps into transforming are also called *postmodern*. And that opens a Pandora's box when it comes to our current social and political climate.

Navigating the Postmodern Terrain

Postmodernism seems to defy definition. Stuart Jeffries, author of *Everything, All the Time, Everywhere: How We Became Postmodern*,[5] offers a few possibilities including "a movement that disdained the modernist vision," "both alibi for and indictment of the neoliberal order," a "rhizomatic approach" with no beginning or end, and "a semiotic black hole, consuming everything but signifying nothing." Just trying to define postmodernism, we start to notice the topsy-turvy quality of this space. And we find we aren't getting very far. Rather, we can find ourselves sucked into that black hole, like the everything-bagel vortex of the Daniels's unrelated but similarly-named smash-hit postmodern film, *Everything Everywhere All At Once*,[6] a film that takes us on a wild adventure into the collapse and integration of perspective and possibility.

The term *postmodernism* has become a bogeyman in certain circles, with serious scholars telling us to turn back as soon as possible. "The humanities have yet to recover from the disaster of postmodernism, with its defiant obscurantism, self-refuting relativism, and suffocating political correctness," writes Steven Pinker in *Enlightenment Now*.[7] In *Death of Truth: Notes on Falsehood in the Age of*

Trump,[8] literary critic Michiko Kakutani considers the intersection of postmodernism with a "post-truth era," and its politically weaponized "fake news" and "alternative facts." In describing postmodernist thinking she writes, "Out with the idea of consensus. Out with the view of history as a linear narrative. Out with big universal meta-narratives. The Enlightenment, for instance is dismissed by many postmodernists on the left as a hegemonic or Eurocentric reading of history, aimed at promoting colonialist or capitalistic notions of reason or progress." And into this vacuum that has emptied itself of consensus and meta-narrative, what crept in, Kakutani believes, is narcissism. Calling out both baby boomer and millennial generations, Kakutani writes, "Relativism, of course, synced perfectly with the narcissism and subjectivity that had been on the rise, from Tom Wolfe's 'Me Decade,' on through the selfie age of self-esteem."

Similarly, independent philosopher Ken Wilber writes in *Trump and a Post-Truth World*,[9] "when there are no binding guidelines for individual behavior, the individual has only his or her own self-promoting wants and desires to answer to—in short, narcissism. And that is why the most influential postmodern elites ended up embracing, explicitly or implicitly, that tag team from postmodern hell: nihilism and narcissism—in short, aperspectival madness. The culture of post-truth."

Although presenting different views on the matter, both Kakutani and Wilber lament this post-truth landscape, and rightly so. In today's world we can feel like we've lost all binding narratives and meaningful beacons, like we're wading through a vast quagmire with no relief on the horizon. In the United States and beyond we find that politics are viciously divided, conspiracy theories abound, and we are no longer clear on how to relate to institutions, or each other. Gallup has found steady declines in US confidence in major institutions since 1980 (the beginning of neoliberalism), each decade seeming to dip to a new all-time low plateau (see Figure 4.2).

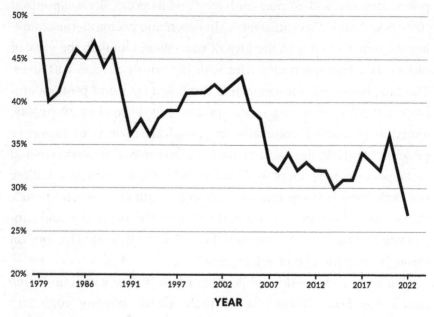

Average confidence in major U.S. institutions

Figure 4.2 Decline in institutional trust

Source: Adapted from Gallup, https://news.gallup.com/poll/394283/confidence-institutions-down-average-new-low.aspx

Alana Newhouse has written about "brokenism," claiming that the most vital debate in America today is not between "liberals" and "conservatives" but "between those who believe there is something fundamentally broken in America, and that it's an emergency, and those who do not."[10] She ties brokenism to "flatness," a concept that seems to overlap with the more problematic aspects of neoliberalism and current expressions of postmodernism. Flatness is characterized by "boundarylessness; speed; universal accessibility; an allergy to hierarchy, so much that the weighting or preferring of some voices or products over others is seen as illegitimate; seeing one's own words and face reflected back as part of a larger current; a commitment to gratification at the push of a button; equality of access

Getting Over Ourselves

to commodified experiences as the right of every human being on earth; the idea that all choices can and should be made instantaneously. . . ." We can hear the *Everything, All the Time, Everywhere* quality of Newhouse's "flatness." Jeffries calls postmodernism the *cultural handmaiden* of neoliberalism, a partnership he sees as presiding over an "erasure of the commons." He writes, "Neoliberalism—rolling back the frontiers of the state, extending corporate control over our lives, and using technology, by turns, to dominate, titillate and exclude the masses—is thriving." I would argue that neoliberalism as a cultural phenomenon is a form of achieverism that takes on some qualities of, but does not truly surrender itself to, postmodernism and the self-questioning mind. Neoliberalism seems like an eddy in the stream that is stuck and swirling in on itself, and on the human self. It's going nowhere, very fast.

Looking out across the flat, disorienting, aperspectival and post-truth terrain of postmodernism, it helps to understand that different forms of mind may be operating at any given time—in others and in ourselves. Our different minds make sense of postmodernism in different ways.

For the opportunist in us, postmodernism is a free-for-all where the rules have disappeared and anything goes. It's a fun-house of instant gratification. Pleasure rules. We can eat the marshmallow now, and then we can eat the whole bag, because it doesn't matter and it's all good. Neoliberalism certainly feeds on these more knee-jerk parts of our brain, finding ways to capture data on our needs and preferences in order to reflect those desires back to us and make them available for purchase with one click of a mouse.

To our socialized mind, the postmodern landscape can appear infuriatingly devoid of direction, a place where we must rapidly zero in on the most compelling guiding light. The decline of trust in major institutions (a trend that certainly has its merits as well as its problems) can lead us into the thrall of modern-day "influencers" and

Wandering at an Apex

dubious sources of authority. In some sectors of society, postmodernism collides with deep suspicion and rigid rejection of traditional sources of authority, which can spiral into the embrace of conspiracy theories based on questionable sources of information that grip the socialized mind. In the case of the QAnon conspiracy, the slogan is not "ask good questions," "think critically," or "check your sources." It is "trust the plan."

One rather confusing phenomenon is that our mind can be socialized to appear as self-authoring. If thinking for oneself and being independent is the "right" way to be, our socialized mind can take on this mantle, adopting slogans of autonomy and self-determination. I found it interesting that during the COVID-19 pandemic, some people indiscriminately labeled those wearing masks as "sheep." What this message really implies is, "if you don't believe the same things I do and act the same way as me, which means never wearing a mask, then you are a sheep." The irony is that this is a conformist mindset, and does not leave room for independent consideration of the information at hand, or authorship of a decision to wear or not wear a mask. The point here is that we cannot infer the autonomy of a person's thought based on their behavior; we have to probe for the reasoning behind that behavior. These days American culture idealizes self-authorship, and the socialized mind can easily glom on. But rejecting traditional authority, thinking for oneself, and going against the grain aren't behaviors that indicate a fully self-authored capacity unless they include the all-important practice of critical thinking. This means considering multiple sources of information, checking the credibility of those sources, and involving reason and scientific knowledge in decision-making.

Here is where our achiever mind thrives and indeed, is critically needed in a "post-truth" world. But our achiever mind will also stop short when it reaches the flat terrain of postmodernism and the further step into questioning itself. Postmodernism, to the achiever mind, looks like a dangerous swamp, full of toe traps and pitfalls. It offers little to no certainty or reassurance, and perhaps most disappointingly, no hill to climb. Nor can the terrain be traversed alone.

In my experience this is an extremely tricky juncture. The achiever mind tends to see the whole developmental journey as an endless climb. It wants to get higher and better. "I'm done with achiever, let's go to transforming!" the achiever mind says. "I'll work as hard, as long, as intensely as I can, because transforming is better!" But this step of the journey offers no new next rung, and the achiever's foot slips again and again into thin air. The only way out is through, and that involves making moves that are deeply counterintuitive to our achiever self.

Neoliberal Quicksand

In October 2018, a painting by the anonymous activist street artist Banksy sold at auction for almost $1.5 million, a tie for the artist's previous auction record. But moments after the sale of "Girl With Balloon," the print passed through the bottom of its frame, emerging half-shredded in an act of self-destruction.[11] Renamed "Love is in the Bin" by Banksy's authentication office, the destroyed art went up for auction again in 2021 and sold for a record-shattering $25.4 million.[12]

"Love is in the Bin" is both a metaphor for and a real-life example of neoliberalism's juggernaut, the same closed-loop cycle we considered in Chapter 1. In an effort to destroy itself, neoliberalism reifies itself; its demise only making it more powerful. This is the great irony in Banksy's work—that a subversive, anti-establishment artist should gain such great capitalist success. As Mark Fisher points out in *Capitalist Realism*,[13] anti-capitalism becomes more fodder for capitalism. Anti-neoliberalism sells, causing the anti-neoliberal act to fold back again into a neoliberal act. It can start to feel that there's no way out, that indeed, as Thatcher said, there is no alternative.

I have experienced this on the individual level as well: I have witnessed myself and others trying to achieve our way out of the achiever mind, efforting to be more transforming, more conscious, more developed. The more we struggle, the more we try to escape the orbit of achieverism, the more entrenched we become. It's like quicksand. As our achiever mind efforts, wrestles, and applies itself to its own development, the more deeply it is caught in its own strife.

I grew up in Maine where we have a saying, "You can't get there from here." It feels relevant at this juncture. The achiever can't achieve its way out of achiever, just as capitalism can't capitalize its way out of capitalism; neoliberalism can't neoliberalize its way to a better place. We need a different path, with different guideposts.

Destroy This Model

We will explore some of these potential guideposts in Part II. Before we move on, I want to say a few things about stage developmental psychology itself. There has been recent lively debate about these models, with some thought leaders pointing out dangerous and even "colonial" applications of developmental approaches.[14] Although we should be careful that this critique not become unilateral and dominating in the exact same fashion to which it objects, it is a very important argument. Stage developmental psychology can be harmfully employed, so let me offer a few cautions. First, if you look at these models, decide you are very developed, and feel like you are better than other people or are entitled to something—you're doing it wrong. Believe me, it is not an advanced part of you that is thinking this way. It's a very tempting trap that I'm sure I've been guilty of at points in my own life. Consider this a fair warning.

Second, in looking at these models I think we need to be careful to stay in the lane of the Euro-American history they issue from, rather than trying to impose them on other cultures or other parts

88

Getting Over Ourselves

of the world. That imposition would indeed be a colonial move, and Euro-American society has done enough of that. If these models are useful in a more widespread way, then that is something that can be discovered, but we should be careful not to make assumptions. There seem to be unique trajectories of growth and development around the world, with different configurations and patterns of autonomy and oneness. True plurality allows us to exchange knowledge and learn from one another, rather than imposing one story on everyone's reality.

Third, there is the matter of how the stages themselves look from the self-questioning mind and beyond. Where our opportunist mind might see some perplexing, suspicious definitions, our socialized mind might see new rules or codes to follow, our achiever mind sees a ladder to climb, and our self-questioning mind sees the limitations of the theory itself. Stage developmental psychology appears as just another grand narrative to impose on the world as mentioned previously. The self-questioning mind may call out, "Destroy this model. It doesn't really even exist."

I don't think we have to go to this extreme. We can let the stages be kaleidoscopic or disappear and reappear depending on how we're looking at things. The models can slip through our fingers. If they're needed they'll come back again. In fact, at this juncture in the developmental arc, letting things slip through our fingers is often the most we can do.

Slipping Through the Cracks

As I've been studying what different people have to say about the circumstances of today's world, I've been struck by the repeated theme of fault lines and cracks. One of my favorite contemporary thinkers, Dr. Bayo Akomolafe, teaches about "the spirituality of cracks."[15] A former clinical psychologist who left a teaching position at a Nigerian university to pursue a path less traveled, Akomolafe describes a crack as a type of "wound" and "an occurrence that exceeds its causes."

"The cracks of today are much more than things that want to be closed up. They reshape our bodies," Akomolafe says. "Our invitation is to listen to those modulations and to share those modulations as experimentations, as new rituals. . . . Instead of just continuing, or getting back to normal . . . how about you stay with those cracks, how about instead of putting things together again, you stay with the fact that things fall apart, but maybe that's how things become in the first place." Akomolafe cautions against the rush to solutions, and instead presents the possibility of "postactivism" which is in part "a study of cracks, fissures, fault lines."

Meanwhile in the United States, writing about brokenism in *Tablet Magazine*, Alana Newhouse says, "we should follow the cracks in the foundations of American society not in the way a pundit follows 'politics' or 'partisanship' or the 'culture wars,' but more like a seismologist tracks sudden slips in tectonic plates."[16] In another article, "Everything Is Broken," she writes, "We should seek out friction and thorniness, hunt for complexity and delight in unpredictability. Our lives should be marked not by 'comps' and metrics and filters and proofs of concept and virality but by tight circles and improvisation and adventure and lots and lots of creative waste. And not just to save ourselves, but to save each other."[17]

Troubling times call for strange measures, for moving in directions that look perilous or unpromising, for challenging our achieverism not with more of the same, but with that which it is not capable of. And this entails challenging our selves in new ways.

Perhaps, like Foster's octopus teacher, we need to lose our shells and become more directly available, gelatinous, vulnerable, yet resilient in our malleability. Perhaps we need to study what it means to shapeshift, change color, and fade into our surroundings, as well as what it means to back ourselves down and burrow into the deepest, darkest caves and cracks. Or perhaps we can be more like sand—shifting, seeping, and slipping through our own grasp. Not struggling in the quicksand, but becoming the sand itself, dropping down into the depths that appear threatening to us. Or maybe there is a different possibility altogether, an alternative we can't currently imagine.

Part II of this book takes the millennial and neoliberal stereotypes explored in Chapter 2 and asks, what happens if we turn them inside out or on their heads? If we don't treat these stereotypes as problems to fix, but rather passageways into different possibilities, what do we find?

The guideposts presented in this book are not intended as life hacks or quick solutions. Rather than self-help I'm calling it un-self help. I present practices for you to experiment with, and I think they are useful for reorienting. But your achiever mind may be disappointed that I'm not helping you do more, better, faster, that there's nothing to accomplish. Nor do I end the book by presenting alternatives to neoliberalism, because I don't think anyone can do that alone. All of that seems to me like falling in synch with achieverism, with heroism, with fixism, with work-harder-and-get-out-of-the-quicksand-ism. More of the same.

Rather, I offer the following chapters as ideas about how we might prepare ourselves for conversations and relationships that could help us find a future together. These are guideposts that can help us sink in, slow down, and really be with each other as we venture across the flat, confusing, and imperiled landscape of our human and more-than-human world. What might happen if we let go—of answers, solutions, hope, and even our selves? What might happen if we learn to slip through the cracks?

Wandering at an Apex

Un-Self Help

"This longing
you express is the return message.
The grief you cry out from
draws you toward union.
Your pure sadness
that wants help
is the secret cup."

Jalal al-Din Muhammad Rumi, "Love Dogs,"
translated by Coleman Barks

"Ring the bells that still will ring
Forget your perfect offering
There is a crack in everything
That's how the light gets in."

Leonard Cohen, "Anthem"

Chapter 5

Selfies and Self-Realization
Guidepost 1: From Self-Perfection to the Wisdom of Humility

Narcissus, son of a demi-goddess, was a young Greek man of great beauty. One day while hunting in the forest, he bent down to drink from a clear fountain and saw his reflection in the water. He was immediately transfixed by his own image.

Narcissus lay beside the pool, pining for the reflection in the water. But every time he reached for his object of desire his arms passed through the surface and came up empty-handed. In recounting Narcissus's tale, the Roman poet Ovid wrote, "He loves a bodiless dream. . . . Fool, why try to catch a fleeting image, in vain? What you search for is nowhere: turning away, what you love is lost! What you perceive is the shadow of reflected form: nothing of you is in it."[1] Immobilized, unable to relinquish the image he loved, Narcissus wasted away beside the mirror-like pool.

Narcissus's myth is an original cautionary tale of the selfie. As we explored in Chapter 2, the search for the perfect selfie can be a dangerous and even deadly endeavor, leading selfie-takers to perform extreme stunts, or to put resources and risk into going under the surgeon's knife. We hear the echoes of Narcissus's tale perhaps most clearly in Danny Bowman's story in Chapter 2, when in his moment of greatest despair, he decides he would rather die than live without the perfect self-image.

We tend to wag our fingers at the word *narcissism* and associate the concept with selfishness. Although this is indeed one dimension of narcissism that can involve harm and abuse of other people, the myth of Narcissus points to something different. Narcissism is not simply selfishness or gluttony. It is forgetting one's real self and falling in love with an image, a two-dimensional representation, what Ovid calls *a bodiless dream.* "Nothing of you is in it," he says. Narcissism is, at its root, a form of dissociation and amnesia, a confused meandering through a hall of mirrors.

Narcissism as Mistaken Identity

So far we have been considering that our modern-day environmental and mental health crises may be linked and can form a destructive feedback loop that keeps us locked on a path of disaster. In *Returning the Self to Nature: Undoing Our Collective Narcissism and Healing Our Planet,*[2] ecopsychologist Jeanine M. Canty describes connections among narcissism, environmental destruction, and the psychological concept of the "false self." She describes the false self as a protective identity that serves to separate a person from painful mis-attunements experienced in childhood. "At the heart of the false self is a deep sense of loneliness and despair," Canty writes. "It is a feeling of lack wherein even the acquirement of things, experiences, and people does not fulfill us. There is a sense—sometimes conscious, but more often unconscious—that something is missing." Canty says that while the false self is distressing on a personal level, it is nonetheless very good for business in a capitalist system. "By keeping people feeling deeply insecure about their worth, corporations are able to prey upon these insecurities, and the result is that we constantly purchase goods to try to feel better about ourselves. . . . We have become a culture of consumers addicted to our self-images," Canty writes. This aligns with Olivia Sagan's observation, referenced in Chapter 2, that in the neoliberal era, we "buy stuff that makes us feel lonelier so we buy more stuff."

By introducing the concept of a false self Canty implies the existence of a real self, and later introduces an "ecological self" and "Self with a capital S" as more connected, expanded alternatives to a false self. Thus, she roots our present-day environmental crises in a basic confusion of identity. She points to "waking up to something deeper and truer that arises within our most authentic selves as well as in the larger world," as a direction of healing and positive growth.

Canty's views align with certain spiritual teachings, including those of spiritual teacher and author A. H. Almaas, who has written extensively about narcissism and spirituality in *The Point of Existence: Transformations of Narcissism in Self-Realization*.[3] Similar to Canty's description of the false self, Almaas explains narcissism as a condition of "not feeling centered in oneself, or authentic and free enough to be oneself" that can lead to self-conscious, self-centered, defensive and exploitative behavior. He describes narcissism as an experience of self that is "disconnected from its core, from the depths of what it is" and as an "identification with superficial aspects of the self" that "results in a feeling of alienation."

Descriptions of a false self and experiences of alienation might sound dramatic. But in Almaas's view, aside from severe circumstances that lead to serious disorder, narcissism is a pretty normal aspect of human life. Most of us know what it means to feel deeply connected and at ease in ourselves, but if we're honest, we probably also relate to feeling off-center, self-conscious, fake, or selfish at least some of the time. Rather than an anomaly, Almaas identifies this kind of disconnection as a natural outcome of human development that begins with the emergence of a self-concept in childhood. "The 'fall' into narcissism happens as the self forms concepts and structures

97

Selfies and Self-Realization

of concepts, and then identifies with them at the cost of awareness of Being," he writes. "This 'fall' is not something unnatural, tragic or avoidable. In fact, what we have just described is normal ego development." In other words, developing a certain level of narcissism, defined as identifying with self-images and self-concepts (basically, ideas about oneself), is just part of growing up. And although it's normal and perhaps even necessary, this everyday narcissism disconnects us from a state of simply being ourselves in a full, relaxed way.

Almaas explains that in the typical and basically healthy process of developing a distinct human identity, we inevitably lose touch with a more essential, "primordial" identity. Like Narcissus staring into the water, we begin to focus on ideas and *images* of who we are, at the "shadow of reflected form," rather than staying in touch with the direct experience of being ourselves. We forget our real self lying on the bank and instead fixate on the illusion at the surface of the water. In this way, we come to have a false self.

We can have inflated, grandiose ideas about ourselves ("I'm the best"), or negative, even degrading ideas about ourselves ("I'm the worst"), and we can have rather mundane or neutral ideas about ourselves as well. From the perspective offered by Almaas, all of these can be called narcissism. Narcissism is any preoccupation with fixed beliefs about ourselves. These self-concepts form a layer through which we see the world, and whether we regard ourselves as wonderful or horrible, we are filtering reality through a veil of false self and through the image of our reflection in the water.

To illustrate I'll give you a personal example. I grew up as the younger of two children and the youngest in my extended family. I was, in effect, the identified "young one." In my family my nickname was the diminutive "Teenie," as in teeny tiny, a moniker my father used for the whole time he was alive (well into my adult years). I still find it an endearing nickname. There's nothing wrong with it. But I also see how deeply that identity affected me, consciously and unconsciously, throughout my life. Even as I moved out of adolescence, I tended to see older people as the "real" adults, who knew better and had more authority. I pursued my interests and had successes but still felt a bit young and inexperienced, like I needed to be deferential to people who had the "real" answers. And I did not feel completely comfortable showing up in all my robustness and maturity.

This self-image has not only affected ways I experience myself and interact with others but also how I move through the world. Interestingly, I have often found myself participating in programs and activities where I am the youngest person in the room, sometimes by decades. I was likely sincerely but also unconsciously drawn into these situations, where it was easy to become the identifiable "young one" and also the "precocious one," another aspect of this self-image.

This is an illustration of how self-images structure the way we experience ourselves and also shape our life. We believe in these self-images; we see the world through them; we expect, and sometimes demand, that they be reflected back to us. If you really think about it, you will probably recognize times you have gone out of your way to reinforce an identity you have, even a painful one. Just as we can be addicted to the idea that we are wonderful and worthy, pursuing prizes and rewards that tell us as much, we can also be addicted to ideas that we are unlovable, valueless, and not enough. In the same way I have lived out the identity of the "young one," I have repeated patterns of relationship where negative authority dynamics or rejection have played out.

I want to be careful here *not* to endorse ideas of being responsible for all the bad things that happen to us, or proposing that we subconsciously "call in" instances of abuse or trauma. That feels to me more like the responsibilization of the neoliberal self, buying into the idea that we can and do control every aspect of our destiny. Rather, I am pointing to how we get stuck in specific and narrow ideas about our false selves, and we act those out, often without being fully conscious of it. When I am experiencing the world through a "young one" identity, for instance, I am captive to all the conscious and unconscious limitations that identity involves. I am not free to be myself, fully, plainly, and authentically. And if I am expecting other people to reinforce that identity, I am looking at them through my own reflection in the water, through a veil of my false self, rather than seeing them simply and authentically, as they really are.

From Almaas's point of view, narcissism is a simple, albeit profound, "case of mistaken identity." It is not the domain of a few troubled and villainous people, but rather, the common territory of the false self in adulthood. "Most of us are consciously and unconsciously identified with self-concepts which greatly limit our experience of ourselves and the world," Almaas writes. Although I have provided one small example, our personalities contain layers on layers of these concepts and identities, layers on layers of this false self. Some are obvious to us and easily recognizable, and others are buried close to the core of what we take ourselves to be.

From this perspective, narcissism is not something to hide or be ashamed of, but rather something to explore with great curiosity. And we can rest assured that we will find our true self lying there on the shore, if only we know how to look.

Default Mode

In the late 1990s to early 2000s, neuroscientists studying psychological phenomena like visual information processing[4] and working memory[5] started paying attention to what was going on in people's brains when they *weren't* engaged in experimental tasks. They found that when research participants rested between activities, relaxing quietly in the dark interior of the brain scanner, a particular network of brain regions became active. In 2001, neurologist Marcus Raichle and colleagues at the Washington University School of Medicine coined the term *default mode of brain function*[6] and encouraged further investigation of this type of brain activity.

In the years that followed we learned a lot more about the default mode of our human brains. The default network is composed primarily of medial brain regions, meaning areas at the center of our head, including the posterior cingulate cortex (PCC) and the medial prefrontal cortex (mPFC), along with an area toward the outside and back of the head called the angular gyrus, an area of the temporoparietal junction that is involved with language. (See Figure 5.1.) Default mode activity has been linked to "internal mentation," meaning conjuring up mental images and remembering things, as well as planning for the future. And this default brain activity is particularly geared toward content that has to do with the self. Brain areas like the PCC and mPFC are activated when we remember "autobiographical information" as well as when we "reflect on personal preferences, beliefs, values, feelings, abilities and physical attributes."[7] In other words, if we're not otherwise engaged, it seems our brain defaults toward day-dreaming about ideas and images of ourselves, often narrated with self-talk.

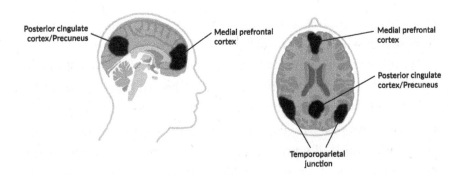

Posterior cingulate cortex/Precuneus

Medial prefrontal cortex

Medial prefrontal cortex

Posterior cingulate cortex/Precuneus

Temporoparietal junction

Figure 5.1 Brain default mode network

Selfies and Self-Realization

Indeed, parts of the brain's default mode network have been more precisely linked with experiences of what is called the *conceptual self* or *narrative self*. The narrative self has been defined in cognitive science as "a more or less coherent self (or self-image) that is constituted with a past and a future in the various stories that we and others tell about ourselves."[8] This narrative self seems to take up a considerable amount of the brain's default activity. And it sounds roughly analogous to the self-concepts and self-images described by Almaas, the self-images Jeanine Canty says we are addicted to, that are a normal part of ego development, yet also contribute to the false self and its sense of alienation. Our discoveries about the default mode network suggest that our mental status quo is indeed our own self-preoccupied story.

The narrative self is a very important and seemingly central mode of experiencing ourselves. But it's not the only possibility.

Narrative Versus Minimal Self

Most of us can recognize a sense of "me" that is based on past experiences as well as a desired future. It is "me," but more specifically, it is the *story* of me. It is the "me" that arises from what happened in my childhood; who my parents, siblings, and friends were; where I grew up; the good and bad events that took place; the good and bad ways I responded. It is also a "me" based on what I am doing in my life now and where I see myself going.

We all have a narrative self, and we may relate to this self differently based on different forms of mind. From our socialized mind, for example, we may feel rather fused with and driven by the stories of our narrative self. The experience is more like one of being *narrated*. For example, if I am living from my "young one" identity in an unquestioned way, I am more or less authored by it. From our self-authoring achiever mind, however, we can start to examine our story, hold it at arm's length, and recognize our ability to shape the plot. We can pick up the pen and become the narrator—writing a story that may be informed by where we've been and who we've known our self to be, but not limited by it. To use the language of modern self-help, we can decide what to give a fuck about, and exactly how many fucks we give. Self-authorship provides the exhilarating opportunity to shape and reshape one's own biography, the vision and goals we pursue, and thus our entire narrative sense of self.

Regardless of the form of mind we're coming from, our narrative self feels important and valuable to us, and it is. It enables us to tell a rich personal story and can imbue our life with meaning. It is not wrong to have a coherent narrative self; to the contrary, it's quite important to have what is sometimes referred to as a "functioning ego" or a "healthy self-image." The condition of schizophrenia, for example, is characterized by disruptions in the narrative self that can cause suffering. "Recovery narratives" that help people experience "an effective sense of self as a social agent and a restored life narrative"[9] have been identified as key to helping people navigate this condition. Schizophrenia has also been found to be associated with differences in functioning of the default mode network of the brain, and the same goes for other challenging conditions like anxiety, depression, and attention deficit.[10] Further, childhood difficulties and traumas can cause painful distortions in the stories we tell about ourselves, and we may benefit from particular forms of therapy to examine and reauthor these narratives. Coaching is also a place that often provides people the opportunity to refine the narrative self.

Although cultivating a healthy narrative self is valid and important, it's possible to have too much of a good thing. If our narrative self is *all* we take ourselves to be, it can become a false self. When we are completely sucked into ideas and images of ourselves, like Narcissus at the water's edge, this preoccupation can be our downfall. Because although our stories about ourselves are valuable, they are not what is most real. Even neuroscientists, like Gregory Burns in his book *The Self Delusion*,[11] acknowledge that the narrative self is a kind of "simulation." Burns writes, "the notion of who we are is a confabulation that stems from the existential need to connect versions of ourselves across time." We don't need to reject or villainize this existential need, but we can also see how the construction of self through story and image is on some level not real; it is false and fake.

Further, in our captivation with these constructed self-images, we can enter the trap of toxic achieverism. From this mindset we attempt to improve and perfect our self-image, and thus our false self. We try to narrate the ultimate story of self and in the neoliberal context, this pursuit becomes an end in itself. We can be consumed with what we believe is both the power and the responsibility to create the perfect narrative, which we take to be the perfect self. In *Pain Generation*,[12] L. Ayu Saraswati points to the two-dimensionality of such a pursuit, writing, "The neoliberal self(ie) should thus be understood *not as a person, but a practice; not as a figure, but figurative; not as a subjectivity, but as a performativity*." She calls the selfie "a shadowy projection," a description that might make us think once again of Narcissus.

The neoliberal self and the selfies it generates are so often a play-acting of self, rather than real, authentic expression. At some level we can't help but feel fake. In the pursuit of the perfect neoliberal narrative self, we reach like Narcissus into the water, hoping to capture the reflection staring back at us, the perfect selfie. We furiously move the pen, but we're writing on water. It's hopeless. The words disappear as soon as we get them down. And we always feel that something is missing, flat, empty. Success is just out of reach. And the cycle continues. In this turbulent neoliberal whirl of self-production and self-consumption, we miss the bigger picture of other people and the planet.

In cognitive science, the narrative self is contrasted with another sense of self that seems to present an important possibility when it

Getting Over Ourselves

comes to seeing through the false self. This experience is called the *minimal self*. Philosopher Shaun Gallagher defines the minimal self as "a consciousness of oneself as an immediate subject of experience, unextended in time."[13] The minimal self is you, here and now, in your direct experience, unmediated by self-images and stories. It is an analogue to what Almaas describes in *The Point of Existence*, writing, "Our experience of ourselves can be transformed from identifying with our mental self-images to having awareness of less contingent, more fundamentally real aspects of the self." He continues, "It is possible to arrive at a place where we can experience ourselves as the actual phenomenon, the actual ontological presence that we are, rather than as ideas and feelings about ourselves. The more we know the truth of who we are, the more we can be authentic and spontaneous, rather than merely living through concepts of ourselves." He is pointing to the minimal self as an entryway into a different kind of experience compared to our default day-to-day self-narration—to one that is clear, vibrant, and full of potential.

Becoming familiar with our minimal self means getting out of our ideas, out of our heads, and into the directly felt experience of being alive. It is the practice of being grounded and centered in the present moment. It is Narcissus breaking the trance, awakening from his bodiless dream, and finding himself shivering with his shirt soaked, pants muddied, knees and elbows sinking into the soft earth of the water's bank.

The True Meaning of Humility

Years ago I was helping facilitate a mindfulness and personal growth retreat that involved slowing down, quieting down, and being present. We stayed at an aging manor in the West Virginia countryside, surrounded by old hardwood forests and sprawling lawns. I remember one afternoon after several hours of silence and contemplation, a participant broke down in tears, recognizing how long it had been since they had walked barefoot across grass.

It's painful to acknowledge our disconnection from direct experience and grounding on the earth. Yet this is what brings us back to our senses and erases our narcissism, our alienation. It opens our hearts and makes us humble. In fact, this connection and grounding is the real meaning of humility.

Much is said about humility, and many of us would like to be known for this quality. We may believe we *should* have this quality. After all, servant leadership and humble leadership conjure much better images than arrogant leadership. We may feel shame about the obvious traces of our narcissism, and attempt to hide them. We might try to shrink down or undermine ourselves, thinking this will make us appear modest. Or we might try replacing some grandiose self-images with some humble ones. But try as we might, despite our good intentions, in the end all we're doing is fiddling around with our self-concepts, two-dimensional representations that aren't real in the first place. So it never seems to work. In truth, we have not yet come back down to earth.

If you look up the root word for *humility* you find *dhghem-*, an ancient Indo-European[14] term that means "earth." Humility isn't about being small or self-effacing. It actually means "of the earth."

Humility shares an origin with the words *humane* and *human*, which means "kind" as well as "earthling." So humility simply means being human, which means having humanity, which means to be of the earth. In fact the *homo* in *homo sapiens* issues from the same root meaning as humility, with *sapien* meaning "to taste," as well as "wise." A true human is the wise one who knows the earth intimately, one who tastes the earth.

Now we see what it really means to come back down to earth and embrace our humanity, what it means to be humble. And we see the connection to Canty's "ecological self," which she says "develops our understanding that we are connected to nature, building our recognition that we feel compassion and even love for nature." Canty attributes the concept of ecological self to Norwegian philosopher Arne Næss and writes, "Næss would also refer to it as the process of self-realization, as it means maturing from the small ego self to a sense of self that is in relationship with the more-than-human natural world."

This brings us to the topic of *self-realization*, which, as we have been alluding to, must be more than some kind of struggle to perfect our self-image and autobiography. Let's look more carefully at what self-realization might mean.

The Richness of Self-Realization

The word *realization* means both "to be fully aware of" and "to bring into concrete existence." So it is about waking up, and it is also about becoming real. Clearly, self-realization moves in a different direction from the false self. It does not seem to be about improving our stories or self-images, hacking life, or engaging in "self-help" in any way. Self-help and self-realization appear to be two different things.

In writing about the ecological self in his essay "Self-Realization: An Ecological Approach to Being in the World,"[15] Arne Næss makes clear that our problem stems from a case of mistaken identity, and that there is a difference between a small self and more expanded Self. "We underestimate ourself. And I emphasize 'self,'" he writes. "We tend to confuse our 'self' with the narrow ego." In explaining the ecological self, which he sees as a greater alternative to this narrow ego, Næss describes an expansion of identity. He sees the potential for the self to encompass all that is, in humanity and in nature. Canty relates this to moving from a small sense of self to a "Self with a capital *S*," which she writes, "extends into all aspects of the seen and unseen world, from all beings on Earth, to all places, to our psyches, to our shared psyches, to our dream world—it reaches everywhere." In a similar vein, Almaas describes, "Full self-realization means the complete realization of the fullness of Being. By fullness of Being, we mean Being in its totality and completeness, including all its dimensions and aspects. . . . This attainment is so profound and radical that no book can do it justice." He talks about the "richness and subtlety" of Being, which we can experience when we know our real identity, our "essential identity." In describing just how big this identity can feel, Almaas writes, "We feel all-loving, all-knowing, and all-powerful. There is a sense of completeness and totality."

These descriptions may sound exciting and perhaps they resonate with some knowing deep inside of you. They may also start to sound a bit esoteric, intimidating, or complicated. Don't worry about it. First, we can see that self-realization is described as an expansion, a wealth of potentiality, a richness. If you consider the root of the word *real*, similar to the way we looked at the word *humility*, we see that *real* comes from *rē-*, which means wealth, as well as *reg-*, which means royalty.[16] So being real—*really* being real—invokes some kind of richness, fullness, and regalness, as Almaas describes.

Based on our exploration thus far, we also know that a critical step in self-realization involves waking up from our self-images and getting in touch with the immediate experience of our minimal self. This simpler, more direct experience of self is paradoxically a doorway to enrichment and expansion. We might call it a *true self.* And all we have to do to get started on this exploration is click our heels and wake up.

In humility, Narcissus gains the opportunity to pull himself away from his self-image and come back to the river bank, back to his senses, back to his direct experience, back to his real self. He is able to know himself as a being of the earth. And the first step in such a realization is quite literally getting his feet on the ground, and being directly in touch with his body.

Anchoring in the Practice of Embodiment

Enlightenment principles encouraged people to think for themselves and construct their own narratives, rather than depending on others' beliefs. This is an important step in the movement from the socialized to the self-authoring mind. The self-authoring mind can continue to examine these narratives, and in some cases rewrite the script.

However, in the hyper-individualistic context of neoliberalism, we have become fixated on perfecting our scripts and self-images. In his book *What About Me? The Struggle for Identity in a Market-Based Society*,[17] clinical psychology professor Paul Verhaeghe explores the connections between neoliberal ideology and mental health, writing, "Around the turn of the millennium, the focus on discovering oneself shifted to perfecting oneself." Verhaeghe says, "First individuals were expected to perfect their minds; soon, they were also expected to perfect their bodies; and last, but certainly not least, they were given the message to perfect themselves in a socio-economic sense. . . . this period has also seen a spectacular rise in certain psychiatric ailments, such as self-mutilation and eating disorders, and depression and personality disorders. The former two are all about the body; the latter two, all about identity." The freedom and responsibility to author our own story has given way to pressures to *perfect* that story, with unhealthy consequences.

Self-authorship can help us improve our life scripts, but the next step is to question the need for any script at all, to make room for improvisation and spontaneity, for aliveness in the moment. In describing the self-questioning mind, Cook-Greuter writes that people become "newly focused with being and feeling rather than with doing and achieving. . . . Meaning making has shifted from an analytical-intellectual to a more organismic, somatic and holistic mode of understanding."[18]

Selfies and Self-Realization

Our body, our soma, is where we know firsthand our aliveness. It's where the action is happening, here and now. It is our port of connection to the earth and, as we'll see in the next section, everything else. When I am in my body, sensing directly, I am not in an idea or image of myself. I am in experience, immediately, here and now. I know myself and feel myself as real in this moment. This is the wisdom of the ocean diver exploring without a wetsuit, the shell-less octopus undulating with the currents, and the direct, living contact between the two.

We find humility by getting our feet directly on the ground, by getting our body directly into the water. We anchor our selves by anchoring in the body. Embodiment is something that can be practiced anytime, anywhere. In my own spiritual journey as a student of the Diamond Approach (a spiritual path originated by A. H. Almaas), I have learned a foundational practice of sensing my arms and legs. This is an incredible support to being present, being here, and acknowledging but not getting lost in ideas or self-images. It supports my ability to remember who I am, not as a concept, but as a direct experience. This has enabled me to see more clearly, think more clearly, to know what I'm feeling, to enjoy the immediate experience of being alive, and to be present. Presence is always right here, right now, direct and palpable.

Practicing embodiment brings us close to life, close to the real experience of ourselves. Embodiment brings us to the cutting edge of what is real, what is actually happening, rather than our *thoughts* about what is happening. Of course, our bodies can also be sources of suffering. First there are all our ideas and concepts about bodies— how our body is supposed to look and function. These ideas can bring a great deal of pain, and it takes time to see through them. Then there are the physical realities of the body. We may be hungry or wounded. We may find aches and pains, chronic tightnesses and numbnesses. And we all are aging, a reality we can't escape that affects our body over time. Still, our body is an anchor into the present moment. We can be with what is, what's here, what's true.

I offer you a practice you can engage with, to support your embodiment. You may need to modify this exercise to meet your particular circumstances. If your body is different or your ability to physically sense parts of your body diverges from what I describe, please consider the spirit of the exercise, then adapt the words to be appropriate to you. You can do this practice standing up, sitting down, laying down, or however you find yourself. And you can make it your own. (Please see "Try This: Being the Body" on the next page.)

*****

As we saw in Chapter 2, selfie has become a millennial stereotype that makes perfect sense in a self-interested, self-centered neoliberal world. We might think we need to "kill" this stereotype (which millennials should be good at doing), but what if we did the opposite, and instead turned toward our narcissism to explore it further? What if narcissism is a crack, an opening we can walk into, to find out what's on the other side?

Arnie Næss says our mistake is identifying with a small sense of self rather than a much more real, expanded reality of who we are. And Almaas writes about the "truth of the grandiose self," explaining that our narcissism actually contains a kernel of reality. Although it takes time to work through our myriad self-concepts and images, seeing through them enables us to glimpse our "essential identity," where "we feel that we are completely wonderful, completely able, and totally indestructible," according to Almaas. This sense of self sounds like a great support for facing the world's current challenges, especially compared to our insecure, self-obsessed, self-perfecting, and isolated neoliberal identities.

Practicing embodiment enables us to experience ourselves directly and move toward a path of self-realization. But it is not a practice to benefit the individual alone. Just as getting out of our self-images

Try This: Being the Body

Start by sensing your feet on the ground. See if you can slow down and feel each toe from the inside and outside. Put all of your awareness there. See if you notice ideas and images of your toe. Then come back to sensing the toe itself. You can do this with each toe if you like. Then move to the ball of your foot, slowing down, taking your time and really sensing into it . . . the arch, then the heel. . . . Be in your feet. Let yourself land. Feel your connection to the floor, or ground, or earth. Now move up into your ankles and the long shin bone on the front of your legs . . . then the flesh of your calf . . . and the back and front of your knees. Sense into your thighs, the back and the front. Sense your hips and hip bones, your butt. Now sense your hands wherever they are resting. Sense each finger . . . your wrist . . . and into your forearm . . . your elbows, and into your upper arms. Now sense your shoulders, all the way across the shoulder girdle. Take some deep breaths and a few moments to sense your whole body, in its totality. Now listen— what do you hear? Letting your eyes relax and also see, look around you. What is here now?

This kind of focused practice can help us sense our body in all types of situations. You can notice being in your body while you're taking a walk, washing the dishes, talking to your child, or writing an email. See what happens when you really inhabit your body in day-to-day activities.

can bring expansion and true humility, getting out of our images of other people helps us to see them more clearly and to be present. Just as we have images of self, we have images of other people that we overlay on the world. We also have collective images of "good" bodies and "bad" bodies, and these ideas have been and continue to be sources of misunderstanding, suffering, and some of our worst human violences. Just as our narcissism is a trance that prevents us from connecting deeply with our selves, practicing embodiment and presence can help break these collective trances and open different potentialities in relationship.

As we know, our culture has become incredibly socially and politically polarized, such that groups of people can hardly walk into the same room without experiencing high blood pressure. We start boxing ourselves and others in before anyone opens their mouths. Although it's necessary to have boundaries around actions such as hate speech and blatant disinformation, we also cancel speakers and ban books because the very existence of the given perspective perturbs something in our own identity. "Left" defines itself against "right," and "right" defines itself against "left," without recognizing that the very contours of these groups are delineated by the other.

This is where the window of self-realization can open into another type of realization, which is the truth of interdependence. As we will explore more deeply in the next chapter, embodiment can support us in recognizing the interwoven, entangled nature of people and planet. The author and activist Sonya Renee Taylor writes about the connection between embodiment and interdependence in her book *The Body Is Not an Apology: The Power of Radical Self-Love.*[19] Radical self-love as Taylor sees it is not simply the development of body positivity, self-acceptance, or self-esteem. It gets to the "root or origin of our relationship to ourselves." And it is "interdependent," Taylor writes, moving beyond the "flimsy ethos of individualism, and operates at both the individual and systemic levels. Radical self-love is about the self because the self is part of the whole. And therefore, radical self-love is the foundation of radical human love. Our relationships with our own bodies inform our relationships with others. . . . Radical self-love invites us to love our bodies in a way that transforms how we understand and accept the bodies of others."

113

Taylor shows us that our own embodiment, how we relate to our bodies and show up in them, shapes how we interact with and affect other bodies. And her practice of radical self-love is one avenue for clearing the veils that obstruct our experience of self and other.

We are entangled with other people, as well as with the planet. This truth is known by the ecological self, the Self with a capital S, that can see itself in and as nature. One contemporary writer who articulates this powerful reality is Sophie Strand. In her book *The Flowering Wand: Rewilding the Sacred Masculine*, Strand offers a retelling of the myth of Narcissus, one in which she allows a reframed version of his fall. Pointing to the confused activity of our disembodied, narrative selves, as well as the urgency of our environmental crises, she writes:

> We have no more time for abstraction. And we have no more time for moralizing. Species collapse every day, bringing down other beings they have been mutualistically involved with for millennia. But, conversely, the emergency of our situation does not call for the manic techno-narcissistic death dance of trying to "fix" the world. It calls for slowing down. For sitting next to the pool. And looking into the water. If we are lucky, we will see ourselves. But not as an isolated subject in the abstracted blank space of phenomenological ontology. Or in the metaverse of digital binaries. We will see that we are in the pool. We are not outside of the life forms that we are damaging and polluting. We are intimately of them. The real narcissism is to believe we can stand apart philosophically, or morally. And yes, let us, like Narcissus fall in love with this more complex reflection. A reflection that contextualizes our being inside of, and dependent on, many other modes of being.[20]

Strand's "manic techno-narcissistic death dance of trying to 'fix' the world" sounds to me like the frenzied, self-referential whirl of the neoliberal narrative self, the self that is always trying to move faster, to improve, to "hack," to solve. As we break the trance of these self-images, ground in the here-and-now and, paradoxically, glimpse a much greater sense of self than before, something else begins to happen. We start to see through the fundamental separateness that has quietly plagued our frantic neoliberal false self. And we begin to recognize the truth of our interconnection, our entanglement with all that is, our interdependence.

Chapter 6

Loneliness and Oneness

Guidepost 2: From Separateness to the Wisdom of Interdependence

I'm inviting you into a thought experiment but first, fair warning—it involves your certain death as you hurtle through outer space.

Imagine one day you are suddenly catapulted from the surface of earth, beyond the confines of the atmosphere, into the black expanse of the cosmos. How long will you live? In the absence of oxygen, it will be only 90 seconds until you asphyxiate. I'm sorry, but you are dead.

Now consider that at the moment of your unfortunate departure, you happen to be wearing an air tank and breathing apparatus. This buys you precious time, but not much. Even if you could carry an infinite supply of oxygen, without the protective properties of the atmosphere you have enjoyed close to earth's surface, your body will boil, burn, or freeze quite quickly, depending on where you are positioned in space. Unfortunately, you are dead.

But wait, against all odds, perhaps you are wearing not only breathing equipment but also a carefully engineered spacesuit at the time of launch. Breathing easily, shielded from heat, cold, and space debris by your high-tech suit, you nonetheless have little time to live. With a body composed of a whopping 60 to 70% water, you rapidly grow thirsty and dehydrated. Within about three days, you are dead.

And even if you lift off with all of the resources I've described, along with an unending water source within your suit, you don't have long to live in space. You might last one or two months without food, but not more than three. Without the nutrients from plants or other animals you enjoyed on earth, your cells run out of fuel and energy. Your body fails. You are dead.

The idea of the "ecological self" can seem abstract or metaphorical, but it is in fact practical and real. As human beings we are of the earth, quite literally. We are bodily systems entangled within other, larger ecological systems, without which we do not exist. Our thought experiment shows us that although we can create some artificial conditions that prolong our ability to survive apart from the earth, our dependence on our planet is profound—we cannot and do not live in a vacuum. As human bodies, we really are humble earthlings. And beyond these physical contingencies, as we'll explore in this chapter, even our emotions, thoughts, and behaviors are entangled with greater forces. Contrary to our typical way of thinking, it is not the ecological self that is a fantasy. It is the separate, solitary self that is an invention.

In this chapter we'll consider the truth of interdependence, not as a new age concept but as a basic reality. Physically, emotionally, socially, and spiritually, we are not isolated entities bouncing off one another here and there. We are interwoven, interpenetrating phenomena that fundamentally depend on one another and the larger whole.

Physical Interdependence: Bodies of Multitudes

In early 2023 Brazilian geologists made what they called a "terrifying" discovery on Trindade Island, nearly 700 miles off their country's coast. They found "plastic rocks," meaning rocks composed of plastic debris, mainly from fishing nets that have melted in the heat and melded with natural material. Trindade Island is a remote, largely uninhabited conservation area where members of the Brazilian navy protect endangered green sea turtles, yet synthetic materials are now entangled with its shores. "We talk so much about the Anthropocene, and this is it," said geologist Fernanda Avelar Santos, noting that plastic is becoming "preserved in earth's geological records."[1]

It's easy to think of pollution as a one-way street, to imagine humans as the perpetrators of pollution and earth as the vulnerable recipient. But this plays into the mirage of the separate self. Just as plastic rocks litter earth's coasts, we know that plastic entangles our own human bodies. In addition to melting fishing nets, a whole range of plastics end up in the oceans and other waterways, gradually breaking down into tiny particles called microplastics.[2] When plastic materials degrade to a small enough size, they can be inhaled and ingested by animals including humans.

A 2019 review by the World Wildlife Foundation reported that plastic fibers are found in over 94% of US drinking water,[3] and they are just as ubiquitous in bottled water as tap water.[4] By some estimates, you and I are ingesting the equivalent of one plastic credit card every week.[5] Studies have now found trace plastics in human feces,[6] breastmilk,[7] organs such as the liver,[8] and in our blood.[9] Although the health effects of microplastics are not yet well understood, previous research on particles from air pollution suggests these plastic granules may enter our cells, causing inflammation and disease.[10]

Similarly, we have discovered that "forever chemicals" that leak into the ground also inevitably leak into our bodies. Substances known as PFAS that have been used on everything from nonstick pans to dental floss are detected in water, air, fish, soil,[11] and also the blood of most of the US population.[12] We still have a lot to learn about the effects of PFAS, but current studies point to a host of potential consequences including low birth weight and developmental delays in children, increased risk of certain cancers, and reduced vaccine response.[13]

The chemical stability of PFAS and their accumulation in the environment have been compared to DDT,[14] the synthetic insecticide widely used in the 1940s and 1950s that was later banned from agricultural use due to its harmful properties. DDT was found to cause eggshell thinning in birds, leading to near-destruction of bird populations including the bald eagle, and it is a known disrupter of hormone activity in humans. Based on the ubiquity and endurance of DDT, scientists state, "No living organism may be considered DDT-free."[15] Clearly that includes you and me. Disturbingly, researchers have suggested that DDT exposure can affect human reproductive cells and transmit its health effects across multiple generations. A 2021 study found that levels of DDT in a grandmother's blood serum was related to her *granddaughter's* early menstruation and obesity, both of which are outcomes associated with DDT exposure.[16]

All of this reflects the reality that we are not only producers, users, and dumpers of plastic material and forever chemicals. We are imbibers of them. We are not only the polluters, but the polluted. Our assault on the environment is an assault on our own physical selves.

Our human bodies are symbiotic, communal with our surroundings. As shown in the thought experiment that opens this chapter, we are embedded within greater systems of air, water, and food on which we are dependent, and from which we cannot truly extract ourselves. Ecopsychologist Theodore Roszak writes, "As nature around us unfolds to reveal level upon level of structured complexity, we are coming to see that we inhabit a densely connected ecological universe where nothing is 'nothing but' a simple, disconnected isolated thing."[17] Our physical interdependence is obvious yet invisible, expansive while microscopic.

Indeed, just as we are contaminated with synthetic materials that may cause harm, we know we are contaminated and interpenetrated with a whole host of natural phenomena. Some of these threaten our bodily system with forms of organic attack and pollution, and others are essential to maintaining our health. Mites known as demodex (basically, microscopic spiders) almost certainly live in the pores of your face right now.[18] A "friendly fungus" called *Pichia* is keeping other fungi inside your mouth in check.[19] And as we have discovered through an explosion of recent research on the human microbiome, each of us is home to between 10 and 100 trillion single-celled organisms representing thousands of different species,[20] mainly bacteria in our gut, with whom we live symbiotically.

The microbes in our bodies lend us an incredible level of genetic diversity. Left on our own, human beings are nearly genetically identical: we share 99.9% of genetic material from one person to the next, drawing from a pool of just 22,000 unique human genes. Even our closest cousins, chimpanzees, are 99% genetically overlapping with humans.[21] The gut microbiome, however, is characterized by more than three million genes that can vary by as much as 90% between individuals,[22] a pattern that runs directly counter to the similarity of our human genome. And astonishingly, we are just as much "bacterial" beings as we are "human" beings: although microbes are relatively small and take up only a few pounds of body weight, our bodies are composed of a 1:1 ratio of human cells to microbes.[23]

These tiny creatures cover our skin, coat our digestive and urinary tracts as well as our genitals, and inhabit our respiratory system. They depend on our bodies as environments where they can survive and thrive. Equally, we depend on them for health and survival. Although we may think of our bodies as relatively independent and self-sufficient, the truth is that we don't have everything we need to break down and absorb nutrients from our food. We are dependent on our microbiota for help. The microbes in our gut provide critical enzymes to aid digestion, while also producing vitamins and anti-inflammatories that our human bodies can't produce on their own.[24]

121

Science shows us that microbial and human life is delicately intertwined. Our real self *is* our microbial self. It is our ecological self. As biological beings we are interdependent with the oceans, trees, animals, and the tiny organisms inhabiting our bodies. We are also porous and extended into the world. Ed Yong writes in *I Contain Multitudes: The Microbes Within Us and a Grander View of Life*, "Every time we touch an object, we leave a microbial imprint upon it. Every time we walk, talk, scratch, shuffle, or sneeze, we cast a personalized cloud of microbes into space. Every person aerosolizes around 37 million bacteria per hour. This means that our microbiome isn't confined to our bodies. It perpetually reaches into our environment."[25] Toward the close of his book he states, "Every part of the world is full of partnerships that have been playing themselves out for hundreds of millions of years, and that have affected all the flora and fauna we know."

These partnerships are present within our body and as Yong describes, also in our immediate surround. In his book *Never Home Alone* Rob Dunn writes, "The tap water that flows into your house . . . is alive,"[26] replete with everything from benign bacteria to, in some cases, tiny shrimp. Although we may be bothered by the thought of ingesting or bathing in microorganisms from tap water, Dunn's overarching message is that these relationships are more often healthy than harmful. It is actually our myopic focus on sterilization that get us into trouble. "Our increasing human efforts to kill the life in homes have unintended and yet very predictable consequences," he writes. "The use of pesticides and antimicrobials, along with ongoing attempts to seal off homes from the rest of the world, tends to kill off and exclude beneficial species that are also susceptible to such assaults." For example, Dunn has found that treating water with chlorine kills certain bacteria, but leaves chlorine-tolerant strains like mycobacteria to thrive, putting some humans at risk of infection.

Dunn also describes research on the "biodiversity hypothesis," a theory that posits a strong relationship between ecological and human health. The hypothesis was originally formulated by a team of Finnish researchers, one of whom had noticed that increasing chronic inflammation in humans seemed to coincide with declines in the health of the butterflies he studied. This observation led ecologist Ilkka Hanski to write a 2009 paper called "Allergy Is Rare Where Butterflies Flourish in a Biodiverse Environment."[27] In the biodiversity hypothesis, Hanski proposed that when people are deprived of contact with a variety of organisms in natural environments, their microbiota become imbalanced, leading to immune disturbances and risk of disease.[28]

Hanski teamed up with epidemiologist Tari Haahtela and microbiologist Leena von Hertzen to test the hypothesis by measuring relationships among exposure to plant diversity, the presence of bacteria, and allergies in teenagers. They found that teens living amidst more diverse plants had more diverse bacteria on their skin, which was in turn related to less likelihood of atopy, another word for the exaggerated immune response that characterizes an allergy. The team concluded, "the present results demonstrate that biodiversity can be surprisingly strongly associated with atopy, a common immune dysfunction of the modern era."[29] In other words, the less we are exposed to diverse natural environments, the less diverse are the microbes that inhabit our body, and this can lead to increased health problems such as allergies.

Indeed, multiple studies have shown that children living on rural farms are at lower risk for asthma and allergies than their urban counterparts. This and other research leads scientists to identify a clear "association between the rise of allergic diseases and increasingly modern Westernized lifestyles, which are characterized by increased urbanization, time spent indoors, and antibiotic usage."[30]

The science suggests that shrinking back from our interdependent selves, our ecological selves, has real implications for well-being. When we imagine ourselves as separate entities with limited connection to the natural world, when we attempt to cut ourselves off, disinfect our lives, and enclose our bodies in sterile environments, we end up weak and sick. No wonder our modern lives are full of malaise.

Moreover, our bodily interdependence reaches beyond the physical, directly into the realm of emotional and mental health. The microbes that allow us to digest food have intricate connections with our nervous systems, communicating from our intestines to our brains along what has been dubbed the *gut-brain axis* (Figure 6.1). This axis depends on the vagus nerve, the longest nerve to emerge directly from the brain. The vagus nerve runs down the body like a superhighway, transferring information between the brain and other areas including neck, heart, stomach, and intestines. The gut-brain axis also involves the "enteric nervous system" (ENS), a network of

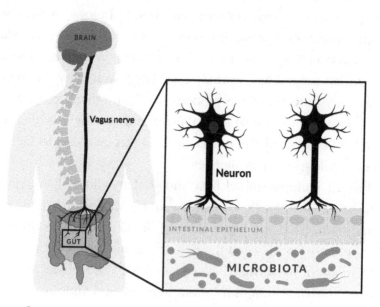

Figure 6.1   Gut-brain axis

over 100 million nerve cells that line the entire digestive tract. The ENS is so extensive it is sometimes called the "brain in your gut." We are only beginning to study the implications of this extended nervous system.

The gut-brain axis facilitates "crosstalk"[31] between our brain and the activity in our gut. This means that psychological distress can disrupt what goes on with digestion (as most of us have experienced through a "knot" or "butterflies" in the stomach); conversely, disruptions in our gut health, including our microbiome, can affect mental health. Experiments with animals show that gut inflammation from bacterial infection is accompanied by anxious behaviors. When infected animals are treated with probiotics, also known as "good bacteria," the anxious behaviors subside.[32] As for humans, there is a growing body of evidence that probiotics can assist in alleviating symptoms of depression.[33] In one study, people diagnosed with major depressive disorder had significantly decreased depression symptoms after eight weeks of taking a probiotic containing *Lactobacillus* and *Bifidobacterium*, compared to peers who were given a placebo pill. They also showed signs of improved metabolism and reduced inflammation.[34] We are, as Rob Dunn says, "never home alone," and the company we keep in our gut microbiome may be one important factor in assuaging discontent and loneliness.

Of course, gut bacteria are only one source of interdependence when it comes to our psychological health. As we'll see in the next section, just as our physical body is embedded and extended into a greater oneness, so too is our psychological experience.

Psychological Interdependence: The Resonant Brain

The adult human brain is a roughly three-pound organ that extends from the head into the entire body in an intricate network of nerves.

Our brains are constantly processing and responding to information in the environment. The brain is electrical and chemical, capable of coordination and computation. Our brains are also organs of resonance and synchrony with our wider surround.

Brain synchrony is important from the very outset of our lives, when we are born helpless and dependent on our first caregivers. We need attuned interaction to survive and thrive. The pediatrician D. W. Winnicott once exclaimed "There's no such thing as an infant!"[35] Winnicott, well-known for his contributions to psychology in the mid-1900s, originated the idea of a "holding environment," originally a reference to a mother's (or parent's) attuned holding of her child, that was later extended to describe the space a skilled psychotherapist can hold for a client. Winnicott is also responsible for writing at length about the "true self" and "false self." Canty's descriptions of the false self referenced in Chapter 5 are based in part on his work.

When Winnicott denied the existence of the infant, he was pointing to the fact that wherever he found a baby, he also found a care giver. Winnicott amended his statement to say, "without maternal care there would be no infant,"[36] challenging the idea that a baby could really be considered apart from the context of its primary relationships.

Winnicott's statement was corroborated by mid-1900s observations of infants who lost their familial caregivers and ended up in orphanages. Psychoanalyst René Spitz studied babies who were physically well cared for with nutritious food, proper bathing, and medical care, but were deprived of close one-to-one relationships. In 1947 he created a heartbreaking silent film called *Grief, A Peril in Infancy*[37] that shows these lonely children lying passively, rocking themselves in distress, staring perplexedly at their own hands, and grabbing at the empty air. Another of Spitz's films[38] states, "In 37.3% of the cases observed, the progressive deterioration of the total personality led eventually to marasmus [malnutrition and weight loss] and death by the second year of life." In other words, in nearly 40% of the cases in which the infant was physically cared for but had little human interaction, the baby wasted away and died. Without a loving holding environment, there eventually was in fact no infant.

More recent research has explored differences in brain structure and activity depending on a child's access to close caregiving. When children are raised in institutions where one-to-one attention is limited, their brains just don't grow as much. They have smaller heads and brains than those raised at home, and their brains function differently than family-raised children in a variety of ways.[39]

Extreme examples emerged from Romania in the 1990s, where many children had been orphaned in the wake of pro-population growth policies such as taxation of childless adults. Encouraged to have children but struggling to support them, it was common for parents to put babies into state institutions where individualized attention was scarce at best, and conditions were inhumane at worst. The Bucharest Early Intervention Project starting in the 2000s allowed researchers to study the impact of moving children from these overwhelmed orphanages into high-quality foster care. A baby who was accustomed to mechanical handling by busy nurses and eating meals from a bottle propped against the bars of a crib,[40] entered an environment of close and ongoing interaction with foster parents. Researchers found that for foster children, the white matter of the brain that connects one region to another appeared to increase and catch up to the brains of their never-institutionalized peers. Their default mode brain activity also began to look more like their family-raised peers, shifting from duller, seemingly suppressed levels of activity to a more typically active default mode.

All of this reinforces our understanding that brain development is not only a physical process. It is a deeply relational, contextual process. These kinds of observations have led to a whole field of "interpersonal neurobiology," pioneered by psychiatrist and neuroscientist Daniel Siegel, who states, "the mind develops at the interface between human relationships and the unfolding structure of the brain."[41] As youngsters our bodies and brains are nourished not only by the food we eat and physical tending we receive, but the relationships and social environment in which we are held. And we cannot truly extract ourselves from this interdependence.

Scientists point to the importance of early "serve and return" interactions between babies and their caregivers, where a child's movements, facial expressions, and noises are responded to in kind.[42] Serve and return, as the name implies, is mutual and reciprocal. Different behaviors from a baby elicit different responses from a caregiver, and the caregiver's actions influence the baby's behaviors. Serve and return interactions are part of what is called *synchrony*, a "dynamic and reciprocal adaptation of . . . behaviors between interactive partners."[43] Synchrony has been shown to be critical for child development, with greater levels of synchrony between parents and children relating to better functioning of the heart and vagus nerve in infancy,[44] higher scores on measures of toddler IQ,[45] and smoother adjustment to school.[46]

Brain scanning is now showing us how synchrony works within and between our nervous systems. Researchers have developed technologies for "hyperscanning," meaning they can measure the brain activity of two or more people at the same time and see whether this activity is related. Scientists have found that the day after a baby is born, the pain that registers in their brain during a blood draw synchronizes with their mother's brain activity, with signals from the baby's brain seeming to pull the mother's brain into this resonance.[47]

Studies with older children have shown that brain synchrony does not occur when playing a game with a stranger or during a competitive game with a parent. However, when a child plays a cooperative game with a parent, areas of the brain's dorsolateral prefrontal cortex begin to synch between parent and child. The dorsolateral prefrontal cortex, an area of the outermost layer of our brain that is located toward the front of the head, is associated with "executive functions" that include our ability to plan, make decisions, and regulate our emotions (dorsolateral prefrontal cortex is adjacent to but distinct from the medial prefrontal cortex, the brain area involved in the default mode network described in Chapter 5). Researchers found that not only does the dorsolateral prefrontal cortex synch between parent and child during a cooperative game but also the degree of synchrony predicts their cooperative behavior, and also explains the relationship between the parent and child's emotional regulation. The scientists conclude, "brain-to-brain synchrony may represent an underlying neural mechanism of the emotional connection between parent and child," and may also reflect the child's development of emotion regulation.[48] A parent's stress has been shown to reduce this kind of prefrontal brain synchrony with a child.[49]

Brain synchrony is important between adults, too. Similar to parents and their children, romantic partners synchronize an area of prefrontal cortex during a cooperative game, and the better their synchronization, the better they perform the task. Strangers don't demonstrate this brain synchrony, nor can they perform the cooperative task as well as couples.[50] And there is evidence that this type of synchrony may actually lead to romantic partnerships in the first place—in another study that measured brain activity during speed dating (with participants who were willing to speed date while wearing a funny-looking brain-reading cap), scientists found that synchronization of the prefrontal cortex predicted whether a person wanted to go on a second date.[51] In other words, brain synchrony may be an important factor in choosing a life partner.

Brain synchrony is now thought to be a way we can help change one another's brains for the better. Synchrony occurs during psychotherapy between therapist and client, and experienced therapists are better than brand-new therapists at developing this resonance. For

129

experienced practitioners, stronger brain synchrony translates into a stronger therapeutic relationship, according to the client. These findings, along with other research on brain synchrony, have led scientists to propose a model of "inter-brain plasticity" in psychotherapy. They suspect that when a client repeatedly experiences strong synchrony with their psychotherapist, this sets them up to have better synchrony with others and improved relationships outside the therapist's office.[52]

Our resonant brains may open doors for healing and positive change, but they can also get us into trouble. Neuroscientists have found that although strong synchrony between brains is tied to stronger relationships, more efficient cooperation, and even therapeutic efficacy, it can also pull us toward riskier behavior and extremism. In one study, brain researchers found that stronger brain synchrony among groups of three was related to bigger swings in the riskiness of their collective decision-making. And risky group decisions were characterized by less activity in those areas of the prefrontal cortex associated with higher-order decision-making.[53] Other brains can draw us into healthy attunement, but it seems they can also lull us into dangerous groupthink. So, be careful whom you synch with.

Another study showed that brain synchrony is related to political polarization—while watching a political debate, self-identified conservatives synched with the brains of conservatives whereas liberals synched with liberals. However, the extent of this polarized brain activity was determined by a character trait that had nothing to do with political affiliation: the degree to which a person could tolerate uncertainty. Those who were less tolerant of uncertainty tended toward more polarization and more in-group synchrony, regardless of whether they were liberal or conservative.[54] We discuss tolerance of uncertainty more extensively in Chapter 8.

The research on between-brain synchrony suggests that psychological experience is related to our brains, but it is not just in our heads. Emotions have long been considered "contagious," with scientists defining emotional contagion as "the tendency to automatically mimic and synchronize expressions, vocalizations, postures, and movements with those of another person's and, consequently, to converge emotionally."[55] The contagiousness of emotions means we are influenced in an ongoing way by the mood of our surround. In her book *Between Us: How Cultures Create Emotions*, social psychologist Batja Mesquita describes how emotions are just as much interdependent as they are personal, shaped by the cultural cues and demands we experience. "The fabric of our emotions is woven by interactions with others," Mesquita writes.[56]

Psychological experience is transmitted in relationships and culture—and it can travel quite literally in the air. An entire body of research on "emotional chemosignals" looks at how body odors can transfer mood and emotion from one person to another. Believe it or not, there is evidence that smelling the sweat of someone experiencing fear can make you feel more afraid, and the sweat of a happy person can make you happier.[57] "Air can be happy or fearful or angry in the sense that people have those experiences and leave chemicals in the air with that information," writes Jeannette Haviland-Jones and her research team. "People are always part of the ecology in an invisible way and emotions in the air become part of us every time we breathe."[58]

Even more surprising, psychological states waft to us directly from the environment. Smelling baby powder can help an infant settle and focus,[59] and the fragrance of flowers can stimulate positive emotions and prosocial behavior in adults.[60] Further, environmental dysregulation shows up in our human psyches and behaviors. Researchers have found that air pollution is related to more negative emotion and decreased trust between people.[61] There is also evidence that air pollution increases risk for dementia.[62] Coming full circle from the previous section on physical interdependence, we

131

Loneliness and Oneness

now have plenty of evidence that our biological health is intertwined with our mental health, which is intertwined with other people in our social and cultural surround, which is intertwined with the health of the environment.

Science continues lending support to Einstein's statement that "a human being is a part of the whole, called by us 'Universe,' a part limited in time and space. He experiences himself, his thoughts and feelings as something separated from the rest—a kind of optical delusion of his consciousness."[63] Although we can conceptualize ourselves as isolated particles, we are in many ways more like waves; although we may feel lonely at times and disconnected, the reality is that we are like drops of water in an expansive sea of physical and psychological phenomena.

If this sounds less like something out of a science lab and more like something from a place or worship or spiritual text, you are not off the mark. Modern science is teeming with evidence of interconnection, but the interweaving and oneness of all things is a theme that has been explored for millennia, running strongly through sources of ancient wisdom.

Spiritual Interdependence: The Garment of Destiny

In 2015 Pope Francis shared a letter "to every single person in the world"[64] entitled *Laudato Si', On Care for Our Common Home*. In one section, after quoting biblical stories he writes, "These ancient stories, full of symbolism, bear witness to a conviction which we today share, that everything is interconnected, and that genuine care for our own lives and our relationships with nature is inseparable from fraternity, justice and faithfulness to others." In a closing prayer, Pope Francis says, "Give us the grace to feel profoundly joined to everything that is."

In the anthology *The Oneness Hypothesis: Beyond the Boundary of Self*,[65] philosopher Owen Flanagan references this letter from Pope Francis. He also writes, "Hinduism, Buddhism, Jainism, Daoism, and neo-Confucianism endorse wide compassion and selflessness for reasons of a noninstrumental kind. And the philosophies of indigenous people in the Americas, Africa, and Oceana emphasize the intrinsic significance of harmonious relations with all between heaven and earth."

Oneness permeates a variety of spiritual traditions from around the world and throughout human history. There are, of course, important distinctions and nuances from one tradition to the next, but the truth of interdependence echoes across diverse cultural and spiritual worlds. In his book *Native Science: Natural Laws of Interdependence*, professor Gregory Cajete writes, "The Native American paradigm is comprised of and includes ideas of constant motion and flux, existence consisting of energy waves, interrelationships, all things being animate, space/place, renewal, and all things being imbued with spirit. . . . The constant flux notion results in a 'spider web' network of relationships. In other words, everything is interrelated."[66] From the other side of the world, the ancient Confucian *I Ching* emphasized the "unity of heaven and humanity."[67] Interdependence is a basic principle in certain forms of Buddhism: Zen monk Thich Nhat Hanh wrote, "If a teaching is not in accord with Interdependent Co-arising, it is not a teaching of the Buddha"[68] and the Dalai Lama of Tibet has written about the "all-pervasive nature of interdependence."[69] Rabbi David Hartman wrote, "The idea that divine perfection is a relational category involving interdependence begins in the biblical story of creation."[70] And the seventh principle of Unitarian Universalism, a religion emerging from Christianity, is "Respect for the interdependent web of all existence of which we are a part."[71] Unity is a fundamental principle of Islam, with the Qur'an teaching that all human beings were created from a single soul.[72]

133

The spiritual implications of interdependence can translate into moral and practical matters. The Reverend Doctor Martin Luther King Jr. famously wrote in his "Letter from Birmingham Jail," "Injustice anywhere is a threat to justice everywhere. We are caught in an inescapable network of mutuality, tied in a single garment of destiny. Whatever affects one directly affects all indirectly."[73] He also said, "For some strange reason I can never be what I ought to be until you are what you ought to be. And you can never be what you ought to be until I am what I ought to be—this is the interrelated structure of reality."[74] I'm always amazed that King made these statements when he was only in his mid-30s.

King is telling us that interdependence is not just a metaphysical or philosophical issue. It is a practical issue. Interdependence means we are interwoven with one another, and what one does has a ripple across a single garment of destiny. What we do matters. Who we are matters. This means that what we give our energy to, and the partnerships we invest ourselves in are matters of critical importance, and deserve our conscious reflection.

Anchoring in the Practice of Connection

During the Enlightenment, intellectual pioneers challenged Westerners to separate from the crowd, to stand apart and think independently. This is an important step in moving from the socialized to self-authoring mind. But over the course of hundreds of years, this human separateness has become exaggerated in the hyper-individualized, hyper-privatized context of neoliberalism. It has led us to distorted dynamics of responsibility. It has exacerbated isolation and loneliness. Our hyper-individualism needs to be questioned and seen through in its false forms. George Monbiot writes in his *Guardian* article "Neoliberalism Is Creating Loneliness. That's Wrenching Society Apart," "Why are we engaging in this world-eating, self-consuming frenzy of environmental destruction and social dislocation, if all it produces is unbearable pain? . . . This does not require a policy response. It requires something much bigger: the reappraisal of an entire worldview. Of all the fantasies human beings entertain, the idea that we can go it alone is the most absurd and perhaps the most dangerous."[75]

Cook-Greuter observes that moving into the post-conventional, transforming worldview opens up a systems view of reality, where interdependence and the importance of context are recognized. We can engage in a practice of observing interconnection in our own lives.

Try This: Living Connection

We've seen in this chapter that we are constantly connected with and embedded within our physical, psychological, and spiritual environments. This practice invites you into close observation of interdependence. In any expression of this practice, it helps to begin by anchoring in embodiment as introduced in the previous chapter. Bring your attention here and now, so you can notice the impact of various interconnections.

You can begin with the simple mindfulness practice of noticing the breath. Observe breath flowing into and out of your body. Sense the air entering your nose or mouth, filling your lungs, then leaving your lungs, your entire body moving and expanding, then emptying and contracting with the breath. Feel the air all around you, outside and inside the body. Take your time. What is the impact of noticing the breath?

If it feels right you can bring this practice to eating—notice what it's like to take in food and water. You can also practice in your interactions with other people. Slow down and notice what it's like

---

to relate with another person. You might start with someone familiar to you, someone you interact with day-to-day. Notice how your experience is affected by that person's presence, whether positive and uplifting, challenging, neutral, or anything in between. What does this show you about interdependence? Notice your state when you are with people you know less well or when you find yourself in a crowd. Pay attention to how your own experience changes in different social situations.

Finally, you can observe how different environments affect your thinking, your emotions, and sensations. It can be as simple as noticing what it's like to be in your bedroom, then your kitchen. Or you can pay attention to moving from inside to outside. If possible, spend time in nature, whether a city park or deep in a forest. Notice the impact of water, trees, and animals. How does this shape your experience, your sense of self?

In any expression of this practice, pay attention to whether there is a sense of separateness. Where is that separateness coming from? Is it a sensation, feeling, a thought, a belief?

Now notice, is there a sense of connection or interdependence? Where is that connection coming from?

In Chapter 2 we looked at the separateness and isolation that plagues the neoliberal identity, which has created an entire "lonely generation." But as we can see, this hyper-individualism is based on a misunderstanding. From biology, to psychology, to spirituality, it's clear that we contain multitudes, that we are never home alone, that we are resonant, permeable beings constantly caught up in connections and partnerships of all kinds. Each person functions as a single node in a vast web. We can't escape this web, because it is not a trap. Our connection is also what delineates us, sustains us, and gives rise to who we are. If we can recognize ourselves within this web, there doesn't need to be a struggle because this web is also a kind of safety net. We can lean back and relax into the fundamental support of oneness.

When Einstein described human separateness as a "delusion of consciousness," he continued, "This delusion is a kind of prison for us, restricting us to our personal desires and to affection for a few persons nearest to us. Our task must be to free ourselves from this prison by widening our circle of compassion to embrace all living creatures and the whole of nature in its beauty."[76] Interconnection can free us from this prison and help us relax, but it requires more than our minds. As Einstein says, we need compassion. We need our heart. This is the topic we'll explore in the next chapter.

Chapter 7

Burnout and Wholeheartedness
Guidepost 3: From Rationality to the Wisdom of Vulnerability

The first time I heard a counterintuitive remedy for burnout I was lying in a sleeping bag on the floor of a tent, staring into the darkness of the canopy. My tent mate was a new friend, a woman who had offered lodging in advance but who I'd just met that day at a friend's wedding. We chatted as we settled in to rest. I was in my 20s at the time and she was a bit older, moving into a second phase of her career. Having recently completed training as a therapist, she was happy about embarking on a new and different vocation.

I, however, was feeling a bit lost. I was working in brain science, a long-held dream of mine that I'd been able to realize after college. I worked at a top-notch institute, on interesting projects, with good people. But something within me wasn't right. When I looked at myself in the mirror I was pale and depleted, like a shadow of what I knew as the real me. I had lost my oomph. I was burning out.

"Have you ever heard that the solution to burnout isn't rest?" my companion asked, her question filling the darkened space. "It's wholeheartedness." Her words stayed with me as I drifted off to sleep.

It would be some time before I located the original source of my friend's reference, a passage in David Whyte's book *Crossing the Unknown Sea: Work as a Pilgrimage of Identity*. Whyte describes that before devoting himself fully to writing, he held a job at a nonprofit in Washington state. The organization was involved in good work, but Whyte had become, in his own words, "incredibly busy." "My arrogance took the form of busyness," he writes, seeming to give voice to the achiever mind. "I had lots of meetings, courses to run, people to accommodate, budgets to meet. . . . Speed was my essence and, I thought, my true savior."[1]

One evening, feeling particularly burned out and deflated, Whyte met with another David, an Austrian monk with whom he enjoyed poetry and wine. He asked Brother David to talk about exhaustion. Here, Brother David gives us the line: "You know that the antidote to exhaustion is not necessarily rest? The antidote to exhaustion is *wholeheartedness*."

To Brother David, wholeheartedness meant finding work to which one could commit with passion. It also had to do with courage. "The word *courage* in English comes from the old French word *coeur*, heart," he told David Whyte. "You must do something heartfelt, and you must do it soon."

When Your Heart's Not in It

Burnout involves weariness, but that is not its defining feature. Talk to someone who has just finished running a marathon and they will say they are tired. They will not say they're experiencing burnout. Burnout occurs when something is off at the core and has been for a while, when a person is not necessarily dealing with physical exhaustion, but rather "emotional exhaustion." Burnout indicates that a person is losing heart.

The 1990s were declared the "decade of the brain" in the United States, and we seem to be living in this age still. With the development of brain imaging technologies and the rapid advancement of neuroscience, we are understandably fascinated with the complex organ inside our heads. Meanwhile, the heart has become more of a second-class citizen. This is a shift from ancient times, when some cultures revered the heart as the most sacred organ of the body. The ancient Egyptians, for example, saw the heart as the seat of intelligence, personality, memory, emotions, and wisdom. According to their belief system, when a person died their heart was placed on a scale to be weighed against the feather of Maat, the goddess of truth. A heavy heart, indicating a lack of gratitude and harmony in one's life, meant banishment from the afterlife and instant destruction.[2]

Aristotle was also partial to the heart, identifying it as the seat of the soul and the human intellect.[3] But over the centuries more attention was paid to the brain, and by the time of the Enlightenment Descartes was writing, "I have plainly found out that that part of the body wherein the soul immediately exercises her function is not a jot of the heart."[4] He was fascinated instead by the brain's pineal gland. Although Descartes's specific focus lost support in the modern age, our attention has remained fixated on the brain when it comes to understanding human nature.

Poetically, however, we have never abandoned the supreme status of the heart. Even after centuries of interest, no one talks about the brain's yearning, or the post-breakup pain of a broken mind. Love songs have little use for neuroscience. As we'll see, there may be good reason for this, as the heart has secrets for us still.

In Chapter 6 we talked about the enteric nervous system, the millions of neurons that create a "brain in the gut." The heart also has a "little brain." Officially called the *intrinsic cardiac nervous system*, the heart's brain is smaller than the gut's, composed of only about 40,000 neurons. Like the brain in the gut, the cardiac nervous system uses the vagus nerve to crosstalk with the brain, sending more information up to the brain than it receives.[5]

The implications of this little brain in the heart, along with the heart-brain axis in general, are not fully understood, especially when it comes to emotions and personality. The most startling suggestions about the brain in the heart come from research on personality changes in heart transplant patients, some of whom notice significant differences in their preferences, emotions, identity, and memories following surgery.[6] For example, a woman who identifies as gay receives a heart transplant from a woman whose family described her as "man-crazy." The recipient reports feeling as if she received a "gender transplant" and becomes engaged to a man. A five-year-old heart recipient decides to name his organ donor "Timmy" and says "He got hurt bad when he fell down." He also develops an aversion to the Power Rangers. Unbeknownst to the young recipient, the donor was a boy who died when he fell from a window while reaching for a Power Rangers toy, and his family did indeed call him "Tim."[7] In her book *A Change of Heart*, Claire Sylvia describes developing an unfamiliar craving for chicken nuggets after receiving a heart and lung transplant, to the extent that she drives to KFC as soon as she can leave the hospital. She later discovers this was the favorite food of her donor, a teenage boy who at the time of his fatal motorcycle accident had chicken nuggets in his jacket pocket.[8] These stories sound unbelievable, but accounts from heart transplant recipients are full of these anecdotes. Maybe someday we'll learn they are related to the heart's brain and its ability to store memories.

More typical research on the heart-brain axis shows relationships between psychological experience and heart rate, as well as heart rate variability. Although we might think that a steady, consistent heartbeat is a sign of health, medical researchers have actually found that a "complex and constantly changing heart rate"[9] is an indicator of a system that is well-equipped to adapt to sudden change. As one team of researchers puts it, "A healthy heart is not a metronome."[10] Therefore, higher heart rate variability is a sign of well-being.

Research shows that low resting heart rate is related to antisocial behavior. Lower heart rate variability has been linked to depression, anxiety, and stress. Conversely, higher heart rate variability is associated with better emotional and behavioral regulation, as well as performance on tests of executive functioning.[11] Based on research that connects heart rate variability with functioning in the brain's prefrontal cortex, neuroscientist Julian Thayer and colleagues have proposed that heart rate variability may be used as an indicator of a biological "super-system" that supports a person's adaptive responses to life.[12]

This sign of healthy adaptation along with other measures of heart health are also directly related to burnout. Low heart rate variability has been found in patients with clinical burnout,[13] which is characterized by emotional exhaustion, feelings of indifference or cynicism, and reduced experiences of accomplishment.[14] Personal burnout has been linked with a patient's poorer heart rate variability one year after a heart attack,[15] and burnout has also been shown to increase the risk of irregular heartbeat, also called atrial fibrillation (A-fib), by 20%.[16] Burnout really does involve a struggling heart.

Beyond research on the physical heart, we know the heart area is crucial in the experience of emotions, including burnout. A team of scientists led by Lauri Nummenmaa[17] has studied how emotions map onto the body, and they have found consistent emotional body topography across West European and East Asian research volunteers. The researchers asked nearly 800 participants to color a picture of a human body with the corresponding location of their own sensations while they were reading short emotional stories, watching emotional movies, or looking at emotional facial expressions.

Responses were then combined across participants and analyzed to create statistically significant "emotional body maps." These maps confirm what most of us know from experience—that many emotions are closely associated with sensations in the heart.

When we look at these body maps (see Figure 7.1), we see that love, happiness, and togetherness "light up" the heart. Stress and exhaustion (a proxy for burnout) show a busy head and a dimming heart. In depression, the lights go out completely.

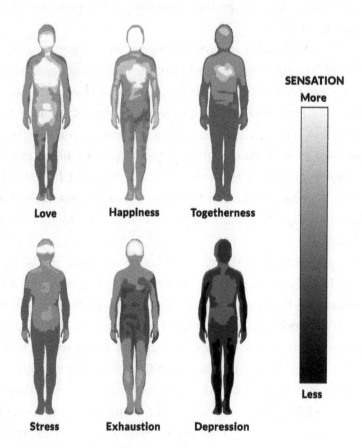

Figure 7.1 Emotional body maps

I imagine many of us relate to the experience of burnout that is depicted—a racing mind coupled with a flagging heart. We keep on working, thinking, efforting, but something is off. Our heart's not in it.

We tend to see burnout as something to rid ourselves of; something to fix. We try to buck up and get back in the saddle. But what if we looked at it in a different way? What if rather than trying to keep up the activity and productivity, we viewed burnout as a red flag warning, a signal to stop, slow down, and investigate the fading heart? And what if burnout was actually a way out of certain kinds of modern suffering?

Heart as Escape Hatch

When Anne Helen Petersen wrote her 2019 "Burnout Generation" article in *Buzzfeed*, she acknowledged that the antidote to burnout is not necessarily rest. She wrote, "You don't fix burnout by going on vacation. You don't fix it through 'life hacks,' like inbox zero, or by using a meditation app for five minutes in the morning, or doing Sunday meal prep for the entire family, or starting a bullet journal. You don't fix it by reading a book on how to 'unfu*k yourself.'. . . You can't optimize it to make it end faster."

The rush to fix, to hack, to get back to a normal level of busyness is so compelling, and it's often how we find ourselves trying to address burnout. But the quick fix is also the portal back into the neoliberal self. It is the way neoliberalism consumes and spits itself back out.

To the neoliberal self, the threat of burnout is incredibly dangerous and incredibly necessary. Burnout must be kept at bay at all costs, with shortcuts and productivity tools and at the very least, constant activity. We can feel the franticness in Petersen's list of tactics, the desperate scrambling of the neoliberal identity to hold on to itself.

145

At the same time, as we learned from Thomas Teo in Chapter 2, stress and burnout are not just results of the neoliberal identity. They are its ammunition. The neoliberal self's stress and its quest to relieve that stress are intrinsic—they are how the neoliberal self *knows* itself. The neoliberal self is on the brink of burnout, by its very nature. And it must keep itself on that brink. This identity must keep pushing, striving, bringing itself closer to burnout. But succumbing to that burnout, burning out completely, would mean cessation of productivity, activity, forward motion and, of course, achievement. Therefore, although pushing to the brink of burnout is required, succumbing to burnout is not an option.

Further, from the neoliberal perspective of responsibilization, each of us is accountable for our own productivity, for our destiny, and for our exhaustion. To burn out is an individual issue. To lose heart is a personal failing. It makes sense that we do anything to get "back on track" and avoid burning out completely. Our head becomes busy, desperate, trying to find a solution and perk us up, get us back in the game, and return to the wheel of busyness.

This keeps up our efforting, which holds up the neoliberal system. Our striving helps preserve a world where striving is required. And so, we really can't resolve burnout through productivity hacks, more efficiency or optimization. We only heal burnout by getting over our neoliberal selves.

I propose that when we arrive at the juncture of burnout, there is an opportunity to engage in a wider, more self-questioning form of mind. From our self-questioning mind, we can let go of the ruse. And we can do something incredibly counterintuitive. We can give up. We can surrender. We can lean into the exhaustion and ask what it is telling us. We can ask our heart what ails it and what it's really longing for.

The heart is an escape hatch for the neoliberal self. It can lead us out of an old world, the world of burnout, and into the new.

Mark of the Valkyries

As Brother David suggests, turning to the heart is an inherently courageous act. Courage means heart. And one of the reasons it takes courage is because it requires that scary *v* word—vulnerability.

Brené Brown, a researcher and a reigning queen of wholeheartedness, has a lot to say about vulnerability, as well as courage. She writes in her book *Daring Greatly: How the Courage to Be Vulnerable Transforms the Way We Live, Love, Parent, and Lead*:

> The perception that vulnerability is weakness is the most widely accepted myth about vulnerability and the most dangerous. When we spend our lives pushing away and protecting ourselves from feeling vulnerable or from being perceived as too emotional, we feel contempt when others are less capable or willing to mask feelings, suck it up, and soldier on. . . . Vulnerability isn't good or bad: It's not what we call a dark emotion, nor is it always a light, positive experience. Vulnerability is the core of all emotions and feelings. To feel is to be vulnerable. To believe vulnerability is weakness is to believe that feeling is weakness. To foreclose on our emotional life out of a fear that the costs will be too high is to walk away from the very thing that gives purpose and meaning to living.[18]

Brown defines vulnerability as "uncertainty, risk, and emotional exposure." She also says, "Vulnerability sounds like truth and feels like courage." Living vulnerably is dangerous, Brown tells us. It entails real risk. Yet living without vulnerability is the greater hazard, as we risk missing out on our purpose: on life itself.

The root word for vulnerability is *welǝ-*, and its definition might surprise you. It means "to strike" or "to wound."[19] It's also related to *Valkyrie*, the name for the female figures in Norse mythology who swooped down over battlefields and marked certain soldiers for death. The Valkyries rendered those men wounded and vulnerable, and sealed their fate.

It may sound bleak, but vulnerability in the Norse tradition did not signal an ending. It was actually the beginning of a new journey. Those selected for death by the Valkyries were transported to a higher realm called Valhalla, a name that also comes from the root word for vulnerability. In Valhalla these men feasted with the gods and prepared for a much bigger battle to take place during *Ragnarök*, a future series of events that would destroy the old world and give rise to the new. The mark of the Valkyries did not just mean these men were wounded; it meant they were chosen. Vulnerability was a path of losing a small fight in service of a much bigger and more important battle.

From the perspective of the neoliberal self, we can't help but get caught up in the small fights of the day-to-day grind. This makes sense if what we are most interested in is perfecting the self and preserving particular self-images. We keep difficult emotions at bay, avoid tough conversations, and try to make ourselves look good, in our own eyes and the eyes of other people. We work on optimizing the small, separate sense of self that is disconnected, alone, and burdened with responsibility.

But working on our self-images this way keeps us in our heads, and on the surface. It means we don't get to know our true self, our expanded self, our interconnected self. We're unable to perceive who we really are and what we are uniquely marked for; what is our destiny. For that, we have to turn to the heart and go down through the escape hatch, not knowing exactly what we'll find. We have to get to know ourselves, wounds and all. We have to show up in our vulnerability.

Let me be clear that when I talk about vulnerability, I do not mean we tell every stranger our life story or walk down dark alleys at night. Real vulnerability doesn't come with a side helping of naiveté. This is one of the mistaken ideas we might have—that vulnerability means becoming wide-eyed, indiscriminate, and over-disclosing. Vulnerability doesn't mean we put on rose-colored glasses and start thinking everyone in this world is acting in our best interest. In fact, most people are largely caught up in their own unexplored hurt, protecting themselves and their self-images, and some people are out to hurt others. Knowing our own wounds doesn't mean we immediately expose them for everyone else to see.

Brené Brown emphasizes that real vulnerability is not about "letting it all hang out." Rather, it involves appropriate boundaries. Brown writes, "Vulnerability without boundaries leads to disconnection, distrust, and disengagement. In fact . . . boundaryless disclosure is one way we protect ourselves from real vulnerability. And the TMI (too much information) issue is not even a case of 'too much vulnerability'—vulnerability is bankrupt on its own terms when people move from being vulnerable to using vulnerability to deal with unmet needs, get attention, or engage in the shock-and-awe behaviors that are so commonplace in today's culture."

Knowing ourselves through and through means knowing our wounds. It also means knowing our intelligence, our discrimination, our boundaries, and our strength. As we'll discuss later in this chapter, it means knowing our no just as much as our yes.

Real vulnerability begins as a personal, private act. We begin by looking into our heart ourselves, or with a trusted companion. To start this exploration we need courage, along with another quality of the heart: compassion.

Real Compassion

We might think of compassion as the ability to feel sorry for someone else or ourselves, to be nice or cheer things up. We might think compassion is treating ourselves to some ice cream when we feel bad, or watching a rom-com, or thinking positive thoughts to replace the dark ones.

Any of those actions may indeed be helpful, but the real meaning of compassion is "to hurt." Compassion means feeling our pain as it truly is, and not trying to change it. This is what our heart often wants most—to be seen, understood, appreciated for its sensitivity. We have all been hurt. And we will be hurt again, especially if we are courageous enough to fully engage life, to move into uncharted territory and risk failure.

Full engagement *is* risky. Putting ourselves out there means taking a chance, and we truly don't know how it's going to turn out. In fact, trying something novel or creating something new almost certainly involves failure. Some attempts will flop. Deficiencies will be exposed. It will hurt. It will hurt in a real way.

Compassion provides a space to feel the truth of hurt. And there is a power that comes from drawing close to pain and soft spots. In the teachings of Buddhism, compassion is sometimes defined as "the heart that can tremble in the face of suffering."[20] It is a heart that can face pain as it is, that can face the world as it is and stay present. Zen monk Thich Nhat Hanh wrote about "looking with the eyes of compassion and listening deeply to the cries of the world."[21] The Tibetan Buddhist teacher Chögyam Trungpa taught that the heart awakens through sadness and tenderness, and that this sensitivity is part of being a "warrior." He wrote "this experience of sad and tender heart is what gives birth to fearlessness. Real fearlessness is the product of tenderness. . . . You are willing to open up, without resistance or shyness, and face the world."[22]

Our neoliberal self is too busy to face the world in this vulnerable way. It doesn't want to open up, feel things, and find out what's in the heart. The neoliberal self is very busy getting a whole bunch of things done; it doesn't have time to go to Valhalla and feast with the gods. So it stays stuck, dangling between heaven and earth, with no feet on the ground and no greater purpose to fill the heart.

It's clear that wholeheartedness, courage, vulnerability, and compassion are all tied together. When we move away from pain we cover our heart, cut ourselves off from feeling, and disengage. This keeps us safe in one sense, but also keeps us in a comfort zone of familiarity. Facing suffering, although difficult, can take us deeper into the heart and deeper into life. It's a way to open the escape hatch and find out what is waiting for us.

Vulnerable Confidence

If you look at the root word for courage you find *coeur*, "heart." You also find *credere*, which means "to believe" and "to place trust." In other words, taking heart involves having faith. As we touched on previously, the heartfulness and courage we're discussing here is not about having blind trust or believing everything is always going to turn out okay. But it does involve taking leaps of faith.

Trust is also related to confidence, a topic on which I used to have quite a bit of confusion. I heard the expression "confidence comes from competence," and made the error of thinking that my shaky confidence was an indicator of incompetence, which of course just eroded my confidence further. I marveled at how some people could have so much confidence, and I noticed that some could appear more confident than me even when I knew more than them about a particular topic or had more experience. At some point I realized that my competence probably wasn't at the root of the problem.

When I looked more deeply into the topic of confidence, I learned that what it really means is to trust in oneself and one's own experience. But this trust can come on either side of vulnerability, on either side of the heart, which yields different kinds of confidence.

On the one hand, it's possible to put a great deal of trust in our narrative self—in the stories we author about ourselves and the images we create. This is the purview of many self-help speakers, books, and programs—think positive thoughts about yourself, believe in yourself, and have confidence in that self. This isn't necessarily a bad thing. As we discussed in Chapter 5, reauthoring our story can be a critical step in our health and maturity.

The problem is that when we travel unendingly in this direction, we may develop a polished veneer of confidence, but there always remains a deeper insecurity. This is because we're putting faith in ideas and images, rather than coming back down to earth. We haven't become humble and vulnerable. We're not being really real. And we haven't escaped fully through the portal of our true heart.

A powerful depiction of invulnerable confidence appears in Paul Thomas Anderson's film *Magnolia*.[23] Tom Cruise plays the fictional Frank T. J. Mackey, a particularly toxic and misogynistic self-help icon. Mackey appears full of confidence and bravado as he tells men to take charge, "seduce and destroy," and to "fake like you are nice and caring," all of which sounds like a twisted form of self-authorship. "I am what I believe!" Mackey declares backstage, making clear his investment in his ideas and self-images.

When a shrewd reporter confronts Mackey with the reality of his painful past we see him begin to break open, first into violent defensiveness, then confusion, and eventually vulnerability and tears at his dying father's bedside. We witness the dissolution of the carefully crafted veneer, and the emergence of the wounded, but more real and authentic man within.

In other cases, vulnerability means stepping out from behind false stories of who we are or what we're capable of. Consider the story of Katherine Johnson and other Black female NASA mathematicians of the 1960s depicted in *Hidden Figures*.[24] The film shows how these women had to show up, keep their hearts in the game, and destroy the masks they'd been told to stay behind. "We needed to be assertive as women in those days—assertive and aggressive—and the degree to which we had to be that way depended on where you were. I had to be," the real Katherine Johnson said.[25] That sounds like uncertainty, risk, and emotional exposure to me.

True vulnerability does not erode confidence. To the contrary, it opens the door to real confidence. It takes us through layers of brittle esteem that are based on ideas, images, and beliefs, until we hit the bedrock of who we really are, warts and all, wounds and all. It removes false confidence and just as powerfully it burns up ideas and images that might be blocking real confidence and keeping us small.

In real confidence there can be a sense of fearlessness, because there's nothing left to expose. We see ourselves fully and clearly, so we can show up fully and clearly. This fearlessness invites us to take smart risks and jump in. With vulnerable confidence, we can surrender to the heart as a compass and a guide.

The Heart of Yes and No

As Brené Brown describes, vulnerability is often mistaken for weakness. We think that if we feel our feelings, become acquainted with our own pain and the pain of others, that we'll be left with a lack of strength. But if courage is wholeheartedness, and wholeheartedness is vulnerability, then the idea of vulnerability as weakness must be off the mark.

Most of us know the feeling of the heart saying yes. The heart longs for what it longs for, and loves what it loves. We can relate to the phrase "follow your heart," and although it sometimes creates difficulty or gets us into trouble, we have probably experienced the heart leading us to some of the best things in life.

But just as the heart can indicate the strongest kind of yes, it is also the most reliable voice of no. Heartfulness sometimes stops us in our tracks. David Whyte, whose writing originated the title for this chapter, describes saying no as a "path to soul." He writes in *The Heart Aroused*, "If we have little idea of what we really want from our lives, or what a soulful approach to our work might mean, then often the only entrance we have into soul comes from the ability to say a firm *no* to those things we intuit lead to a loss of vitality. This way is traditionally known as the *via negativa*, or negative road. . . . But in the continuous utterance of the *no* is a profound faith that the *yes* will appear."[26]

One important element to pay attention to and say no to is our own critic. Some of us have a very strong inwardly turned critic that is mean and ruthlessly attacking toward us. It keeps us deflated and hemmed in. Others of us have an outwardly turned critic that is constantly judging others, getting us into trouble in our relationships and cutting us off from heartfelt connection. And some of us are lucky enough to have strong versions of both of these!

The true heart says no when it sees violence, injustice, and abuse. It says no to perpetrating on others, and it says no to having these things perpetrated on us. Our heart can help us learn to say no to attacking ourselves, as well as sharply judging others. There are many wonderful books and resources on working with the critic, such as *Soul Without Shame* by Byron Brown.[27]

Burnout is, in a way, the ultimate statement of no. It is our heart telling us to stop, pay attention, reassess. It takes strength to rein in the neoliberal self, to have compassion and take this kind of pause. And it takes courage.

Anchoring in the Practice of Courage

Descartes helped kick off the Enlightenment with his words, "I think, therefore I am." Enlightenment thinkers encouraged people to turn away from faith in external authorities, and use their own reason to discover the truth. This movement in history brought a revolution in scientific knowledge; it led to democratic forms of government and free-market economies. The Enlightenment helped to secure the place of critical thinking in Western education, a capacity that remains crucial for navigating the world, particularly a "post-truth" world.

At the same time, not all human questions can be answered using rationality alone; in fact, many cannot. And in the context of neoliberalism, rationality seems to have gotten a bit out of hand. Paul Verhaeghe writes in *What About Me?* "these days, the word 'science' conjures up images of banks of computers operated by white-coated boffins—men as hyper-rational as Mr. Spock, albeit without the pointy ears. There is no room for passion; the official thinking is that science must be value-free and objective. . . ."[28] Reason can bring us a wealth of knowledge, but without the passion and sensitivity of the heart, we lose something essentially human. We start to feel like robots, like emotionless cogs in the machine. And we get a world where the principle of rational self-interest starts to look ugly—where time with family is not a priority,[29] where companies distribute record profits to shareholders while laying off thousands of employees amidst a global pandemic,[30] where "pharma bros" milk sick people for all they're worth,[31] where our personality profiles, covertly gleaned from Big Data on social media, are auctioned off to the highest bidder.[32]

According to Cook-Greuter, from the self-questioning mind, we can begin to "bridge rational thought with non-linear approaches to getting information."[33] When we stay in our heads, and particularly when we are caught in the endless stress and spinning of the neoliberal self, we end up burning out. We need to practice integrating our heart's knowing into how we operate.

The heart is a muscle that needs exercise and training. Courage takes practice; we can't sit around waiting for it to arrive. Buddhist

155

nun Pema Chödrön teaches about the sweet spot of the "learning zone," which falls between our "comfort zone" and the zone of "excessive risk."[34] Similarly, leadership professor Ron Heifetz teaches about a "productive zone of disequilibrium,"[35] where we move ourselves out of avoidance, but not so far that we are beyond our "limit of tolerance." Courage means pushing ourselves just enough. We can't sit back and stay comfortable, but we don't have to completely freak ourselves out, either.

It's rare that courage manifests as a grand act for the history books. More often we find our courage in the small gestures of every day. Maybe our heartfulness is practiced when we look the cashier at the grocery store in the eye; when we give an employee, colleague, or friend a sincere "thank you"; when we say "I'm sorry" for something stupid we did; or we say no to an event or activity that really

---

Try This: Stretching the Heart

Identify an area of your life where you could apply additional courage. Notice what falls in your learning zone—between your comfort zone, and a zone of intolerable risk.

It may feel funny at first, but this exercise is best supported by connecting directly with the heart. It can help to put your hand on your heart while asking the questions, or to breathe directly into your heart, as if the air is moving in and out through the chest.

Ask yourself:

- What area of my life could use more courage?
- What is my heart saying no to?
- What is my heart saying yes to?
- What action will I take?

---

doesn't feel right. Sometimes it's pushing a little further—starting a conversation on a topic we've been scared to broach; standing up to someone who has been inappropriate; saying no to a big opportunity that just isn't landing in our heart; saying "I love you" without knowing what we'll hear in return. We can find our own way into courage, as a personal practice. (Please see "Try This: Stretching the Heart" on the next page)

※※※

Howard Thurman, a minister, educator, and advisor to Martin Luther King Jr., famously said, "Don't ask yourself what the world needs. Ask yourself what makes you come alive, and go do that, because what the world needs is people who have come alive."[36] Coming alive takes courage. It takes heart.

Coming alive can help us bridge our practice of courage with finding our place and our work in the world. When we're involved with something we truly care about, we access a fundamental vitality that carries us along. We need time to rest and restore, but we don't lose that fundamental momentum. Even if we have to quit a particular job or leave a particular situation, the flame for what we love does not burn out. If we hit a barrier we find a way through, over, or around, or else we turn around and go find somewhere else to burn brightly. We feel capable, resilient. We might feel bold, expansive, even larger than life. In the best moments we are entirely engaged, entirely involved, finding ourselves in flow, absorbed in our work and unselfconscious.

When we're engaged in real work and truly aligned, we can endure failure and withstand opposition. We adjust our situation as necessary so we can keep on coming back to the work. Our heart supports us so we can stay with it. This is the true strength and the true confidence that enables us to show up and do what needs to be done, even when times get tough. It is the heartfulness that expands beyond boundaries, real and imagined, and takes us into new territory. It can catapult us from the orbit of the status quo and take us off the map completely—into ideas, feelings, and experiences we've never known before, that open life unexpectedly. Courage propels us into adventure.

The problems we face today will be solved through this kind of boldness, adventure, discovery. Wholeheartedness is necessary. Of course, we can't embark on this type of journey without our minds. Engaging with big thorny problems calls for minds that are creative, insightful, and open. We turn to this topic next.

Chapter 8

Lost and Liberated
Guidepost 4: From Progress to the Wisdom of Openness

The first time I remember being lost was when I was about nine-years-old. I was at the Bangor Mall with my friend and her father, and at some point we found ourselves alone, adult-less, unsure of which direction to turn. I don't remember how it happened. Maybe we saw something interesting and wandered off, or perhaps he stepped away thinking we'd stay put for a minute. What I do remember is the feeling of a racing heart and clenching throat, the desperation that mounted with every moment we still had not found our way. Although it seems unreasonable looking back now, I think we were afraid the situation would never end, that we may remain lost forever.

Getting lost can be scary. It's often associated with strife and basic survival. "Midway upon the journey of our life / I found myself within a forest dark, / For the straightforward pathway had been lost," Dante begins the *Divine Comedy*,[1] just before his descent into the underworld. The straightforward path is the known path, the trajectory of moving from A to B, where B is in some way an improvement. It's the path of progress. When we lose our sense of that known target, of point B, we feel lost. The *Divine Comedy* seems like a parable for what we call today the midlife crisis, when people question their accomplishments and their purpose as they contemplate mortality, and sometimes in their confusion buy a flashy car.

I read recently that most millennials won't be able to afford a traditional midlife crisis.[2] But maybe it balances out. We were, after all, the first generation for whom the quarterlife crisis was an acknowledged phenomenon. I was in my 20s when *Quarterlife Crisis*[3] was newly published, a book about the challenges of young adulthood by Alexandra Robbins and Abby Wilner, young Gen Xers born close to the millennial threshold.

I don't know if I'll have a midlife crisis, but I definitely had a quarterlife crisis. I remember the dread I felt when I turned 25 and had not yet accomplished anything that felt grand or significant. In my mind, 25 was somehow a critical deadline for success; my birthday came and went and I was sure I had peaked. I read *Quarterlife Crisis* and *20 Something, 20 Everything: A Quarter-life Woman's Guide to Balance and Direction*,[4] looking for answers, looking for help. The problem was, I couldn't learn very much because I spent the whole time comparing myself to the authors. I wished it was me who had written those books. Here were young women, just a little older than me, who had lived through a quarterlife crisis and made something out of it—who turned their pain and tragedy, their crisis, into success. That's what I wanted.

I was no stranger to making lemonade from life's sour lemons. A defining event of my young adulthood was the death of my mother, one month after I turned 20. In late 2000 my mother traveled by herself from Maine to the Midwest for a parents' weekend with my college field hockey team. She attended all of the games and events; she laughed, clapped, and cheered with gusto. She looked good, if a little thin.

The next month I arrived home to find her confused, nearly comatose, my sister's friend trying to help her back into bed after she fell. Cancer had spread to her brain. Hospice was making visits. She died a few days after I got there, right before Christmas.

I had known for two years that my mother had cancer, but my parents hadn't shared all the details or the prognosis, and I didn't ask too many questions. When it came to difficult topics, my family had a strong culture of polite avoidance. So I didn't have enough information to see her death coming. When she passed away I was shocked and confused. I didn't know how to orient without my mom. Our weekly phone check-ins, her interest in my latest projects and successes, were an anchor in my life that I had not recognized until it was gone. I found myself unmoored, lost.

I dealt with all of this by overcompensating. Rather than facing into the extent of my personal tragedy, I neoliberalized the shit out of it. I went right back to college at the end of January break and took on a full course load. I wore my best clothes and tried to always look put together, a type of revenge dressing for life's betrayal. I earned some of my highest grades yet.

Of course, I was not really okay. I would get drunk and break down sobbing, I picked fights with friends, I was once in such a state that my roommate took it upon herself to walk me to the counseling center.

I would continue running from the pain of my mom's death for a few years, until I quit a job in Boston and moved back to my father's house in my mid-20s, burned out and lost yet again, unsure of what work I really wanted to pursue. I called it a *quarterlife sabbatical*, which was code for quarterlife crisis. I worked as a substitute teacher in my childhood school district and did some odd jobs. I had lost my point B. I did not know how to make progress.

I was fortunate to have the option to live with my father at that point, but moving home was also hard because it was a stark confrontation of my mom's absence. The house was much darker and colder than when my mother was alive. My dad did his best to carry on normally, but he was struggling too, dealing with the ultimate stressor of having lost his spouse. We couldn't keep up with a leak in the roof. We also had a bit of a mouse problem.

I remember once in the middle of the night I heard a mouse rustling in a small live trap I had set. I decided to transfer it to a metal trash can until morning. I lined the can with a plastic bag so that I could easily throw away the mouse poop the next day, then opened the trap and released the mouse into the trash can. It looked at me for a moment with its big, terrified eyes. Then it swiftly climbed the plastic bag and disappeared into the darkness.

Somehow that moment was a window into hopelessness. I was utterly defeated. Even this mouse knew what it was doing. I, however, was stuck, confused, adrift.

That's the whole story I want to tell you. That I suffered loss, that I was disoriented, and I was bested by a mouse. We need the freedom to tell such stories. If there is any "win," any "growth" to this story, it is that this moment of hopelessness and defeat did open a window to something beyond the neoliberal self. I couldn't really recognize it at the time, but it was a start.

The neoliberal self likes to squeeze those lemons and add lots of sugary optimism; likes to create some triumph porn, and give everybody hope that this terribly awful thing that is happening or has happened is actually this amazingly wonderful thing that is going to lead to some outstanding success. Our achiever self needs forward motion, needs progress. Difficulty is just fodder for a really great comeback story.

Real openness isn't like that. It's both simpler than the neoliberal success fantasy and more complex. Openness has room for paradox. If you ask me about my own tragedy, I can say that on the one hand I didn't stay stuck forever. I did find a way forward, sometimes in ways that surprised me, and there were important things that grew out of the experience of my mother's death. If my mother hadn't died when I was 20, I'm sure I would have made very different choices with my life. I wouldn't have learned many of the things I've been fortunate to learn; I wouldn't have had a lot of the amazing experiences I've had;

I wouldn't be writing the book you're reading now. I likely would not have traveled the path that led me to meet my husband, so we wouldn't have the same kid, and I wouldn't trade them for anything. My mother's death helped turn me into the person I am today, and I don't wish to change that. In fact, I wouldn't change a thing.

On the other hand, I would change everything if I could. I would go back and take away my mother's cancer. I would turn into somebody else, even if it meant doubling down as my own expert or achiever self; I would grow less as a person and maybe be less happy. I would change all of this, if it meant seeing her live. Not wanting to change a thing, and wanting to change everything—these realities are both true. Real openness has room for all of that.

In this chapter we'll talk about being lost, and we'll talk about curiosity, insight, and liberation. Liberation means the freedom to live fully, outside of demands for perfection or progress. Openness doesn't mean everything is great all the time; it means everything is possible. In the introductory poem to this book, Rilke does not say, "Let wonderful things happen to you." He says, "Let everything happen to you."

Don't translate this into taking a submissive posture and letting life trample who you are. Rilke isn't saying you should make impulsive choices, or allow other people to take advantage of you or treat you poorly. What he is offering is an invitation to live spaciously, boldly, without reassurance of a perfect result. Brené Brown tells us that avoiding vulnerability is a foreclosure on a full emotional life—without the most difficult emotions, we can't really experience the most wonderful ones. The same is true when it comes to openness, and a willingness to lose our way. Refusal to live into our dark, confusing moments puts limitations on our experience of the light. True liberation is the freedom to experience reality as it truly is, in its totality. This opens us to difficulty, but also clears a trail for adventure.

Beyond our neoliberal striving is the opportunity to walk into the wild unknown. Openness is standing at point A without the expectation of reaching point B, and instead letting the destination find you.

Dare to Not Know

Immanuel Kant's motto of the Enlightenment, *Sapere aude* is often translated as "dare to know!" Kant and other Enlightenment pioneers challenged people to use their reason, to find out the truth for themselves rather than relying on external authorities.

Knowing is important. There are a lot of things we need to know in order to live effectively each day. A. H. Almaas, the originator of the spiritual path I've studied for a while, calls this "ordinary knowledge,"[5] which is knowledge based on all the facts and concepts we've learned before, including our self-images. It's our standard, habitual way of orienting in the world. I wake up in the morning knowing who I am, where I am, how to walk, talk, and more or less what I need to do. I know my narrative self and how that self relates to the world around me. Ordinary knowledge is important for leading a functional life. From the achiever mind, we can even assemble our ordinary knowledge in unique and personal ways. We dare to know and to author life for ourselves.

But according to Almaas there is another kind of knowledge, which is "direct knowledge in the moment—the stuff of our immediate experience." He calls this *basic knowledge*. Basic knowledge is not based on concepts or past events; rather, it's the knowledge that's right here in our experience, right now. It's what the minimal self observes, free from images and self-concepts. You might look around at this moment and think, "That's stupid. Not much is happening right now." But many spiritual teachers challenge us to look again. We might start to recognize how we overlay the present moment with our existing ideas, our ordinary knowledge. This overlay makes things look familiar, and also perhaps a bit stale.

A. H. Almaas writes, "Taking the position that we know the present manifestations constrains these manifestations to appear within the conceptual confines determined by this old knowledge." In other words, we keep shoehorning our present experience into the known terrain of our past. This, Almaas says is how we get into "fixed, rigid, repetitive patterns. It destroys the freshness of the moment and separates us from the wonder of the mystery that is always confronting us." Our ordinary knowledge can create a kind of barrier to perceiving things directly and dynamically. It constrains our mind to the world of the known. To perceive things in a more fundamental way, we ultimately must have an emptier, more open mind.

These ideas are found in a variety of wisdom traditions. You've probably heard the concept of "beginner's mind" from Buddhism. According to influential Zen teacher Shunryu Suzuki, "If your mind is empty, it is always ready for anything; it is open to everything. In the beginner's mind there are many possibilities; in the expert's mind there are few."[6] Suzuki also said, "When we have no thought of achievement, no thought of self, we are true beginners. . . . This is also the real secret of the arts: always be a beginner." Suzuki's words seem to challenge both our expert and achiever forms of mind. From the expert mind, we find reassurance in bodies of knowledge and codes of conduct we have dedicated ourselves to. From the achiever mind, we have generated our own code of conduct to live by. Suzuki is pointing to something beyond expertise and achievement to a space that is more open and available to possibility.

Tibetan Buddhist teacher Chögyam Trungpa talked about "nowness" as "the magic of the present moment."[7] Like Almaas, he suggested that focusing on familiar, ordinary knowledge cuts off our contact with this magic. "Normally, we limit the meaning of perceptions . . . we fit what we see into a comfortable or familiar scheme," Trungpa writes. "We shut any vastness or possibilities of deeper perception out of our hearts by fixating on our own interpretation of phenomena. . . . We always have a choice: we can limit our perception so that we close off vastness, or we can allow vastness to touch us." This vastness, according to Trungpa and other spiritual teachers, is not found in some faraway secret place, but rather is so close that we don't tend to see it. It's right here in the openness of the moment.

Similar themes on ordinary knowledge and mystery appear in Western religion, for example, in the medieval Christian text "The Cloud of Unknowing," written by an anonymous mystic to his student. The author encourages the student to put all knowing under a "cloud of forgetting," and to "go after experience rather than knowledge"[8] in order to encounter God. These ideas inform modern practice of Christian centering prayer.

If this all seems a bit too esoteric for you, consider that modern descriptions of critical thinking also invoke openness and not-knowing. Philosophy professor Jack Kwong has defined open-mindedness as "a willingness to take a novel viewpoint seriously."[9] A novel viewpoint is, by definition, something that is fresh and unfamiliar. And professor Harvey Siegel calls open-mindedness a "necessary but not sufficient condition of critical thinking."[10] He writes, "If one is not openminded, one lacks the critical spirit, and so lacks a central, necessary component of critical thinking."

We must dare to know, to question authority and find out for ourselves. Although knowing is essential to having a functioning world, we must also dare to *not* know, to suspend our habitual categorizations and judgments and be surprised. Letting go of our preconceptions about the world, ourselves, and how everything works opens doorways to the new.

Staying with Uncertainty

Not knowing is challenging. Most of us have minds that like to know. Clarity feels supportive. Certainty looks like safety.

Getting Over Ourselves

But life is full of uncertainty, whether we acknowledge it or not, and our ability to tolerate that ambiguity has implications for other parts of our life. "Tolerance of uncertainty" is a somewhat slippery psychological term, with a working definition of "the set of negative and positive psychological responses—cognitive, emotional, and behavioral—provoked by the conscious awareness of ignorance about particular aspects of the world."[11] When we know that we don't know, we can either stay with that ignorance, or we can follow the rising anxiety that propels us toward some kind of firm knowing, some kind of certainty. But unwillingness to stay with ambiguity can close the doors too quickly.

Researchers have found links between intolerance of ambiguity and experiences of burnout in the medical profession.[12] Intolerance of uncertainty during the COVID-19 pandemic was associated with less effective coping strategies and increased health anxiety.[13] And as we saw in Chapter 6, lower tolerance for uncertainty is related to stronger black-and-white, polarized political views on both sides of the aisle, as well as increased brain synchrony with like-minded, in-group individuals.

Comfort with ambiguity, however, has been shown to tap a wellspring of creativity. In one study with French adolescents and their parents, greater comfort with uncertainty was related to generating more ideas and more unique ideas during a divergent thinking task, in which participants were asked to write as many titles as possible for a sample of ambiguous text.[14] In another study with architectural design students, tolerating ambiguity did not necessarily make students better designers overall, but it was correlated with a measure of original, divergent thinking.[15] So tolerating uncertainty seems to unleash a flow of creative ideas and generate more unique options to choose from.

Rather disturbingly, tests of creative, divergent thinking showed declines for younger children from 1990 to the mid-2000s, even as

IQ scores rose. This led researchers to wonder whether "hurried life-styles and a focus on academics," along with less unstructured play was zapping the emergence of creativity.[16] The progress of the neo-liberal lifestyle, always moving from a clear point A to B, always pro-ducing and achieving, may hone certain types of intelligence while also narrowing young minds.

Of course, it's normal to want clarity and reassurance. We can't just snap our fingers and do a better job of tolerating uncertainty, nor can we criticize ourselves into creativity. It's important to be compas-sionate with ourselves while also exploring what might help us be resilient and creative in the face of an uncertain world. We find one remedy in the exercise of curiosity.

The Cure in Curiosity

We've made a habit in this book of looking at root words to find their true meaning. We'll do this one more time, with the word *curiosity*. The Indo-European root of *curious* literally means "to care for." It's also related to the word *cure*.

Curiosity is, in its basic form, medicinal. This is backed by sci-ence. Research has linked curiosity to overall life satisfaction,[17] and curiosity and openness are shown to be protective against high blood pressure and diabetes,[18] as well as posttraumatic stress disorder.[19] In a five-year study with older participants greater curiosity even pre-dicted survival, regardless of a participant's smoking habits, blood pressure, or cholesterol levels.[20] There does seem to be some kind of cure in curiosity. It keeps us vital.

Curiosity is understood to be a prime motivator for learning, and psychology professor Todd Kashdan calls it an "engine of growth." In his book *Curious? Discover the Missing Ingredient to a Fulfilling Life* he writes, "Curiosity is about recognizing and reaping the rewards of embracing the uncertain, the unknown, and the new. . . . By being curious, we explore. By exploring, we discover. When this is satisfying, we are more likely to repeat it. By repeating it, we develop competence and mastery. By developing competence and mastery, our knowledge and skills grow. As our knowledge and skills grow, we stretch and expand who we are and what our life is about. By dealing with novelty, we become more experienced and intelligent, and infuse our lives with meaning."[21] In this way, curiosity creates a virtuous spiral, with our openness leading to more curiosity and learning.

Curiosity lightens things up, opens things up, and it can cure and protect against languishing. One thing curiosity is most protective against is judgment. Judgment hardens the mind. It shuts down care and circumvents cure. It closes down possibilities.

Although it's important to go forward with certainty at particular times, judgment can move us too quickly toward the known. If we're trying to make progress, we often diagnose our point A, then try to move to the vision of B. Our achiever mind believes it knows where we need to go and tries to move there, in a straight line, as quickly as possible. Sometimes this is exactly the right thing to do. But if our curiosity is tempered, there isn't much openness. This doesn't leave room for the new and novel, for the element of surprise. It doesn't leave room for the magic of insight.

Relaxing into Insight

One way we solve problems is through analysis: by using our logical mind and plodding steadily toward a solution. As psychology researchers John Kounios and Mark Beeman describe, "analytic solving taps well-known procedures and your current understanding of the problem. As you work on a problem in a deliberate, step-by-step fashion and pass each milestone, you can tell that you're getting closer and closer to the solution."[22] We move from A to B based on familiar, ordinary knowledge. We make progress.

However, as Kounios and Beeman have studied and explained in their book *The Eureka Factor*, there is another kind of problem-solving that involves the aha moment we call insight. In this situation, we first are working on a problem. We immerse ourselves in the material, learn everything we can about it and struggle with it, looking for a solution. But analysis fails us. We can't find an answer and, alas, we hit an impasse. Although we may feel stuck and lost in uncertainty, things are secretly incubating in the subconscious. It's when we stop and step away from the problem to engage in a diversion—a walk, a meal, a shower—then suddenly the light bulb goes off. When it comes to insight the mind and brain must first work hard, then put aside the task and relax in order for incubation to succeed. It's when the brain is at ease that, Eureka, the insight arrives.

Historically, many psychologists suspected that insight was not so different from analytical problem-solving. They thought it was probably just good old-fashioned progress accompanied by a burst of feeling good. Others were not so sure. In the 2000s, Beeman and Kounios thought they could better address the question of insight by looking at the brain. Using imaging technology to measure blood flow and EEG recordings to detect electrical activity, they and their colleagues identified a distinct brain signature of insight. The team found that aha moments are characterized by increased blood flow to an area of the brain behind the right temple called the right anterior superior temporal gyrus, along with a "sudden burst"[23] of high-frequency electrical activity in this same region, just before the insight occurs. Additionally, the researchers found that about one and a half seconds before an insight, the area at the back of the brain that processes visual information has a sudden decrease in activity. The researchers called this a *brain blink*, where the brain briefly shuts out visual input to allow the insight to spring forth.

If the left side of the brain is known as the logical, talkative one, the brain's right hemisphere—where Beeman and Kounios located that distinct flash of insight—has gained a reputation as the more intuitive, more creative, and mysterious sibling. Although this contrast is often oversold, specialization of the brain's hemispheres, also called *lateralization*, is a well-established phenomenon. Areas for understanding language (Wernicke's area) as well as expressing language (Broca's area) are located for most people on the left side of the brain, whereas processing of visual-spatial and nonverbal language cues takes place on the right. For example, both sides of the brain have an area called the *fusiform gyrus*, but it is specifically the right fusiform gyrus that is associated with recognizing faces.[24]

One incredible story related to brain lateralization comes from Dr. Jill Bolte Taylor, a neuroanatomist who suffered a massive stroke on the left side of her brain. After years of recovery Taylor went on to give a TED Talk and write about her experience in the book *My Stroke of Insight*.

Taylor was on her exercise machine one morning in 1996 when a strange, detached feeling came over her. As she was having a stroke, the left side of her brain bleeding and progressively losing function, she began oscillating between an experience of pain and alarm, and a profound sense of connection, bliss, and peace. She glimpsed a life that was absent of the left brain's language commentary and sense of orientation, a life mediated entirely by the brain's right hemisphere. This seemed to bring Taylor beyond judgment and open her to the "nowness" that the spiritual teachers referenced previously in this chapter describe. She writes:

> In the absence of my left hemisphere's analytical judgment, I was completely entranced by the feelings of tranquility, safety, blessedness, euphoria, and omniscience. . . . Instead of having my moments prematurely stunted, they became open-ended, and I felt no rush to do anything. Like walking along the beach, or just hanging out in the beauty of

nature, I shifted from the doing-consciousness of my left brain to the being-consciousness of my right brain. I morphed from feeling small and isolated to feeling enormous and expansive. I stopped thinking in language and shifted to taking new pictures of what was going on in the present moment. I was not capable of deliberating about past or future-related ideas because those cells were incapacitated. All I could perceive was right here, right now, and it was beautiful. . . . My entire self-concept shifted as I no longer perceived myself as a single, a solid, an entity with boundaries that separated me from the entities around me. I understood that at the most elementary level, I am a fluid. Of course I am a fluid! Everything around us, about us, among us, within us, and between us is made up of atoms and molecules vibrating in space. Although the ego center of our language center prefers defining our self as individual and solid, most of us are aware that we are made up of trillions of cells, gallons of water, and ultimately everything about us exists in a constant and dynamic state of activity. My left hemisphere had been trained to perceive myself as a solid, separate from others. Now, released from that restrictive circuitry, my right hemisphere relished in its attachment to the eternal flow. I was no longer isolated and alone. My soul was as big as the universe and frolicked with glee in a boundless sea.[25]

We can feel the awe, wonder, and peace in Taylor's expansive experience. It sounds a lot like the self with a capital S we explored in Chapter 5, as well as the interconnected reality we considered in Chapter 6. This view is imbued with the present-moment awareness and freedom of an open mind. Indeed, Taylor likened her right-brain experience to entering "Nirvana."

172

Getting Over Ourselves

Most of us will never have an experience exactly like Jill Bolte Taylor's, nor should we wish to. Although she expresses gratitude for what her brain hemorrhage revealed, we shouldn't forget that Taylor suffered a massive stroke from which it took many years and great effort to recover. But as she describes in her book, practices like meditation and prayer that are associated with spiritual experiences seem to have overlapping impacts on the brain and can help us access different ways of perceiving reality.

The Mindful Brain

Researchers have identified a number of brain structures related to religious and spiritual experiences. The temporal lobes of the brain are associated with spiritual visions and moments of déjà-vu. Self-transcendence and out-of-body experiences are tied to the temporo-parietal junction, where the brain's temporal and parietal lobes meet, located just above the temples and toward the back of the head. Experiences of ego-dissolution during the use of psychedelics have been related to reduced activity in the mode network of the brain, which we discussed in Chapter 5.[26]

In recent decades we have seen a surge of research on the impact of mindfulness on the brain, as a "mindfulness revolution" has swept through Western culture. Between 2012 and 2017, the CDC reported a tripling of meditation practice among adults[27] and a ninefold increase among children.[28] The trend has been propelled in part by scientific evidence that mindfulness practices can positively affect health outcomes and create measurable changes in the brain and body, down to the DNA.[29]

When I worked in brain research in the 2000s I supported a study at Massachusetts General Hospital, Harvard Medical School that looked at whether mindfulness could change the brain of new practitioners. For this research, authored by Dr. Britta Hölzel and conducted in the

173

lab of Dr. Sara Lazar, we enrolled participants who were healthy but stressed, and had signed up for an eight-week mindfulness-based stress reduction (MBSR) course. Two weeks before they started the program each participant came to the brain imaging center so we could measure their brain structure using MRI. They returned two weeks after completing the course, so we could slide them back into the scanner and measure their brain structure once again. Then we could look for changes.

We found that, compared to a control group that was waiting to take an MBSR class, these new mindfulness practitioners had a few areas of increased gray matter concentration in their brains. These included the left hippocampus, an area deep inside the temple in the brain's emotional "limbic" system that is associated with memory and emotion regulation; the temporo-parietal junction; the posterior cingulate cortex, a part of the brain's self-referential default mode; and the cerebellum and brainstem in areas related to body movement, emotional regulation, and mood.[30] This was one of the first studies to provide evidence that mindfulness practice could change the brain (See the Notes at the end of the book for more about this research).

Since the time of that study, converging evidence from multiple laboratories has shown that meditation practice affects the brain. One area that is implicated time and again is the hippocampus. The hippocampi are seahorse-shaped structures located toward the core of the brain, one in each hemisphere. They are covered with receptors for stress hormones, making them particularly vulnerable to stress. Research with animals has shown that chronic stress causes hippocampal cells to atrophy,[31] and the hippocampus has been found to be 10 to 20% smaller in people with stress-related conditions like posttraumatic stress disorder and depression.[32]

At the same time, the hippocampus seems to be the most impressive structure in the brain when it comes to change and growth.

In 1998 Peter Eriksson and colleagues overturned the dogma that the adult human brain cannot regenerate, showing that new neurons were still being produced in the hippocampi of cancer patients who were in their 50s, 60s, or 70s at their time of death.[33] Since then, we have found that exercise,[34] learning challenging new skills,[35] and mindfulness practice are all potential ways to promote growth of brain cells in the hippocampus.

In addition to the hippocampus and other brain areas, mindfulness practice has been found to affect the brain's default mode activity. One team of scientists looked across various studies on mindfulness and resting state brain activity and found strengthened connection between activity in the posterior cingulate cortex, a main hub of the default mode network located toward the back of the head, and the dorsal anterior cingulate cortex, an area that is part of the same brain structure but more toward the front of the head. They proposed that this functional connection may reflect self-regulation that helps a practitioner remain alert and focused during mindfulness practice, as well as "observe internal states with open awareness."[36] A study with experienced practitioners of Insight meditation, who had more than 10 years of experience and 5,000 to 15,000 hours of practice, found this same coordination of activity between posterior cingulate cortex and dorsal anterior cingulate cortex, compared to non-meditators. Interestingly, this coordination was present whether the meditators were meditating or not. The researchers also found less overall activity in the default mode network in the experienced meditators compared to non-meditators. The researchers wrote, "meditation practice may transform the resting-state experience into one that resembles a meditative state, and as such, is a more present-centered default mode."[37] In other words, brain research suggests that meditation practice may turn down the self-centered chatter of our brain's default mode and allow us to anchor more firmly in the moment.

Further, this kind of default mode deactivation has been linked with creativity. In one study, long-term mindfulness practitioners scored higher on divergent thinking than non-practitioners, and the longer a person had been meditating, the higher their creative fluency scores. Greater creativity was also related to decreased default brain wave coordination between the posterior cingulate and prefrontal areas of the brain. The researchers speculated, "the less self-focused one is during the resting state, the more creative one will be during a divergent thinking task."[38] Another study found that learning mindfulness improved students' ability to solve problems with insight.[39]

Taken together, the research suggests that mindfulness practice may alter the brain—protecting us from stress, helping us to be more creative and insightful, and potentially opening us to the magic of beginner's mind the meditation masters describe.

But what happens when you bring such powerful practices into a neoliberal context? As we've seen, neoliberalism has a sneaky way of ensnaring anything that attempts to escape its grasp, of making meals out of its friends and even bigger meals out of its enemies. Mindfulness, too, can fall into this trap.

The Modern Mindfulness Trap

In the United States, corporations have been quick to adopt mindfulness to promote stress reduction and productivity among employees. The phrase "search inside yourself" echoes the ancient maxim of the Temple of Apollo at Delphi, but these days is associated with employee wellness programs at Google. It looks as if wisdom has found its way into modern corporate life. Or has it?

The mindfulness revolution seems to have many benefits, but it may not be taking us as far as we think. In his uncompromising critique, *McMindfulness: How Mindfulness Became the New Capitalist Spirituality*, management professor and ordained Zen teacher Ron

Purser asserts the movement is "complicit in maintaining the status quo of corporate capitalism and neoliberal government." He states: "The so-called mindfulness revolution meekly accepts the dictates of the marketplace. Guided by a therapeutic ethos aimed at enhancing the mental and emotional resilience of individuals, it endorses neoliberal assumptions that everyone is free to choose their responses, manage negative emotions, and 'flourish' through various modes of self-care. Framing what they offer in this way, most teachers of mindfulness rule out a curriculum that critically engages with causes of suffering in the structures of power and economic systems of capitalist society."[40]

Purser's premise is jarring: mindfulness in its current form is not necessarily waking people up to the greater systemic impacts of neoliberalism, and it may actually be lulling them to sleep. Mindfulness programs can be cloaked in responsibilization and ideals of self-reliance, telling people that stress management is an individual problem, not a structural one. It can play into the middle-class time squeeze described in Chapter 1, when people blame themselves for pervasive, systemic struggles. Purser asserts that rather than moving practitioners toward greater engagement, the aims of stress reduction and increased acceptance simply create "better-adjusted cogs in the capitalist machinery." In the land of McMindfulness, these ancient practices are fed into a closed loop that reinforces the neoliberal self and traps us in an outmoded ideology, rather than liberating us into a new one.

Reading *McMindfulness* spurred my own insights that led me to begin writing this book. When I looked into neoliberalism to better understand Purser's arguments, I recognized what a tremendous shift had begun taking place in the United States the year I was born, the year that marked the beginning of the millennial generation. I saw connections between neoliberalism and the millennial stereotypes described in Chapter 2. And I noticed connections between those stereotypes, my own suffering, and some of the real antidotes I had learned as a spiritual student over the years. Things further clicked into place when I noticed that neoliberalism, with its "end in itself" individuality, seemed like some exaggerated form of the self-authoring stage of psychological development. And I recognized the impact of this worldview on my own mindsets and life experience.

Purser's views challenged me to look at my own spiritual practice, and my work and contributions in the field of mindfulness. I began to see my neoliberal self more clearly, the one that believes in endless self-perfection, self-reliance, rationality, and progress. And I saw the part of myself that, if I wanted to contribute to real change in the world, needed to lean into the questioning space more strongly; I needed to worry less and engage more; I needed to *get over my self*.

Purser writes, "A truly revolutionary mindfulness would challenge the Western sense of entitlement to happiness irrespective of ethical conduct. . . . Instead, the practice is being sold to executives as a way to de-stress, improve productivity and focus, and bounce back from working eighty-hour weeks. . . . Even if individuals become nicer people, the corporate agenda of maximizing profits does not change. Trickle-down mindfulness, like trickle-down economics, is a cover for the maintenance of power."

Purser is highlighting the fact that we can sink into the peace and stillness of mindfulness practice, then open our eyes and act in ways, conscious and unconscious, that maintain an unsavory status quo. What if we let open-mindedness open up all the questions, all the seeing that is possible? This can be supported by having our feet on the ground in humility, acknowledging our interconnection, and leaning into the heartfulness of courage. It also calls for a mind that dares to know but also to not-know, a mind that is willing to get lost, that is open to insight and creativity, a mind that is available to wonder.

Anchoring in the Practice of Wonder

A quick web search left me impressed with the number of nonfiction books on the topic of awe and wonder that have been published in the past few years. In 2020 there was *World of Wonders: In Praise of Fireflies, Whale Sharks, and Other Astonishments* and *Wonder: The Extraordinary Power of an Ordinary Experience*, along with *Awestruck: How Embracing Wonder Can Make You Happier, Healthier, and More Connected*, and *In Awe: Rediscover Your Childlike Wonder to Unleash Inspiration, Meaning, and Joy. Tracking Wonder* was published in 2021. And already in 2023, we have seen *Awe* by Dachner Keltner, *The Power of Awe* by Jake Eagle and Michael Amster, *The Awe of God* by John Bevere, *The Power of Wonder* by Monica C. Parker, and *Enchantment: Awakening Wonder in an Anxious Age* by Katharine May. I guess this topic is on our minds.

In describing the movement from the achiever to the self-questioning mind, Susanne Cook-Greuter indicates a shift from progress to wonder. She writes, "Instead of marching into the future, individuals become now-oriented as they infuse experience in the present with importance. The past is gone and the future cannot really be known." She also describes a mind that is liberated into openness: "There is a perception that sudden insights and breakthroughs are possible. Playful exploration and imagination are set free. Life is fresh and enticing."[41]

Sometimes insight and creativity catch us unawares, piercing our default functioning with something unexpected and new. We can also make ourselves available to this freshness. Practicing wonder allows play and exploration in the way Cook-Greuter describes.

Wonder invites us into the open moment, to see with fresh eyes, hear with fresh ears, feel with a fresh heart, and think with a fresh mind. These are capacities we need when we're lost. Wonder can help us transform lostness into liberation.

Try This: Opening to Wonder

Let your mind rest and relax. You can support this practice by first relaxing your body. Try tightening then releasing your muscles, first in your feet, then calves, then thighs, your butt; try clenching and unclenching your hands, then arms, then shoulders—bring them to your ears, then drop them. Try scrunching then relaxing your face. You may want to stretch out the muscles around your eyes, moving them in big slow circles. Then let them rest in your head.

Drop into your experience, as if entering a body of water. Let yourself see, hear, and feel your experience. Notice your mind—is there chatter, judgment, worry? You can take note and be curious about that, too.

Try practicing openness out in the world. You might hike a new trail or take a walk in an unfamiliar neighborhood. See what happens when you let your mind relax, just perceive, and be open.

You can practice openness and wonder with people, too. It can be quite fascinating to interact with a person you know well, coming from a place of wonder. Notice your thoughts and feelings. How are you open to this person? What closed ideas do you have? Try looking at this human being as if seeing them for the first time. What do you see? Try listening to their words from a place of presence and openness. What do you hear? Can you see this person as fresh and new, right now?

In Chapter 2, we considered millennials as a "lost" generation. This lostness manifests psychologically. But we are lost systemically as well. Our neoliberal systems, although probably not entirely broken, are exacerbating environmental destruction, stress, and inequality. As professor and thought leader Otto Scharmer says, "Collectively, we create results that no one wants."[42]

If the current system isn't working, then getting lost might not be such a bad thing. Getting lost could be the first step in stumbling onto something new.

When I say this, I don't mean to downplay the suffering and stress that many people are experiencing. I'm not saying it's good that people are stretched and having trouble navigating an individualized, pull-yourself-up-by-your-bootstraps world. And I'm definitely not saying it's your job, personally, to take everything in this book and put the responsibility of changing the system on your shoulders. I'm not suggesting that if you simply do the practices I've offered, then poof, everything will be great. That would just be more responsibilization, more "you're suffering from an idea problem." It would be more of the same.

As I said previously in this book, I don't think anyone can traverse the postmodern landscape alone. The neoliberal self, in its stress and isolation, can't find its way out of neoliberalism. We have a group project on our hands. So, in our next and final chapter, we'll consider how we might come together to wonder, wander, and courageously adventure into new possibilities and new systems.

Lost and Liberated

Concluding and Beginning

"Put down the weight of your aloneness and ease into the conversation. The kettle is singing even as it pours you a drink, the cooking pots have left their arrogant aloofness and seen the good in you at last. All the birds and creatures of the world are unutterably themselves. Everything is waiting for you."

David Whyte

From the Daniels's film *Everything Everywhere All at Once:*

"The only thing I do know is that we have to be kind. Please, be kind. Especially when we don't know what's going on."

Ke Huy Quan as Waymond

"We're all useless alone. It's a good thing you're not alone."

Michelle Yeoh as Evelyn

Part III

Concluding and Beginning

Chapter 9

Friends Between Worlds

T here is much discussion these days about being between worlds, or at the end of the world we currently know. In the first chapter of this book we looked at a world on edge, as we seem to be reaching a breaking point of environmental and human exhaustion.

Steven Pinker presents scores of graphs in *Enlightenment Now* that show positive trends in the modern world, and there's no need to deny the legitimacy of this view. But obviously not every modern trend is moving in a good direction. In *The Bridge at the End of the World: Capitalism, the Environment, and Crossing from Crisis to Sustainability*, James Gustave Speth shows us a set of graphs that depict exponential growth in water use, atmospheric CO_2 concentration, loss of rainforests and woodlands, and species extinction. Speth writes,

> Many of our deepest thinkers and many of those most familiar with the scale of the challenges we face have concluded that the transitions required can be achieved only in the context of what I will call the rise of a new consciousness. For some, it is a spiritual awakening—a transformation of the human heart. For others it is a more intellectual process of coming to see the world anew and deeply

embracing the emerging ethic of the environment and the old ethic of what it means to love thy neighbor as thyself. But for all it involves major cultural change and a reorientation of what society values and prizes most highly.[1]

Sometimes I feel we are on a bridge between worlds. Many of our status quo ways of doing and being are no longer effective or satisfying. We are looking for something new. Although plenty of people are working hard on the various issues we face, we seem to need some kind of breakthrough, an insight that bursts forth from the depths of our being, rearranges the way we look at our problems, and offers novel, unexpected solutions.

From our modern achiever way of looking at things, we might imagine this as a solo endeavor, an opportunity to find our individual genius and heroically come forth with an answer. Maybe it will happen this way. I'm aware this could be the part of the book where I try something like that myself—where I present concrete ideas and persuade my reader toward clear action. But I'm not going to do that. First of all, I'm as lost as anyone. And second, trying to come up with ideas alone seems like falling back into my neoliberal self.

The truth is, this chapter isn't really mine to write. It's ours to discover. So I will not create a conclusion with neat answers, but rather offer an invitation into conversation.

Given where we are, in the flat, disorienting landscape of postmodernism, I think insights will most likely emerge *between* people, and also between people and the more-than-human world. We need to be in dialogue with nature and with each other. We need to see what happens, not only when we think novel thoughts but also when we venture toward novel interfaces and ways of relating. This will take humility, recognition of interconnection, courage, and creativity. And it will take commitment and passion to fuel the work of building something new.

Calling All Builders

In February 2023, author and philosopher Sean Illing spoke with Alana Newhouse on his *Vox* podcast "The Gray Area." They discussed Newhouse's writing on brokenism in America, referenced in Chapter 4 of this book, in which she argues that the defining debate in the United States is not between "liberal" and "conservative" or political parties, but between those who continue to have faith in established systems and those who think they are irreparably cracked. Illing described his own concerns that a brokenist view could turn to fatalism or nihilism and the tearing down of existing institutions without anything to take their place. Further, Illing noted, we should keep in mind "how hard it was to build the society we have, however screwed up and flawed it might be, and no doubt is."[2]

"When I talk about brokenism," Newhouse responded, "I don't mean that we should burn things to the ground. I mean we should imagine more, imagine that there's more opportunity, imagine there were more options, imagine there were more ways of getting people better, safe, happier, richer in whatever way you want to think about it, lives." She continued, "A friend of mine said, 'You know, you don't actually mean brokenist, you mean refounders. Or another friend was like, 'I'm a brokenist, but I call myself a buildist. I want to build stuff.'" Illing and Newhouse seemed to resonate about the idea of moving through brokenism into "buildism."

I, too, resonate with the idea of building the new. But if we try to build strictly from the perspective of our achiever, neoliberal selves, we can only hope to build something incrementally different, incrementally better. We won't be able to create outside of the status quo. And we will build essentially more of the same.

Therefore, we must not only come together to build but we also need to pay attention to who we are being when we come together. And together, we might usher one another into the new.

Power in Diversity, Diversity in Power

There are areas of California where almond trees stretch as far as the eye can see. Almonds are a nutrient-dense superfood, packed with vitamins, minerals, fiber, and healthy fat.[3] But they are also super-consumers of water: by some estimates, almond crops use up as much water as all residents of California combined.[4] And although these single-crop orchards allow for greater farming efficiency, they also create monocultures that require rather perverse practices to remain productive. Every year, nearly 70% of the United States' commercial honeybee population is transported to California's almond groves where they pollinate blossoms while risking exposure to disease and pesticides. About a third die in the process.[5]

There is a place for monocultures. But nature shows us that too much of the same is often not a good thing. In nature, monocultures are vulnerable to blight, they can be destructive to soil, and they require drastic, sometimes exploitative, measures to survive, as in the case of almonds with honeybees. Monocultures can wreak havoc on the wider interdependence of ecosystems. As we saw in Chapter 6, reducing biodiversity—in plant life and in microbiota—seems to weaken the human immune system.

These days we hear a lot of talk about diversity, specifically human diversity. There is growing awareness that monocultures—particularly cultures of disenfranchisement or oppression—in human society are suboptimal. For example, you might be familiar with the statistic that in 2016, more CEO's of large US companies were named John than were female.[6] By 2023, clear progress had been made: now, rather than John alone, the numbers favor a combination of the names David and Michael over femaleness.[7] I do not mean to knock on men named John, David, or Michael—I'm sure people with these names are needed in building the solutions of tomorrow.

But these observations should provoke questions about why such a seemingly uniform group of people is leading the business community. What are the strengths of this uniformity, and what are the real limitations, blind spots, and vulnerabilities?

Too often, diversity is framed as a feel-good issue. Even framing diversity as an issue of justice is inadequate. We need to start considering diversity as a matter of resilience and survival, as a matter of real thriving. And real change.

We need to engage in conversations that are diverse from the start, where power is examined from the start. We need to look around the room and ask, who is here? Who is not here, why not, and is that acceptable? We need to learn to explore perspectives from different angles—different ages, genders, races, cultures, nationalities, religions, socioeconomic situations, educational backgrounds, abilities, and so on; different experiences and walks of life.

It's easy to write this in a few sentences and much more challenging to enact it. But it's important that we pay attention and try. This is not because we "should"; it's because diverse views lead to a more complete picture, greater wholeness, more health, more wisdom. Of course not every conversation will look this way. I'm also sure these kinds of conversations are already happening. And I believe we need more of them. We need safe and effective systems of social interaction, so that real cross-pollination can happen and greater potential for thriving can emerge. I think there are a few principles—including moving slowly, listening deeply, and loving fiercely—that can help us come together in these ways.

Moving Slowly

Our achiever selves orient toward efficiency and productivity. And our neoliberal identities know themselves through stress, through almost-but-not-quite burnout, through pressure and speed. Therefore, we need to find spaces where we can be courageously unproductive and willfully meandering. As contemporary thought leader and proponent of "postactivisim" Bayo Akomolafe says, "The times are urgent; let us slow down." We need to slow way, way down. And we need ways of slowing down in relationship with one another.

The Trappist monk and early proponent of interfaith understanding Thomas Merton foresaw neoliberal dangers in the 1960s when he wrote a collection of reflections called *Conjectures of a Guilty Bystander*. He cautioned that even meaningful, seemingly selfless work could be co-opted by toxic achieverism. Merton observed, "There is a pervasive form of modern violence to which the idealist . . . most easily succumbs: activism and over-work. The rush and pressure of modern life are a form, perhaps the most common form, of its innate violence. . . . The frenzy of the activist neutralizes his (or her) work. . . . It destroys the fruitfulness of his (or her) . . . work, because it kills the root of inner wisdom which makes work fruitful."[8]

Taking a stand against the rush and pressure of modern life, sitting down, and refusing to be swept away in a neoliberal frenzy is an act of courage. It takes tremendous strength. And it calls for good company, good friends to sit with, breathe with, go slowly with.

A problem I have experienced in some communities that identify as conscious is that people seem to want to move quickly. People want to be developed, advanced, enlightened. Indeed, the achiever in us can't orient any other way.

I know I have fallen into this trap myself. Earlier in my life when I was participating in communities organized on the type of developmental philosophies and psychologies described Chapters 3 and 4, I very much wanted to be at a "high" level of consciousness. I wanted to be "transforming"; I was trying to prove that I was, and I was threatened by the possibility that I was not. I now see that this was not only stressful, it also kept me rather embarrassingly focused on myself. Thinking back on those communities, I don't think I was alone in that experience.

In the postmodern space, we can let all of this striving, worrying, and comparing settle down. We can let our selves relax. We can rest into our hearts. We can see people for who they are, beyond any measurements or categorizations. We can slow down and just be. And we can let others be.

The better I understand the potential of postmodernism, the more fully I appreciate that it's not a competition. Or if it is, it's a race in which all our legs are tied together. Anyone, at any moment, could fall in such a way that impedes the rest. And anyone, at any moment, could hold a spark, an insight of utmost importance. We need to slow down. We need time for rest and stillness. And we need to listen to each other.

Listening Deeply

In her book *Emergent Strategy: Shaping Change, Shaping Worlds*,[9] thought leader adrienne maree brown writes, "To a certain degree, our entire future may depend on learning to listen, listen without assumptions or defenses." She goes on to say, "I am listening now with all my senses, as if the whole universe might exist just to teach me more about love. I listen to strangers, I listen to random invitations, I listen to criticisms, I listen to my body, I listen to my creativity and to the artists who inspire me, I listen to elders, I listen to my dreams and the books I am reading."

We tend to hear others, and even interpret our own experiences through the filter of our false self. We track another person's story while holding our own story and self-images front and center, looking for how they do or do not match up. This listening takes place mostly in our head, where the things we hear bump around in a cluttered space of existing ideas.

When we practice listening via the minimal self, with openness, we are able to hear through presence. We can bring our heart online and listen at the level of emotions. We can listen with all our senses, as brown describes, noticing what is registering in our body. We can hear what the other person is telling us not only through words but also through movement, gesture, and posture. Our listening expands in this tuning of presence. We can notice more layers of complexity and more simplicity in the here-and-now directness of being together.

Our achiever self tends to have plenty of ideas, goals, and talking points. Many of these are useful, but we also need space around them. We need quiet. And we need deep listening, so that we can fully affect and learn from one another. This means not only theorizing, but feeling and sensing our way into interdependencies, interconnection, and possibilities for collective wisdom.

Loving Fiercely

Good things don't happen in the absence of love. There's not a lot more to say about it.

Of course, much is said about love. It's what everybody fundamentally wants, and what not enough people get enough of. Love is at the heart of things, and it is the heart of things.

It's important to be bold in what we care about and what we stand for, to let our love be fierce, and in a sense all-consuming. When you know something deep and true in your heart, you may need to say it once, or a million times, until people hear you. Standing strong, speaking bravely, doing what's right when it isn't easy— these are all things fueled by love's power.

There's also a great power that comes from looking for friends rather than villains. The achiever self is interested in its own agenda and way of authoring things. We can fall into a trap of seeking only alignment and agreement, of defining ourselves against opposition, of drawing energy from conflict, rather than love and prioritization of what matters most. In so doing we miss a wider view, different ways of seeing, knowing, and solving difficult problems.

People don't open up in the absence of love. We need to be aware of when we're listening to make a point or even to attack the other, versus when we're truly listening to understand. We need to be aware of whether we're appreciating another person's point of view and way of life, and we need sensitivity to whether our own heart is open. People relax when they feel respected and understood. We need to let our hearts widen to touch the vast and diverse chorus of life.

I Don't Want to Move to Mars

The *overview effect* is the experience some astronauts report after seeing earth from the distance of outer space. Astronauts describe it as a shift or expansion of identity, and movement toward a more global consciousness that sounds congruent with experiences of ecological self, interconnectedness, and openness we explored in Part II. Edgar Mitchell, the sixth person to walk on the moon, explained the overview effect as an "explosion of awareness" and an "overwhelming sense of oneness and connectedness . . . accompanied by an ecstasy." Russian cosmonaut Yuri Artyukhin said, "The feeling of unity is not simply an observation. With it comes a strong sense of compassion and concern for the state of our planet and the effect humans are having on it. It isn't important in which sea or lake you observe a slick of pollution or in the forests of which country a fire breaks out, or on which continent a hurricane arises. You are standing guard over the whole of our Earth."[10]

The overview effect sounds like an awe-inspiring expansion of identity and awareness. But astronauts are also prone to something else. Annie Murphy Paul writes, "Psychologists who study the psyches of astronauts—many of whom already spend months at a time on space stations orbiting Earth—use a telling word for the malaise that many experience: such individuals, they say, are 'homesick.'"[11] Indeed, it's reported that astronauts orbiting earth spend most of their free time looking out the window at our home planet.[12]

Due to rigorous screening and selection processes, astronauts are by definition among the hardiest, most well-adjusted people in the world. If *they* battle homesickness during space travel, I don't even want to consider what that means for the rest of us. As a rather anxious and sensitive person, I know I am not cut out to be an astronaut. I can hardly wear a turtleneck, let alone a spacesuit.

So, it makes sense that I'm not lining up to colonize Mars, a place where temperatures dip hundreds of degrees below zero, and earth appears as a distant pinpoint in the night sky. I admire the boldness and vision of those working toward sending a group of humans to the red planet, and I don't think the project is wrong. But I worry that too much focus on outer space takes us in the exact wrong direction. We need to touch back down onto earth, not lift off.

From our achiever selves, we can't help but climb and strive. We are, as we heard from Brigid Schulte in Chapter 1, "always behind and always late," in a constant state of pressure, trying to catch up, get ahead, and catapult ourselves into the progress of the future. Humility, however, plants us firmly on earth. We surrender to the reality that we are certainly *of* the earth.

To think we can extract ourselves from the ecological systems from which we have emerged is an ultimate form of hubris. In humility, we can reexamine what it means to live well, and die well. We can reexamine what structures and ways of organizing might support a humble wellness, as well as how we might transform the damage that has been done to the interdependent systems of earth into which our human lives are inextricably woven.

Room for Alternatives

One of the great ironies of neoliberalism is that proponents have claimed there is "no alternative." It's a real conundrum to endorse an ideology as an ultimate form of freedom, while simultaneously declaring there is no other option and no way out. Of course, from the neoliberal point of view, this is true. As Mark Fisher explained in *Capitalist Realism*, and as we have seen in this book, neoliberalism has ways of harnessing even forms of opposition and subversion, as demonstrated by Banksy's *Love Is in the Bin*. Likewise, the neoliberal self only knows how to work harder in an effort to become something else, and thus becomes a stronger and stronger version of the very thing it is trying to transform. It's like the saying, often attributed to Einstein, that a problem cannot be solved at the same level of consciousness that created it.

In Chapter 1 we considered that self creates system and system creates self in an ongoing feedback loop. Fisher writes, "What needs to be kept in mind is *both* that capitalism is a hyper-abstract impersonal structure *and* that it would be nothing without our cooperation." How do we actually change this cooperation?

Author of *Emergent Strategy* adrienne marie brown has said that we are in an "imagination battle." "I often feel I am trapped inside someone else's imagination, and I must engage my own imagination in order to break free," she writes. We can free our own imaginations, and we can help free one another's imaginations, by slowing down, listening, and loving.

And we can break free via some of the practices we've considered in this book—humility and embodiment, interdependence and connection, vulnerability and courage, and openness and wonder (Figure 9.1). We don't need more self-help, but rather un-self help.

Another powerful practice is to simply observe when we are being our neoliberal, false selves. We can be curious about what

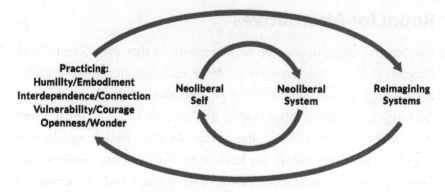

Figure 9.1 Expanded feedback loop

compels us, catches us, and captures our imagination in a spin of self-reference and self-interest. Observing the neoliberal self is a powerful practice, because whatever we can observe, we are not completely subject to. We are at least beginning to hold that self as object, so we can see how it operates. We can lean back into the space that is not completely identified with that neoliberal self. That is a different, fresher, more expanded self. And as we lean into that expanded self, and lean toward others who want to explore, who want to build something together, who knows what we might imagine?

Heroes of Belonging

In Chapter 2 we considered the question of what it might mean to be a hero in today's landscape. Some people say we are in a "post-heroic" age, where the concept of heroism itself can be relinquished. Management scholars write about post-heroic leadership. Filmmaker Scott Drummond writes, "It's time we looked beyond traditional heroic narratives for a more inclusive form of storytelling, a collective narrative that can bring us together to tackle the biggest challenges of our time."[13]

But even the fiercest critics of neoliberalism have not given up on heroics altogether. In *Out of the Wreckage: A New Politics for an Age of Crisis*,[14] George Monbiot calls neoliberalism a "story" that replaced Keynesianism as that economic model fell apart in the 1970s. Monbiot believes we need to tell a new collective story, a story of belonging. His message sounds distinctly "buildist" in the style of Sean Illing and Alana Newhouse. "By rebuilding community, we become proud of our society, proud of our institutions, proud of our nations, proud of ourselves," Monbiot writes. "By coming together we discover who we are. We ignite our capacity for empathy and altruism. Togetherness and belonging allow us to become the heroes of the story." We can be heroes, Monbiot tells us. We can save ourselves and each other by finding our togetherness, by challenging one another's imaginations. We can be heroes of belonging.

I invited you into this book with a poem from Rainer Maria Rilke—a youthful ancestor, a person of paradox. I want to end with a poem from him, as well.

Rilke didn't exactly fit the "hero" stereotype. He was not cut out for military training and left after a year. His marriage didn't work out. He had health problems throughout his life and was often bed-ridden. But Rilke knew something of heroism, deep in his being. In his poem "The Winged Energy of Delight,"[15] he suggests that the zeal of childhood experience can transform, becoming more powerful, more complex, and allowing for an astonishing potential to connect and create. He writes, "Just as the winged energy of delight / carried you over many chasms early on, / now raise the daringly imagined arch / holding up the astounding bridges." He finishes the poem by inviting us into challenge and into paradox, writing, "Take your well-disciplined strengths / and stretch them between two / opposing poles. Because inside human beings / is where God learns." (See the Notes section for the original German.)

What might it mean to lean into this learning? What daring arches and astounding bridges might we build? And how might we build them, not single-mindedly or frantically, but with urgent slowness; with humility in connection to the earth and one another; with vulnerability, courage, and wonder? I believe we have a lot to learn, and a lot to do.

What is yours to learn? What is yours to offer? To whom, and to what, will you give your hand?

Notes

Introduction

Original lines from Rilke's poem in *Das Stunden-Buch*, 159:

> Von deinen Sinnen hinausgesandt, / geh bis an deiner Sehnsucht
> Rand; / gib mir Gewand. / Hinter den Dingen wachse als Brand,
> / daß ihre Schatten ausgespannt / immer mich ganz bedecken.
> / Laß dir alles geschehn: Schönheit und Schrecken. / Man muß
> nur gehn: Kein Gefühl ist das fernste.
> Nah ist das Land, / das sie das Leben nennen. / Du wirst es
> erkennen / an seinem Ernste. / Gib mir die Hand.

Chapter 2: Lost Heroes

Strauss and Howe's model of generations is not without its
problems. Their theory is non-falsifiable, making it impossible to evaluate scientifically. Some have gone so far as to call it
"pseudoscience" (https://qz.com/970646/the-world-has-already-bought-into-steve-bannons-apocalyptic-ideology) and "crackpot"
(https://www.politico.com/magazine/story/2017/04/20/stephen-bannon-fourth-turning-generation-theory-215053/).

Controversial political strategist Steve Bannon has endorsed the
idea of a "fourth turning." References to Strauss and Howe's "prophecy" show up in popular culture, including a 2019 play called "Heroes
of the Fourth Turning," and in the 2022 Netflix drama "The Watcher."

Regardless what you make of their theory, consider the following list of potential events for a "crisis" era (roughly 2005–2025) presented by Strauss and Howe in their 1997 book *The Fourth Turning*, published years before 9/11 and decades before the COVID-19 pandemic and the war in Ukraine:

> A global terrorist group blows up an aircraft . . . the terrorists threaten to retaliate against an American city.
>
> The Centers for Disease Control and Prevention announce the spread of a new communicable virus. The disease reaches densely populated areas, killing some. Congress enacts mandatory quarantine measures . . . mayors resist.
>
> Growing anarchy throughout the former Soviet republics prompts Russia to conduct training exercises around its borders.

Chapter 4: Wandering at an Apex

Different developmental psychologists delineate this model in varying ways. Kegan's stages move from socialized, to self-authoring, to self-transforming. Cook-Greuter, Torbert, and others use finer gradations. For example, Torbert breaks up the socialized mind into diplomat and expert; the self-authoring mind into achiever and redefining (self-questioning), and self-transforming mind into transforming and alchemical. Cook-Greuter clearly points to the transition from modern to postmodern as occurring between the achiever and self-questioning stages of development. I think of self-questioning as a stage where we can begin to hold self-authorship as object, and move into greater interdependence.

In this book, I explore only opportunist, expert, and achiever levels, and then proceed into late self-authorship and early self-transforming meaning-making with the first stages of postmodern development. Cook-Greuter and Torbert describe the transforming space in finer detail, which I have left beyond the scope of this book.

Chapter 8: Lost and Liberated

Importantly, a 2022 study that included two randomized controlled trials with larger sample sizes did not replicate the neural findings from the 2011 Hölzel et al. study, and found no differences in brain structure between participants in a Mindfulness-Based Stress Reduction intervention and another active intervention or a waitlist control (See Kral et al., "Absence of Structural Brain Changes from Mindfulness-Based Stress Reduction: Two Combined Randomized Controlled Trials." *Science Advances* (May 20, 2022). https://doi.org/10.1126/sciadv.abk3316). Research on mindfulness and the brain continues to unfold.

Chapter 9: Friends Between Worlds

Original lines from Rilke's "Da dich das geflügelte Entzücken," Uncollected Poems, 1923–1926, in *The Selected Poetry of Rainer Maria Rilke* by Stephen Mitchell:

> Da dich das geflügelte Entzücken / über manchen frühen Abgrund trug, / baue jetzt der unerhörten Brücken / kühn berechenbaren Bug.
> Deine ausgeübten Kräfte spanne, / bis sie reichen, zwischen zwein / Widersprüchen ... Denn im Manne / will der Gott beraten sein.

References

Introduction

1. Rilke, Rainer Maria. *Rilke's Book of Hours: Love Poems to God*. Riverhead Books, 1996.

Chapter 1: A World on Edge

1. NPR Staff. "Transcript: Greta Thunberg's Speech at the U.N. Climate Action Summit." NPR, September 23, 2019. https://www.npr.org/2019 /09/23/763452863/transcript-greta-thunbergs-speech-at-the-u-n-climate-action-summit.
2. Ballew, Matthew, Jennifer Marlon, Seth Rosenthal, et al. "Do Younger Generations Care More About Global Warming?" Yale Program on Climate Change Communication, June 11, 2019. https://climatecommuni cation.yale.edu/publications/do-younger-generations-care-more-about-global-warming/.
3. UNEP-UN Environment Programme. "Spreading Like Wildfire: The Rising Threat of Extraordinary Landscape Fires," February 23, 2022. https://www.unep.org/resources/report/spreading-wildfire-rising-threat-extraordinary-landscape-fires.
4. Lindsey, Rebecca. "La Niña, Climate Change, and Bad Luck: The Climate Context of Colorado's Marshall Fire." NOAA Climate.gov, January 19, 2022. https://www.climate.gov/news-features/event-tracker/la-ni% C3%B1a-climate-change-and-bad-luck-climate-context-colorado%E2%80 %99s-marshall.

5. Henderson, Rebecca. *Reimagining Capitalism in a World on Fire*. PublicAffairs, 2020, 1–2.

6. Aronoff, Kate. *Overheated: How Capitalism Broke the Planet—And How We Fight Back*. Bold Type Books, 2021, 3.

7. Pinker, Steven. *Enlightenment Now: The Case for Reason, Science, Humanism, and Progress*. Viking, 2018.

8. Hyslop, Gill. "General Mills' Bottom Line Boosted by 75% Hike in Flour, Baking Mix Sales as Americans Release Inner Baker During Lockdown," July 3, 2020. https://www.bakeryandsnacks.com/Article/2020/07/03/General-Mills-bottom-line-boosted-by-75-hike-in-flour-baking-mix-sales-as-Americans-release-inner-baker-during-lockdown#.

9. Lorenz, Taylor. "Stop Trying to Be Productive." *New York Times*, July 13, 2020. https://www.nytimes.com/2020/04/01/style/productivity-coronavirus.html.

10. Daly, Michael, and Eric Robinson. "Anxiety Reported by US Adults in 2019 and During the 2020 COVID-19 Pandemic: Population-Based Evidence from Two Nationally Representative Samples." *Journal of Affective Disorders* 286 (February 26, 2021): 296–300. https://doi.org/10.1016/j.jad.2021.02.054.

11. Schulte, Brigid. *Overwhelmed: Work, Love, and Play When No One Has the Time*. Macmillan, 2014, 4.

12. Kreider, Tim. "The 'Busy' Trap." *New York Times*, June 30, 2012. https://archive.nytimes.com/opinionator.blogs.nytimes.com/2012/06/30/the-busy-trap/.

13. Bellezza, Silvia. "Research: Why Americans Are So Impressed by Busyness." *Harvard Business Review*, December 15, 2016. https://hbr.org/2016/12/research-why-americans-are-so-impressed-by-busyness.

14. Stillman, Jessica. "Science Confirms It: Talking About How Busy You Are Is a Humble Brag." *Inc. Magazine*, December 19, 2016. https://www.inc.com/jessica-stillman/science-confirms-it-talking-about-how-busy-you-are-is-a-humble-brag.html.

15. Ford, Tiffany N., Jennifer M. Silva, Morgan Welch, and Isabel V. Sawhill. "No Time to Spare: Exploring the Middle Class Time Squeeze." Brookings,

February 16, 2021, 2. https://www.brookings.edu/wp-content/uploads/2021/02/FMCi_Mixed_Methods_No_Time_To_Spare_2.16.2021.pdf

16. Burkeman, Oliver. "This 'Busy-Bragging' Epidemic Must Be Stopped. If Only We Could Find the Time." *The Guardian*, February 14, 2018. https://www.theguardian.com/news/oliver-burkeman-s-blog/2014/mar/24/busy-bragging-epidemic.

17. World Health Organization. "Long Working Hours Increasing Deaths from Heart Disease and Stroke: WHO, ILO." Who.Int, May 17, 2021. www.who.int/news/item/17-05-2021-long-working-hours-increasing-deaths-from-heart-disease-and-stroke-who-ilo.

18. Gallup, Inc. "State of the Global Workplace Report-Gallup." Gallup.com, February 20, 2023. https://www.gallup.com/workplace/349484/state-of-the-global-workplace.aspx#ite-393248.

19. American Psychological Association. "Stress in America 2020: A National Mental Health Crisis." Apa.org, October 2020. https://www.apa.org/news/press/releases/stress/2020/sia-mental-health-crisis.pdf.

20. Heckman, William. "42 Worrying Workplace Stress Statistics—The American Institute of Stress." The American Institute of Stress, April 4, 2023. https://www.stress.org/42-worrying-workplace-stress-statistics.

21. Goh, Joel, Jeffrey Pfeffer, and Stefanos A. Zenios. "The Relationship Between Workplace Stressors and Mortality and Health Costs in the United States." *Management Science* 62, no. 2 (February 1, 2016): 608–28. https://doi.org/10.1287/mnsc.2014.2115.

22. Keynes, John Maynard. "Economic Possibilities for our Grandchildren (1930)," *Essays in Persuasion*. Harcourt Brace, 1932, 358–373.

23. Giattino, Charlie, and Esteban Ortiz-Ospina. "Are We Working More Than Ever?" Our World in Data, December 16, 2020. Accessed April 27, 2023. https://ourworldindata.org/working-more-than-ever.

24. Cerullo, Megan. "Most Americans Check in at Work Even While on Vacation, LinkedIn Survey Shows." CBS News, July 10, 2019. https://www.cbsnews.com/news/most-americans-check-work-email-while-on-vacation-linkedin-survey/.

25. NBC Boston. "Do You Experience 'Vacation Guilt?' You're Not Alone," July 29, 2022. https://www.nbcboston.com/news/local/do-you-experience-vacation-guilt-youre-not-alone/2791866/.

26. U.S. Travel Association. "Study: A Record 768 Million U.S. Vacation Days Went Unused in '18, Opportunity Cost in the Billions," August 16, 2019. https://www.ustravel.org/press/study-record-768-million-us-vacation-days-went-unused-18-opportunity-cost-billions; U.S. Travel Association. "Paid Time Off Trends in the U.S.," 2019. https://www.ustravel .org/sites/default/files/media_root/document/Paid%20Time%20Off% 20Trends%20Fact%20Sheet.pdf.

27. Creamer, John, et al. "Poverty in the United States: 2021." Census.gov, September 13, 2022. https://www.census.gov/library/publications/2022/ demo/p60-277.html.

28. Coleman-Jensen, Alisha, et al. "Household Food Security in the United States in 2021." ers.usda.gov, September 2022. https://www.ers.usda .gov/webdocs/publications/104656/err-309.pdf?v=2906.6.

29. Seitz, Amanda. "Number of Uninsured Americans Drops to Record Low." *AP NEWS*, August 2, 2022. https://apnews.com/article/biden-health-us-department-of-and-human-services-government-politics-24684188 cb67c576ed00d01b2f53c09c.

30. Semuels, Alana, and Belinda Luscombe. "The Economy Is Great. The Middle Class Is Mad." *Time*, April 28, 2022. https://time.com/6171292/ middle-class-falling-behind-economy/.

31. Wapshott, Nicholas. *Keynes Hayek: The Clash That Defined Modern Economics*. W. W. Norton & Company, 2011.

32. Hayek, Friedrich A. von. *The Road to Serfdom*. University of Chicago Press, 1944.

33. "Think Tank with Ben Wattenberg S1 E165: The Commanding Heights—with Milton Friedman (1998)." American Enterprise Institute, July 16, 1998. https://www.youtube.com/watch?v=AioZxWwG3JU.

34. Reagan, Ronald. "Inaugural Address, January 20, 1981." The Ronald Reagan Presidential Foundation & Institute. https://www.reaganfoundation .org/ronald-reagan/reagan-quotes-speeches/inaugural-address-2/.

35. Wapshott, *Keynes Hayek*, p. 270.

36. Springer, Simon, Kean Birch, and Julie MacLeavy, eds. *The Handbook of Neoliberalism*. Informa, 2016, 144.

37. Gerstle, Gary. *The Rise and Fall of the Neoliberal Order: America and the World in the Free Market Era*. Oxford University Press, 2022.

38. Ostry, Jonathan D., Prakash Loungani, and Davide Furceri. "Neoliberalism: Oversold?" IMF.org, June 2016. https://www.imf.org/external/pubs/ft/fandd/2016/06/ostry.htm.

39. Monbiot, George. "Neoliberalism—The Ideology at the Root of All Our Problems." *The Guardian*, September 8, 2021. https://www.theguardian.com/books/2016/apr/15/neoliberalism-ideology-problem-george-monbiot.

40. Mitchell, Travis, Ruth Igielnik, and Rakesh Kochhar. "1. Trends in Income and Wealth Inequality." Pew Research Center's Social & Demographic Trends Project, January 9, 2020. https://www.pewresearch.org/social-trends/2020/01/09/trends-in-income-and-wealth-inequality/.

41. Piketty, Thomas. *Capital in the Twenty-First Century*. Harvard University Press, 2017.

42. Reeves, Richard V., Christopher Pulliam, and Ashley Schobert. "Are Wages Rising, Falling, or Stagnating?" Brookings, September 10, 2019. https://www.brookings.edu/blog/up-front/2019/09/10/are-wages-rising-falling-or-stagnating/.

43. Jacobs, Michael, and Mariana Mazzucato. *Rethinking Capitalism: Economics and Policy for Sustainable and Inclusive Growth*. Wiley-Blackwell, 2016, 1.

44. Thatcher, Margaret. "Speech to Conservative Women's Conference." London, May 21, 1980. https://www.margaretthatcher.org/document/104368.

45. Fisher, Mark. *Capitalist Realism: Is There No Alternative?* John Hunt Publishing, 2009, 2, 12.

46. Holton, Robert J. *The Transition from Feudalism to Capitalism*, 1985. https://doi.org/10.1007/978-1-349-17745-5.

47. Kaplan, Louise J. *Oneness and Separateness: From Infant to Individual*. Simon & Schuster, 1978.

48. Silva, Orlando. "Michael Jordan and Kobe Bryant's Responses to 'There's No "I" In Team.'" Fadeawayworld.net, April 27, 2020. https://

fadeawayworld.net/nba-media/michael-jordan-and-kobe-bryants-responses-to-theres-no-i-in-team.

49. Thatcher, Margaret, and Ronald Butt. "Interview for Sunday Times." margaretthatcher.org, May 1, 1981. https://www.margaretthatcher.org/document/104475.

50. Thatcher, Margaret, and Douglas Keay. "Interview for Woman's Own." margaretthatcher.org, September 23, 1987. https://www.margaretthatcher.org/document/106689.

51. Friedman, Milton, and Rose D. Friedman. *Free to Choose: A Personal Statement*, Harvest, 1980.

52. Monbiot, "Neoliberalism."

53. Pauly, Alexandra. "Kim Kardashian Knows Why You're Poor." Highsnobiety, March 30, 2022. https://www.highsnobiety.com/p/kim-kardashian-work-advice-reactions/.

Chapter 2: Lost Heroes

1. Howe, Neil, and William Strauss. *Millennials Rising: The Next Great Generation*, Vintage, 2000, 5–6.

2. Twenge, Jean M. *Generation Me: Why Today's Young Americans Are More Confident, Assertive, Entitled—and More Miserable Than Ever Before*. Simon and Schuster, 2006, 9.

3. Stein, Joel. "Millennials: The Me Me Me Generation." *Time*, May 20, 2013. https://time.com/247/millennials-the-me-me-me-generation/.

4. Taylor, Kate. "'Psychologically Scarred' Millennials Are Killing Countless Industries from Napkins to Applebee's." *Business Insider*, October 31, 2017. https://www.businessinsider.com/millennials-are-killing-list-2017-8#golf-7.

5. Estcourt, Chip Le Grand David. "State Confronts New Millennial Bug as Coronavirus Cases Rise Among Young." *The Age*, June 28, 2020. https://www.theage.com.au/national/victoria/state-confronts-new-millennial-bug-as-coronavirus-cases-rise-among-young-20200628-p5571c.html.

6. Lynch, David J. "Inflation Has Fed Critics Pointing to Spike in Money Supply." *Washington Post*, February 6, 2022. https://www.washingtonpost.com/business/2022/02/06/federal-reserve-inflation-money-supply/.

7. Turak, Natasha. "The Size of the Millennial Generation Is to Blame for Sky-High Inflation, Strategist Says." CNBC, July 15, 2022. https://www.cnbc.com/2022/07/15/millennials-are-to-blame-for-sky-high-inflation-strategist-says.html.

8. Ruggeri, Amanda. "What Everyone Gets Wrong About 'Millennial Snowflakes,'"BBC.com,October2,2017.https://www.bbc.com/worklife/article/20171003-millennials-are-the-generation-thats-fun-to-hate.

9. Bauerlein, Mark. *The Dumbest Generation: How the Digital Age Stupefies Young Americans and Jeopardizes Our Future (Or, Don't Trust Anyone Under 30)*. TarcherPerigee, 2009; Bauerlein, Mark. *The Dumbest Generation Grows Up: From Stupefied Youth to Dangerous Adults*. Regnery Gateway, 2022.

10. Tickell, Josh. *The Revolution Generation: How Millennials Can Save America and the World (Before It's Too Late)*. Atria/Enliven Books, 2018, 175.

11. Alter, Charlotte. *The Ones We've Been Waiting For: How a New Generation of Leaders Will Transform America*. Penguin, 2021.

12. Stein, "Millennials."

13. Harris, Malcolm. *Kids These Days: Human Capital and the Making of Millennials*. Little, Brown, 2017, 4–5.

14. Petersen, Anne Helen. *Can't Even: How Millennials Became the Burnout Generation*. Houghton Mifflin, 2020, ix.

15. BBC News. "'Selfie' Named by Oxford Dictionaries as Word of 2013." BBC News, November 19, 2013. https://www.bbc.com/news/uk-24992393.

16. Pew Research. "Millennials in Adulthood." Pew Research Center's Social & Demographic Trends Project, March 7, 2014. https://www.pewresearch.org/social-trends/2014/03/07/millennials-in-adulthood/.

17. Blow, Charles M. "Opinion | The Self(ie) Generation." *New York Times*, March 8, 2014. https://www.nytimes.com/2014/03/08/opinion/blow-the-self-ie-generation.html.

18. Caligor, Eve, Kenneth N. Levy, and Frank E. Yeomans. "Narcissistic Personality Disorder: Diagnostic and Clinical Challenges." *American Journal of Psychiatry* 172, no. 5 (April 30, 2015): 415–22. https://doi.org/10.1176/appi.ajp.2014.14060723.

19. Twenge, Jean M., et al. "Egos Inflating Over Time: A Cross-Temporal Meta-Analysis of the Narcissistic Personality Inventory." *Journal of Personality* 76, no. 4 (August 1, 2008): 875–902. https://doi.org/10.1111 /j.1467-6494.2008.00507.x.

20. California Task Force to Promote Self-Esteem and Personal and Social Responsibility. *Toward a State of Esteem.* Hippocrene Books, 1990, 4.

21. Storr, Will. "'It Was Quasi-Religious': The Great Self-Esteem Con." *The Guardian*, June 3, 2017. https://www.theguardian.com/lifeandstyle /2017/jun/03/quasi-religious-great-self-esteem-con.

22. eMarketer Editors. "Facebook Is Tops with Everyone but Teens." *Insider Intelligence*, August 28, 2018. https://www.insiderintelligence.com /content/facebook-is-tops-with-everyone-but-teens.

23. Kardashian, Kim. *Kim Kardashian: Selfish.* Universe, 2015.

24. Eler, Alicia. *The Selfie Generation: How Our Self-Images Are Changing Our Notions of Privacy, Sex, Consent, and Culture.* Skyhorse, 2017.

25. Saraswati, L. Ayu. *Pain Generation: Social Media, Feminist Activism, and the Neoliberal Selfie.* NYU Press, 2021, 1.

26. Bansal, Agam, Chandan Garg, Abhijith Pakhare, and Samiksha Gupta. "Selfies: A Boon or Bane?" *Journal of Family Medicine and Primary Care* 7, no. 4 (July 1, 2018): 828. https://doi.org/10.4103/jfmpc.jfmpc_109_18.

27. AAFPRS. "AAFPRS Survey Says the Selfie Endures and Is Stronger Than Ever." American Academy of Facial Plastic and Reconstructive Surgery, n.d. https://www.aafprs.org/Media/Press_Releases/Selfies%20Endure% 20February%2027,%202020.aspx.

28. Hunt, Elle. "Faking It: How Selfie Dysmorphia Is Driving People to Seek Surgery." *The Guardian*, January 23, 2019. https://www.theguardian. com/lifeandstyle/2019/jan/23/faking-it-how-selfie-dysmorphia-is-driving-people-to-seek-surgery.

29. Balakrishnan, Janarthanan, and Mark D. Griffiths. "An Exploratory Study of 'Selfitis' and the Development of the Selfitis Behavior Scale." *International Journal of Mental Health and Addiction* 16, no. 3 (January 1, 2018): 722–36. https://doi.org/10.1007/s11469-017-9844-x.

30. Aldridge, Gemma, and Kerry Harden. "Selfie Addict Took TWO HUN-DRED a Day—and Tried to Kill Himself When He Couldn't Take Perfect

References

Photo." *Mirror*, March 26, 2014. https://www.mirror.co.uk/news/real-life-stories/selfie-addict-took-two-hundred-3273819.

31. Braghieri, Luca, Ro'ee Levy, and Alexey Makarin. "Social Media and Mental Health." *The American Economic Review*, 112, no. 11 (November 1, 2022): 3660–93. https://doi.org/10.1257/aer.20211218.

32. Verduyn, Philippe, et al. "Do Social Network Sites Enhance or Undermine Subjective Well-Being? A Critical Review." *Social Issues and Policy Review* 11, no. 1 (January 1, 2017): 274–302. https://doi.org/10.1111/sipr.12033.

33. Hunt, Melissa, Rachel Marx, Courtney Lipson, and Jordyn Young. "No More FOMO: Limiting Social Media Decreases Loneliness and Depression." *Journal of Social and Clinical Psychology* 37, no. 10 (November 8, 2018): 751–68. https://doi.org/10.1521/jscp.2018.37.10.751.

34. Marche, Stephen. "Is Facebook Making Us Lonely?" *The Atlantic*, May 2012. https://www.theatlantic.com/magazine/archive/2012/05/is-facebook-making-us-lonely/308930/.

35. Ballard, Jamie. "Millennials Are the Loneliest Generation." YouGov, July 30, 2019. https://today.yougov.com/topics/society/articles-reports/2019/07/30/loneliness-friendship-new-friends-poll-survey.

36. cigna.com. "Loneliness and the Workplace," 2020. https://www.cigna.com/static/www-cigna-com/docs/about-us/newsroom/studies-and-reports/combatting-loneliness/cigna-2020-loneliness-factsheet.pdf.

37. Killeen, Colin T. "Loneliness: An Epidemic in Modern Society." *Journal of Advanced Nursing* 28, no. 4 (October 1, 1998): 762–70. https://doi.org/10.1046/j.1365-2648.1998.00703.x.

38. U.S. Department of Health and Human Services. "Surgeon General's Advisory on Our Nation's Loneliness Epidemic | 5.2.2022," May 2, 2023. https://www.youtube.com/watch?v=B8pa506BFk4; "Social Connection—Current Priorities of the U.S. Surgeon General." https://www.hhs.gov/surgeongeneral/priorities/connection/index.html

39. Miller, Greg. "Why Loneliness Is Hazardous to Your Health." *Science* 331, no. 6014 (January 14, 2011): 138–40. https://doi.org/10.1126/science.331.6014.138.

40. Holt-Lunstad, Julianne, Timothy B. Smith, Mark Baker, et al. "Loneliness and Social Isolation as Risk Factors for Mortality." *Perspectives on*

Psychological Science 10, no. 2 (March 11, 2015): 227–37. https://doi
.org/10.1177/1745691614568352.

41. Ewens, Hannah. "What Young People Fear the Most." Vice.Com,
September 21, 2016. https://www.vice.com/en/article/nnyk37/what-
vice-readers-fear-the-most-hannah-ewens-love-loneliness; Bunch, Erin.
"Therapists Say Millennials Worry Most About 5 Specific Issues."
Wellandgood.Com, October 1, 2019. https://www.wellandgood.com
/millennial-anxiety-causes/.

42. Everyday Health. "Special Report: The State of Women's Wellness 2017,"
2017. https://images.agoramedia.com/everydayhealth/gcms/Everyday-
Health-State-of-Womens-Wellness-Survey-PDF.pdf.

43. Cashin, Alison. "Loneliness in America: How the Pandemic Has Deep-
ened an Epidemic of Loneliness—Making Caring Common." *Making
Caring Common*, February 2021. https://mcc.gse.harvard.edu/reports
/loneliness-in-america.

44. Blue Cross Blue Shield. "Millennial Health: Trends in Behavioral Health
Conditions," October 15, 2020. https://www.bcbs.com/the-health-of-
america/reports/millennial-health-trends-behavioral-health-conditions.

45. Blue Cross Blue Shield. "The Economic Consequences of Millennial
Health," November 6, 2019. https://www.bcbs.com/the-health-of-america
/reports/how-millennials-current-and-future-health-could-affect-our-
economy.

46. Trust for America's Health and Well Being Trust. "PAIN IN THE NATION:
Building a National Resilience Strategy: Alcohol and Drug Misuse and
Suicide and the Millennial Generation—a Devastating Impact." Wellbe
ingtrust.Org, June 2019. https://wellbeingtrust.org/wp-content/uploads
/2019/06/TFAH-2019-YoundAdult-Pain-Brief-FnlRv.pdf?utm_source=STAT
+Newsletters&utm_campaign=d90ea217be-MR_COPY_01&utm
_medium=email&utm_term=0_8cab1d7961-d90ea217be-150444909.

47. Killeen, "Loneliness."

48. Alberti, Fay Bound. "This 'Modern Epidemic': Loneliness as an Emotion
Cluster and a Neglected Subject in the History of Emotions." *Emotion Review* 10, no. 3 (July 27, 2018): 242–54. https://doi.org/10.1177
/1754073918768876.

49. Sagan, Olivia. "The Loneliness Epidemic." *Therapy Today* (December 2022/January 2023) November 29, 2022. https://eresearch.qmu.ac.uk/handle/20.500.12289/12669.

50. Becker, Julia, Lea Hartwich, and S. Alexander Haslam. "Neoliberalism Can Reduce Well-Being by Promoting a Sense of Social Disconnection, Competition, and Loneliness." *British Journal of Social Psychology*, July 1, 2021. https://doi.org/10.1111/bjso.12438.

51. Corbin, Ian, and Joe Waters. "What the Surgeon General Missed About America's Loneliness Epidemic | Opinion." *Newsweek*, May 16, 2023. https://www.newsweek.com/what-surgeon-general-missed-about-americas-loneliness-epidemic-opinion-1800045.

52. American Psychological Association. "Stress in America™ 2020: A National Mental Health Crisis." apa.org, 2020. https://www.apa.org/news/press/releases/stress/2020/report-october.

53. Petersen, Anne Hellen. "How Millennials Became The Burnout Generation." *BuzzFeed News*, January 5, 2019. https://www.buzzfeednews.com/article/annehelenpetersen/millennials-burnout-generation-debt-work.

54. Pendell, Ryan. "Millennials Are Burning Out." Gallup.com, July 19, 2018. https://www.gallup.com/workplace/237377/millennials-burning.aspx.

55. Manpower Group. "Millennial Careers: 2020 Vision: Facts, Figures and Practical Advice from Workforce Experts." Manpowergroup.com, 2016. https://www.manpowergroup.com.br/wps/wcm/connect/manpowergroup/68cb4332-a919-4bca-9b49-feff845329e8/MillennialsVision2020.pdf?MOD=AJPERES&CONVERT_TO=url&CACHEID=ROOTWORKSPACE.Z18_2802IK01OORA70QUFIPQ192H31-68cb4332-a919-4bca-9b49-feff845329e8-m8cvvmG.

56. Carmichael, Sarah Green. "Millennials Are Actually Workaholics, According to Research." *Harvard Business Review*, August 22, 2016. https://hbr.org/2016/08/millennials-are-actually-workaholics-according-to-research.

57. Griffith, Erin. "Why Are Young People Pretending to Love Work?" *New York Times*, January 26, 2019. https://www.nytimes.com/2019/01/26/business/against-hustle-culture-rise-and-grind-tgim.html.

58. Teo, Thomas. "*Homo Neoliberalus*: From Personality to Forms of Subjectivity." *Theory & Psychology*, September 10, 2018. https://doi.org/10.1177/0959354318794899.

59. Adams, Glenn, Sara Estrada-Villalta, Daniel Sullivan, and Hazel Rose Markus. "The Psychology of Neoliberalism and the Neoliberalism of Psychology." *Journal of Social Issues* 75, no. 1 (March 1, 2019): 189–216. https://doi.org/10.1111/josi.12305.

60. Hill, Napoleon. *Think and Grow Rich*. The Original 1937 Unedited Edition. Napoleon Hill Foundation, 2012.

61. Schuller, Robert H. *If It's Going to Be, It's Up to Me: The Eight Proven Principles of Possibility Thinking*. HarperOne, 1998.

62. Byrne, Rhonda. *The Secret*. Simon and Schuster, 2006.

63. Hollis, Rachel. *Girl, Wash Your Face: Stop Believing the Lies About Who You Are So You Can Become Who You Were Meant to Be*. Nelson Books, 2018.

64. Teo, *"Homo Neoliberalus."*

65. Wisner, Wendy. "Arrival Fallacy: Will Reaching a Goal Make You Happy?" Verywell Mind, September 14, 2022. https://www.verywellmind.com/what-is-arrival-fallacy-6561079#citation-1.

66. Love, Shayla. "You Don't Have to Work On Yourself Forever." Vice .com, December 7, 2020. https://www.vice.com/en/article/qjpv5v/you-dont-have-to-work-on-yourself-forever-v27n4.

67. Malone, Noreen. "The Age of Anti-Ambition." *New York Times*, February 20, 2022. https://www.nytimes.com/2022/02/15/magazine/anti-ambition-age.html.

68. Petersen, *Can't Even*.

69. Lowrey, Annie. "Millennials Are the New Lost Generation." *The Atlantic*, May 15, 2020. https://www.theatlantic.com/ideas/archive/2020/04/millennials-are-new-lost-generation/609832/.

70. Cook, Alex. "Millennials' Net Worth Has Doubled Since Start of Pandemic." Magnifymoney.com, July 25, 2022. https://www.magnifymoney.com/news/net-worth-of-millennials/.

71. Gale, William G., Hilary Gelfond, Jason J. Fichtner, and Benjamin Harris. "The Wealth of Generations, with Special Attention to the Millennials," May 7, 2020. https://doi.org/10.3386/w27123.

72. Daniel, Will. "Millennials' Wealth More Than Doubled to over $9 Trillion Since the Pandemic Began, but Baby Boomers Are Still Worth Almost 8

References

Times as Much." *Fortune*, March 22, 2022. https://fortune.com/2022/03
/22/millennial-wealth-doubles-during-pandemic-9-trillion-boomers/.

73. Bauluz, Luis, and Timothy W. Meyer. "The Wealth of Generations."
Social Science Research Network, April 26, 2021. https://doi.org/10.2139/
ssrn.3834260.

74. Hoffower, Hillary, and Andy Kiersz. "Home Values Have More than Doubled in the US since 1970—Here's How Much They've Increased in Every
State." *Business Insider*, December 18, 2018. https://www.businessinsider
.com/home-value-home-price-change-in-50-years-every-state-2018-12.

75. "Median Sales Price of Houses Sold for the United States," April 25,
2023. https://fred.stlouisfed.org/series/MSPUS.

76. Bialik, Kristen, Richard Fry, and Travis Mitchell. "Millennial Life: How
Young Adulthood Today Compares with Prior Generations." Pew
Research Center's Social & Demographic Trends Project, February
14, 2019. https://www.pewresearch.org/social-trends/2019/02/14
/millennial-life-how-young-adulthood-today-compares-with-prior-
generations-2/.

77. College Board. "Trends in College Pricing 2016." Research.Collegeboard
.org, 2016. https://research.collegeboard.org/media/pdf/trends-college-
pricing-2016-full-report.pdf.

78. Chien, YiLi, and Paul Morris. "Accounting for Age: The Financial Health
of Millennials." St. Louis Fed, May 16, 2018. https://www.stlouisfed.org
/publications/regional-economist/second-quarter-2018/accounting-
age-financial-health-millennials.

79. Harris, *Kids These Days*.

80. Twenge, Jean M. *Generations: The Real Differences Between Gen Z,
Millennials, Gen X, Boomers, and Silents—and What They Mean for
America's Future*. Simon and Schuster, 2023, 262, 272–76.

81. Twenge, Jean M. "Millennials Are Doing Just Fine." *The Atlantic*, April 17,
2023. https://www.theatlantic.com/magazine/archive/2023/05/millennial-
generation-financial-issues-income-homeowners/673485/.

82. Hobbes, Michael. "Millennials Are Screwed." *Huffington Post*, December 14, 2017. https://highline.huffingtonpost.com/articles/en/poor-
millennials/.

83. Elliott, Alicia. "'Directionless and Lost': What It Means to Be a Millennial." Macleans.ca, January 8, 2020. https://www.macleans.ca/opinion/directionless-and-lost-what-it-means-to-be-a-millennial/.

84. Comer, Cornelia A. P. "A Letter to the Rising Generation." *The Atlantic*, February 1911. https://www.theatlantic.com/magazine/archive/1911/02/a-letter-to-the-rising-generation/536931/.

85. Strauss, William, and Neil Howe. *Generations: The History of America's Future, 1584 to 2069*. William Morrow, 1991, 254, 357–63.

86. Elliott, "'Directionless and Lost.'"

Chapter 3: Spirals of Change

1. Desan, Suzanne M. "Living the French Revolution and the Age of Napoleon." The Great Courses, n.d. https://www.thegreatcourses.com/courses/living-the-french-revolution-and-the-age-of-napoleon.

2. Hayman, Sheila, and BBC Worldwide. "Heroes of the Enlightenment, Episode 1," 2011. https://vimeo.com/93175734.

3. Dupré, Louis K. *The Enlightenment and the Intellectual Foundations of Modern Culture*. Yale University Press, 2004.

4. Kant, Immanuel. "An Answer to the Question: What Is Enlightenment?" *Berlinischen Monatsschrift*, December 1784. https://users.manchester.edu/facstaff/ssnaragon/online/texts/318/kant,%20enlightenment.pdf.

5. Hazard, Paul. *The Crisis of the European Mind: 1680–1715*. New York Review of Books, 2013.

6. Kegan, Robert. *In Over Our Heads: The Mental Demands of Modern Life*. Harvard Press, 1994.

7. "Top 20 Motivational Quotes About Life & Success from Tony Robbins." tonyrobbins.com, April 27, 2022. https://www.tonyrobbins.com/tony-robbins-quotes/inspirational-quotes/.

8. Peterson, Jordan B. *12 Rules for Life: An Antidote to Chaos*. Random House Canada, 2018.

9. Beauchamp, Zack. "Jordan Peterson, Explained." *Vox*, May 21, 2018. https://www.vox.com/world/2018/3/26/17144166/jordan-peterson-12-rules-for-life.

10. Brown, Kelly Williams. *Adulting: How to Become a Grown-up in 468 Easy(Ish) Steps*. Grand Central Publishing, 2013.

11. Manson, Mark. *The Subtle Art of Not Giving a F*ck: A Counterintuitive Approach to Living a Good Life*. HarperOne, 2016.

12. Sincero, Jen. *You Are a Badass: How to Stop Doubting Your Greatness and Start Living an Awesome Life*. Running Press Adult, 2013.

13. TODAY.com. "Cesar Millan: Train Pet Owners, Not Dogs," October 4, 2010. https://www.today.com/popculture/cesar-millan-train-pet-owners-not-dogs-wbna39507041.

14. Supernanny. "The Froebrich Family | Season 7 | Supernanny USA," March 4, 2011. https://www.youtube.com/watch?v=fWYnWA_edTU.

15. Supernanny. "The Hallenbeck Family | Season 6 | Supernanny USA," January 15, 2010. https://www.youtube.com/watch?v=aJoJTx8IMbA.

16. "Self Authoring—What Is Self Authoring?," n.d. https://www.selfauthoring.com/.

17. Eriksson, Per, Ekaterina Perfilieva, Thomas Björk-Eriksson, et al. "Neurogenesis in the Adult Human Hippocampus." *Nature Medicine* 4, no. 11 (November 1, 1998): 1313–17. https://doi.org/10.1038/3305.

18. Loevinger, Jane. "Confessions of an Iconoclast: At Home on the Fringe." *Journal of Personality Assessment* 78, no. 2 (April 1, 2002): 196–208. https://doi.org/10.1207/s15327752jpa7802_01.

19. Larsen, Randy W. "Jane Loevinger (1918-2008)." *American Psychologist* 63, no. 7 (October 1, 2008): 618. https://doi.org/10.1037/0003-066x.63.7.618.

20. Loevinger, Jane. "Completing a Life Sentence." In *Personality Development*, Eva Skoe, Anna von der Lippe, eds. Routledge, 1998, 351.

21. Kegan, Robert. *The Evolving Self: Problem and Process in Human Development*. Harvard University Press, 1982.

22. Cook-Greuter, Susanne R. "Postautonomous Ego Development: A Study of Its Nature and Measurement. (Habits of Mind, Transpersonal Psychology, Worldview)." *Dissertation Abstracts International*, January 1, 1999. http://psycnet.apa.org/record/1999-95024-117.

23. Rooke, David. "Seven Transformations of Leadership." *Harvard Business Review*, April 2005. https://hbr.org/2005/04/seven-transformations-of-leadership.

24. Wilber, Ken. *A Brief History of Everything*. Shambhala Publications, 1996.

25. FloodSanDiego. "The Marshmallow Experiment—Instant Gratification," April 29, 2010. https://www.youtube.com/watch?v=Yo4WF3cSd9Q.

26. Berger, Jennifer Garvey. *Changing on the Job: Developing Leaders for a Complex World*. Stanford Business Books, 2013.

27. RSA. "The Further Reaches of Adult Development—Robert Kegan," July 10, 2013. https://www.youtube.com/watch?v=BoasM4cCHBc.

28. Cook-Greuter, Susanne. "Ego Development: A Full-Spectrum Theory Of Vertical Growth And Meaning Making." ResearchGate, November 18, 2021. https://www.researchgate.net/publication/356357233_Ego_Development_A_Full-Spectrum_Theory_Of_Vertical_Growth_And_Meaning_Making.

29. *The Office*. S4, E1 "Fun Run," September 27, 2007. https://www.youtube.com/watch?v=aBtYlhNXhh8.

30. *The Office*. S2, E5, "Halloween," October 18, 2005. https://vimeo.com/501093440

31. *The Office*. S4, E2, "Dunder Mifflen Infinity," October 4, 2007. https://www.youtube.com/watch?v=DOW_kPzY_JY

32. Milgram, Stanley. "Behavioral Study of Obedience." *The Journal of Abnormal and Social Psychology* 67, no. 4 (October 1, 1963): 371–78. https://doi.org/10.1037/h0040525.; *Obedience;* The Pennsylvania State University, 1969. https://www.youtube.com/watch?v=rdrKCilEhC0.

33. Cook-Greuter, "Ego Development."

34. Petersen, Anne Helen. *Can't Even: How Millennials Became the Burnout Generation*. Houghton Mifflin, 2020, xxvi.

35. Wallace, Jennifer Breheny. *Never Enough: When Achievement Culture Becomes Toxic—and What We Can Do About It*. Penguin, 2023.

36. Ellison, Sandra. "Understanding Vertical Development. www.academia.edu, June 1, 2020. https://www.academia.edu/43225793/Understanding_Vertical_Development.

37. Howe, Neil. "Where Did Steve Bannon Get His Worldview? From My Book." *Washington Post*, February 24, 2017. https://www.washingtonpost.com/entertainment/books/where-did-steve-bannon-get-his-worldview-from-my-book/2017/02/24/16937f38-f84a-11e6-9845-576c69081518_story.html.

Chapter 4: Wandering at an Apex

1. LaRosa, John. "$10.4 Billion Self-Improvement Market Pivots to Virtual Delivery During the Pandemic." MarketResearch.com, August 2, 2021. https://blog.marketresearch.com/10.4-billion-self-improvement-market-pivots-to-virtual-delivery-during-the-pandemic.

2. Cook-Greuter, Susanne. "Ego Development: A Full-Spectrum Theory Of Vertical Growth And Meaning Making." ResearchGate, November 18, 2021. https://www.researchgate.net/publication/356357233_Ego_Development_A_Full-Spectrum_Theory_Of_Vertical_Growth_And_Meaning_Making.

3. Berger, Jennifer Garvey. *Changing on the Job: Developing Leaders for a Complex World*. Stanford Business Books, 2013.

4. *My Octopus Teacher*, 2020. https://www.netflix.com/title/81045007.

5. Jeffries, Stuart. *Everything, All the Time, Everywhere: How We Became Postmodern*. Verso Books, 2021.

6. *Everything Everywhere All at Once*, 2022. https://www.imdb.com/title/tt6710474/

7. Pinker, Steven. *Enlightenment Now: The Case for Reason, Science, Humanism, and Progress*. Penguin, 2018.

8. Kakutani, Michiko. *The Death of Truth: Notes on Falsehood in the Age of Trump*. Crown, 2019.

9. Wilber, Ken. *Trump and a Post-Truth World*. Shambhala Publications, 2017.

10. Newhouse, Alana. "The Real Left Wing vs. Right Wing Debate." *Tablet Magazine*, November 21, 2022. https://www.tabletmag.com/sections/news/articles/brokenism-alana-newhouse.

11. Johnston, Chris. "Banksy Auction Stunt Leaves Art World in Shreds." *The Guardian*, October 7, 2018. https://www.theguardian.com/artanddesign/2018/oct/06/banksy-sothebys-auction-prank-leaves-art-world-in-shreds-girl-with-balloon.

12. Edwards, Jonathan. "Banksy Tried to Destroy His Art After It Sold for $1.4 Million. The Shredded Version Just Went for $25.4 Million." *Washington Post*, October 15, 2021. https://www.washingtonpost.com/nation/2021/10/15/shredded-banksy-painting/.

13. Fisher, Mark. *Capitalist Realism: Is There No Alternative?* John Hunt Publishing, 2009.

14. Dempsey, Brendan Graham. "Metamodern Spirituality | Advancing the Stage Theory Debate (w/ Daniel Görtz & Nora Bateson)," June 20, 2022. https://www.youtube.com/watch?v=8cMnPZ2MJiU.

15. Re-Vision. "Dr Bayo Akomolafe—Question 4: The Spirituality of Cracks and the Gift of Failure at World Endings," February 7, 2022. https://www.youtube.com/watch?v=NYIQa7hWN6Q.

16. Newhouse, "The Real Left Wing vs. Right Wing Debate."

17. Newhouse, Alana. "Everything Is Broken." *Tablet Magazine*, January 14, 2021. https://www.tabletmag.com/sections/news/articles/everything-is-broken.

Chapter 5: Selfies and Self-Realization

1. Ovid. "Metamorphoses (Kline) 3, the Ovid Collection, Univ. of Virginia E-Text Center," n.d. https://ovid.lib.virginia.edu/trans/Metamorph3.htm#476975714.

2. Canty, Jeanine M. *Returning the Self to Nature: Undoing Our Collective Narcissism and Healing Our Planet.* Shambhala Publications, 2022, 69.

3. Almaas, A. H. *The Point of Existence: Transformations of Narcissism in Self-Realization.* Shambhala Publications, 2000, 5, 26, 10, 15, 7, 8, 208.

4. Shulman, Gordon L., Julie A. Fiez, Maurizio Corbetta, et al. "Common Blood Flow Changes Across Visual Tasks: II. Decreases in Cerebral Cortex." *Journal of Cognitive Neuroscience* 9, no. 5 (October 1, 1997): 648–63. https://doi.org/10.1162/jocn.1997.9.5.648.

5. Mazoyer, Bernard, Laure Zago, Emmanuel Mellet, et al. "Cortical Networks for Working Memory and Executive Functions Sustain the Conscious Resting State in Man." *Brain Research Bulletin* 54, no. 3 (February 1, 2001): 287–98. https://doi.org/10.1016/s0361-9230(00)00437-8.

6. Raichle, Marcus E., Ann MacLeod, Abraham Z. Snyder, et al. "A Default Mode of Brain Function." *Proceedings of the National Academy of Sciences of the United States of America* 98, no. 2 (January 16, 2001): 676–82. https://doi.org/10.1073/pnas.98.2.676.

7. Andrews-Hannaa, Jessica R. "The Brain's Default Network and Its Adaptive Role in Internal Mentation." *The Neuroscientist* 18, no. 3 (June 1, 2012): 251–70. https://doi.org/10.1177/1073858411403316.

8. Gallagher, Shaun. "Philosophical Conceptions of the Self: Implications for Cognitive Science." *Trends in Cognitive Sciences* 4, no. 1 (January 1, 2000): 14–21. https://doi.org/10.1016/s1364-6613(99)01417-5.

9. Roe, David, and Larry Davidson. "Self and Narrative in Schizophrenia: Time to Author a New Story." *Medical Humanities* 31, no. 2 (December 1, 2005): 89–94. https://doi.org/10.1136/jmh.2005.000214.

10. Broyd, Samantha J., Charmaine Demanuele, Stefan Debener, et al. "Default-Mode Brain Dysfunction in Mental Disorders: A Systematic Review." *Neuroscience & Biobehavioral Reviews* 33, no. 3 (March 1, 2009): 279–96. https://doi.org/10.1016/j.neubiorev.2008.09.002.

11. Berns, Gregory. *The Self Delusion: The New Neuroscience of How We Invent—and Reinvent—Our Identities*. Basic Books, 2022, 119.

12. Saraswati, L. Ayu. *Pain Generation: Social Media, Feminist Activism, and the Neoliberal Selfie*. NYU Press, 2021, 8, 12.

13. Gallagher, "Philosophical Conceptions of the Self."

14. Watkins, Calvert. *The American Heritage Dictionary of Indo-European Roots*. Houghton Mifflin Harcourt, 2000.

15. Næss, Arne. "Self-Realization: An Ecological Approach to Being in the World." The Trumpeter, 1987. https://trumpeter.athabascau.ca/index.php/trumpet/article/view/623.

16. Gallagher, "Philosophical Conceptions of the Self."

17. Verhaeghe, Paul. *What About Me? The Struggle for Identity in a Market-Based Society*. Scribe Publications, 2014.

18. Cook-Greuter, Susanne. "Ego Development: A Full-Spectrum Theory Of Vertical Growth And Meaning Making." ResearchGate, November 18, 2021, 81 https://www.researchgate.net/publication/356357233_Ego_Development_A_Full-Spectrum_Theory_Of_Vertical_Growth_And_Meaning_Making.

19. Taylor, Sonya Renee. *The Body Is Not an Apology: The Power of Radical Self-Love*, Berrett-Koehler, 2018.

20. Strand, Sophie. *The Flowering Wand: Rewilding the Sacred Masculine*. Inner Traditions, 2022.

Chapter 6: Loneliness and Oneness

1. Mishra, Stuti. "Scientists Sound the Alarm as Plastic Waste Forms Rocks off Coast of Brazil: 'New and Terrifying.'" *The Independent*, March 18, 2023. https://www.independent.co.uk/climate-change/news/brazil-trindade-island-plastic-waste-rocks-b2302739.html; "Plastic Rocks Found on Brazil's Volcanic Trindade Island." NBC News, May 4, 2023. https://www.nbcnews.com/video/plastic-rocks-found-on-brazil-s-volcanic-trindade-island-165398085776.

2. Hale, Robert C., Meredith Seeley, Mark J. La Guardia, et al. "A Global Perspective on Microplastics." *Journal of Geophysical Research: Oceans* 125, no. 1 (January 1, 2020). https://doi.org/10.1029/2018jc014719.

3. WWF International, Dalberg, and The University of Newcastle. "No Plastic in Nature: Assessing Plastic Ingestion from Nature to People." Wwfint.org, June 2019. https://wwfint.awsassets.panda.org/downloads/plastic_ingestion_web_spreads.pdf.

4. Mason, Sherri A., Victoria Welch, and Joseph Neratko. "Synthetic Polymer Contamination in Bottled Water." *Frontiers in Chemistry* 6 (September 11, 2018). https://doi.org/10.3389/fchem.2018.00407.

5. WWF International, Dalberg, and The University of Newcastle. "No Plastic in Nature."

6. Zhang, Junjie, Lei Wang, Leonardo Trasande, and Kurunthachalam Kannan. "Occurrence of Polyethylene Terephthalate and Polycarbonate Microplastics in Infant and Adult Feces." *Environmental Science and Technology Letters* 8, no. 11 (November 9, 2021): 989–94. https://doi.org/10.1021/acs.estlett.1c00559.

7. Ragusa, Antonio, Simona Sabbatini, Alessandro Svelato, et al. "Raman Microspectroscopy Detection and Characterisation of Microplastics in Human Breastmilk." *Polymers* 14, no. 13 (June 30, 2022): 2700. https://doi.org/10.3390/polym14132700.

8. Horvatits, Thomas, Matthias Tamminga, Beibei Liu, et al. "Microplastics Detected in Cirrhotic Liver Tissue." *EBioMedicine* 82 (July 1, 2022): 104147. https://doi.org/10.1016/j.ebiom.2022.104147.

9. Leslie, Heather M., Martin Van Velzen, Sicco H. Brandsma, et al. "Discovery and Quantification of Plastic Particle Pollution in Human Blood." *Environment International* 163 (March 1, 2022): 107199. https://doi.org/10.1016/j.envint.2022.107199.

10. Vethaak, A. Dick, and Juliette Legler. "Microplastics and Human Health." *Science* 371, no. 6530 (February 12, 2021): 672–74. https://doi.org/10.1126/science.abe5041.

11. US EPA. "PFAS Explained | US EPA," April 10, 2023. https://www.epa.gov/pfas/pfas-explained.

12. "PFAS in the US Population | ATSDR," n.d. https://www.atsdr.cdc.gov/pfas/health-effects/us-population.html.

13. US EPA. "Our Current Understanding of the Human Health and Environmental Risks of PFAS | US EPA," March 16, 2023. https://www.epa.gov/pfas/our-current-understanding-human-health-and-environmental-risks-pfas.

14. Lenox, Kelly. "PFAS in the Spotlight Across the Globe (Environmental Factor, October 2018)." National Institute of Environmental Health Sciences, n.d. https://factor.niehs.nih.gov/2018/10/feature/1-feature-pfas.

15. Turusov, V. S., V. N. Rakitsky, and Lorenzo Tomatis. "Dichlorodiphenyltrichloroethane (DDT): Ubiquity, Persistence, and Risks." *Environmental Health Perspectives* 110, no. 2 (February 1, 2002): 125–28. https://doi.org/10.1289/ehp.02110125.

16. Cirillo, Piera M., Michele A. La Merrill, Nickilou Y. Krigbaum, and Barbara A. Cohn. "Grandmaternal Perinatal Serum DDT in Relation to Granddaughter Early Menarche and Adult Obesity: Three Generations in the Child Health and Development Studies Cohort." *Cancer Epidemiology, Biomarkers & Prevention* 30, no. 8 (April 14, 2021): 1480–88. https://doi.org/10.1158/1055-9965.epi-20-1456.

17. Roszak, Theodore, Mary E. Gomes, and Allen D. Kanner. "Where Psyche Meets Gaia." In *Ecopsychology: Restoring the Earth, Healing the Mind.* Counterpoint, 1995, 8.

18. Rather, Parvaiz Anwar, and Iffat Hassan. "Human Demodex Mite: The Versatile Mite of Dermatological Importance." *Indian Journal of Dermatology* 59, no. 1 (January 1, 2014): 60. https://doi.org/10.4103/0019-5154.123498.

19. Skwarecki, Beth. "Friendly Fungus Protects Our Mouths from Invaders." Science.org, March 14, 2014. https://www.science.org/content/article/friendly-fungus-protects-our-mouths-invaders.

20. Leviatan, Sigal, Saar Shoer, Daphna Rothschild, Maria Gorodetski, and Eran Segal. "An Expanded Reference Map of the Human Gut Microbiome Reveals Hundreds of Previously Unknown Species." *Nature Communications* 13, no. 1 (July 5, 2022). https://doi.org/10.1038/s41467-022-31502-1.

21. Broad Institute. "Comparison of Human and Chimpanzee Genomes Reveals Striking Similarities and Differences," August 31, 2005. https://www.broadinstitute.org/news/comparison-human-and-chimpanzee-genomes-reveals-striking-similarities-and-differences.

22. Ursell, Luke K., Jessica L. Metcalf, Laura Wegener Parfrey, and Rob Knight. "Defining the Human Microbiome." *Nutrition Reviews* 70 (August 1, 2012): S38–S44. https://doi.org/10.1111/j.1753-4887.2012.00493.x.

23. Abbott, Alison. "Scientists Bust Myth That Our Bodies Have More Bacteria Than Human Cells." *Nature*, January 8, 2016. https://doi.org/10.1038/nature.2016.19136.

24. National Institutes of Health (NIH). "NIH Human Microbiome Project Defines Normal Bacterial Makeup of the Body," June 13, 2012. https://www.nih.gov/news-events/news-releases/nih-human-microbiome-project-defines-normal-bacterial-makeup-body.

25. Yong, Ed. *I Contain Multitudes: The Microbes Within Us and a Grander View of Life.* Ecco, 2016, 251, 264.

26. Dunn, Rob. *Never Home Alone: From Microbes to Millipedes, Camel Crickets, and Honeybees, the Natural History of Where We Live.* Basic Books, 2019, 3, 77.

27. Haahtela, Tari. "Allergy Is Rare Where Butterflies Flourish in a Biodiverse Environment." *Allergy* 64, no. 12 (December 1, 2009): 1799–1803. https://doi.org/10.1111/j.1398-9995.2009.02246.x.

28. Haahtela, Tari. "A Biodiversity Hypothesis." *Allergy*, April 4, 2019. https://doi.org/10.1111/all.13763.

29. Hanski, Ilkka, Leena Von Hertzen, Nanna Fyhrquist, et al. "Environmental Biodiversity, Human Microbiota, and Allergy Are Interrelated." *Proceedings of the National Academy of Sciences of the United States of*

America 109, no. 21 (May 22, 2012): 8334–39. https://doi.org/10.1073/pnas.1205624109.

30. Murrison, Liza Bronner, Eric B. Brandt, Jocelyn M. Biagini Myers, and Gurjit K. Khurana Hershey. "Environmental Exposures and Mechanisms in Allergy and Asthma Development." *Journal of Clinical Investigation* 129, no. 4 (April 1, 2019): 1504–15. https://doi.org/10.1172/jci124612.

31. Carabotti, Marilia. "The Gut-Brain Axis: Interactions Between Enteric Microbiota, Central and Enteric Nervous Systems." PubMed Central (PMC), June 1, 2015. https://www.ncbi.nlm.nih.gov/pmc/articles/PMC4367209/.

32. Foster, Jane A., and Karen-Anne McVey Neufeld. "Gut–Brain Axis: How the Microbiome Influences Anxiety and Depression." *Trends in Neurosciences* 36, no. 5 (May 1, 2013): 305–12. https://doi.org/10.1016/j.tins.2013.01.005.

33. Chao, Li-Min, Cui Hua Liu, Senawin Sutthawongwadee, et al. "Effects of Probiotics on Depressive or Anxiety Variables in Healthy Participants Under Stress Conditions or with a Depressive or Anxiety Diagnosis: A Meta-Analysis of Randomized Controlled Trials." *Frontiers in Neurology* 11 (May 22, 2020). https://doi.org/10.3389/fneur.2020.00421.

34. Akkasheh, Gudarz, Zahra Kashani-Poor, Maryam Tajabadi-Ebrahimi, et al. "Clinical and Metabolic Response to Probiotic Administration in Patients with Major Depressive Disorder: A Randomized, Double-Blind, Placebo-Controlled Trial." *Nutrition* 32, no. 3 (March 1, 2016): 315–20. https://doi.org/10.1016/j.nut.2015.09.003.

35. Gaddini, Renata, and Anna Chagas Bovet. "Winnicott and Paradox—From Birth to Creation: By Anne Clancier and Jeannine Kalmanovitch. Translated by Alan Sheridan. London and New York: Tavistock Publications. 1987. Pp. 174." *International Review of Psychoanalysis* 5 (1988): 534–35. https://pep-web.org/search/document/IRP.015.0534A.

36. Winnicott, Donald Woods. *The Maturational Processes and the Facilitating Environment: Studies in the Theory of Emotional Development.* Routledge, 1965.

37. *Grief, a Peril in Infancy: A Film,* 1947. https://collections.nlm.nih.gov/catalog/nlm:nlmuid-9505470-vid.

38. Spitz, Rene A. "Psychogenic Disease in Infancy." Archive.org, 1952. https://archive.org/details/PsychogenicD.

39. Bick, Johanna, and Charles A. Nelson. "Early Adverse Experiences and the Developing Brain." *Neuropsychopharmacology* 41, no. 1 (January 1, 2016): 177–96. https://doi.org/10.1038/npp.2015.252.

40. Greene, Melissa Fay. "The Romanian Orphans Are Adults Now." *The Atlantic*, June 30, 2020. https://www.theatlantic.com/magazine/archive/2020/07/can-an-unloved-child-learn-to-love/612253/.

41. Siegel, Daniel J. *The Developing Mind: Toward a Neurobiology of Interpersonal Experience.* Guilford Publications, 1999.

42. Center on the Developing Child at Harvard University. "Serve and Return," January 27, 2020. https://developingchild.harvard.edu/science/key-concepts/serve-and-return/.

43. Leclère, Chloë, Sylvie Viaux, Marie-Françoise Avril, et al. "Why Synchrony Matters During Mother-Child Interactions: A Systematic Review." *PLOS ONE* 9, no. 12 (December 3, 2014): e113571. https://doi.org/10.1371/journal.pone.0113571.

44. Moore, Ginger A., and Susan D. Calkins. "Infants' Vagal Regulation in the Still-Face Paradigm Is Related to Dyadic Coordination of Mother-Infant Interaction." *Developmental Psychology* 40, no. 6 (November 1, 2004): 1068–80. https://doi.org/10.1037/0012-1649.40.6.1068.

45. Feldman, Ruth, Charles W. Greenbaum, Nurit Yirmiya, and Linda C. Mayes. "Relations Between Cyclicity and Regulation in Mother-Infant Interaction at 3 and 9 Months and Cognition at 2 Years." *Journal of Applied Developmental Psychology* 17, no. 3 (July 1, 1996): 347–65. https://doi.org/10.1016/s0193-3973(96)90031-3.

46. Harrist, Amanda W., Gregory S. Pettit, Kenneth A. Dodge, and John E. Bates. "Dyadic Synchrony in Mother-Child Interaction: Relation with Children's Subsequent Kindergarten Adjustment." *Family Relations* 43, no. 4 (October 1, 1994): 417. https://doi.org/10.2307/585373.

47. Bembich, Stefano, Amanda Saksida, Simona Mastromarino, et al. "Empathy at Birth: Mother's Cortex Synchronizes with That of Her Newborn in Pain." *European Journal of Neuroscience* 55, no. 6 (March 9, 2022): 1519–31. https://doi.org/10.1111/ejn.15641.

48. Reindl, Vanessa, Christian Gerloff, Wolfgang Scharke, and Kerstin Konrad. "Brain-to-Brain Synchrony in Parent-Child Dyads and the Relationship with Emotion Regulation Revealed by FNIRS-Based Hyperscanning." *NeuroImage*178 (September 1, 2018): 493–502. https://doi.org/10.1016/j.neuroimage.2018.05.060.

49. Azhari, Atiqah, W. Q. Leck, Giulio Gabrieli, et al. "Parenting Stress Undermines Mother-Child Brain-to-Brain Synchrony: A Hyperscanning Study." *Scientific Reports* 9, no. 1 (August 6, 2019). https://doi.org/10.1038/s41598-019-47810-4.

50. Pan, Yafeng, Xiaojun Cheng, Zhen-Xin Zhang, et al. "Cooperation in Lovers: An FNIRS-Based Hyperscanning Study." *Human Brain Mapping* 38, no. 2 (February 1, 2017): 831–41. https://doi.org/10.1002/hbm.23421.

51. Yuan, Di, Ruqian Zhang, Jieqiong Liu, et al. "Interpersonal Neural Synchronization Could Predict the Outcome of Mate Choice." *Neuropsychologia* 165 (December 1, 2021): 108112. https://doi.org/10.1016/j.neuropsychologia.2021.108112.

52. Sened, Haran, Sigal Zilcha-Mano, and Simone G. Shamay-Tsoory. "Inter-Brain Plasticity as a Biological Mechanism of Change in Psychotherapy: A Review and Integrative Model." *Frontiers in Human Neuroscience* 16 (January 1, 2022). https://doi.org/10.3389/fnhum.2022.955238.

53. Hou, Yingying, Dingning Zhang, Xiaorong Gan, and Yi Hu. "Group Polarization Calls for Group-Level Brain Communication." *NeuroImage* 264 (November 1, 2022): 119739. https://doi.org/10.1016/j.neuroimage.2022.119739.

54. Van Baar, Jeroen, David Halpern, and Oriel Feldman Hall. "Intolerance of Uncertainty Modulates Brain-to-Brain Synchrony During Politically Polarized Perception." *Proceedings of the National Academy of Sciences of the United States of America* 118, no. 20 (May 18, 2021). https://doi.org/10.1073/pnas.2022491118.

55. Hatfield, Elaine, John T. Cacioppo, and Richard L. Rapson. "Emotional Contagion." *Current Directions in Psychological Science* 2, no. 3 (June 1, 1993): 96–100. https://doi.org/10.1111/1467-8721.ep10770953.

56. Mesquita, Batja. *Between Us: How Cultures Create Emotions*. W. W. Norton & Company, 2022, 82.

57. De Groot, Jasper H. B., Monique a. M. Smeets, Annemarie Kaldewaij, et al. "Chemosignals Communicate Human Emotions." *Psychological Science* 23, no. 11 (September 27, 2012): 1417–24. https://doi.org/10.1177 /0956797612445317; De Groot, Jasper H. B., Monique a. M. Smeets, Matt Rowson, et al. "A Sniff of Happiness." *Psychological Science* 26, no. 6 (April 13, 2015): 684–700. https://doi.org/10.1177/0956797614566318.

58. Haviland-Jones, Jeannette, Judith N. Hudson, Patricia D. Wilson, et al. "The Emotional Air in Your Space: Scrubbed, Wild or Cultivated?" *Emotion, Space and Society* (February 1, 2013). https://doi.org/10.1016/j .emospa.2011.10.002.

59. Coffield, Caroline N., Estelle M. Y. Mayhew, Jeannette Haviland-Jones, and Arlene S. Walker-Andrews. "Adding Odor: Less Distress and Enhanced Attention for 6-Month-Olds." *Infant Behavior & Development* 37, no. 2 (May 1, 2014): 155–61. https://doi.org/10.1016/j.infbeh.2013.12.010.

60. Haviland-Jones, Hudson, Wilson, et al. "The Emotional Air in Your Space."

61. Hou, Yubo, Meiqi Gao, Lianqiong Huang, and Qi Wang. "Air Pollution Reduces Interpersonal Trust: The Roles of Emotion and Emotional Susceptibility." *International Journal of Environmental Research and Public Health* 18, no. 11 (May 25, 2021): 5631. https://doi.org/10.3390/ijerph18115631.

62. Wilker, Elissa H., Marwa Osman, and Marc G. Weisskopf. "Ambient Air Pollution and Clinical Dementia: Systematic Review and Meta-Analysis." *BMJ* (April 5, 2023): e071620. https://doi.org/10.1136/bmj-2022-071620.

63. Sullivan, Walter. "The Einstein Papers. A Man of Many Parts." *New York Times*, March 29, 1972. https://www.nytimes.com/1972/03/29/archives /the-einstein-papers-a-man-of-many-parts-the-einstein-papers-man-of.html.

64. Pope Francis. "Laudato Si'," May 24, 2015. https://www.vatican.va/content /francesco/en/encyclicals/documents/papa-francesco_20150524_enciclica- laudato-si.html.

65. Flanagan, Owen. "Hallucinating Oneness." In *The Oneness Hypothesis: Beyond the Boundary of Self*, Philip Ivanhoe et al., eds. Columbia University Press, 2017.

66. Cajete, Gregory. *Native Science: Natural Laws of Interdependence*. Clear Light Publishers, 2000, x.

67. Wang, Zhen, Yi Wang, Huan Guo, and Qian Zhang. "Unity of Heaven and Humanity: Mediating Role of the Relational-Interdependent Self in the Relationship Between Confucian Values and Holistic Thinking." *Frontiers in Psychology* 13 (September 30, 2022). https://doi.org/10.3389/fpsyg.2022.958088.

68. Hanh, Thich Nhat. *The Heart of the Buddha's Teaching: Transforming Suffering into Peace, Joy, and Liberation.* Harmony, 1999.

69. 14th Dalai Lama. "The Sheltering Tree of Interdependence," February 15, 2017. https://www.dalailama.com/messages/environment/buddhist-monks-reflections.

70. Pearl, Ruth, and Judea Pearl. *I Am Jewish: Personal Reflections Inspired by the Last Words of Daniel Pearl.* Jewish Lights Publishing, 2005.

71. "Unitarian Universalism's Seven Principles," UUA.org. https://www.uua.org/beliefs/what-we-believe/principles.

72. "Human Unity for a Sustainable Peace," Al-Islam.org, September 7, 2021. https://www.al-islam.org/articles/human-unity-sustainable-peace-mansour-leghaei.

73. King, Martin Luther. "Letter from a Birmingham Jail," August 1963. https://www.csuchico.edu/iege/_assets/documents/susi-letter-from-birmingham-jail.pdf.

74. King, Martin Luther. "Remaining Awake Through a Great Revolution," June 1965. https://www2.oberlin.edu/external/EOG/BlackHistoryMonth/MLK/CommAddress.html.

75. George Monbiot. "Neoliberalism Is Creating Loneliness. That's What's Wrenching Society Apart." *The Guardian*, October 12, 2016. https://www.theguardian.com/commentisfree/2016/oct/12/neoliberalism-creating-loneliness-wrenching-society-apart.

76. Sullivan. "The Einstein Papers."

Chapter 7: Burnout and Wholeheartedness

1. Whyte, David. *Crossing the Unknown Sea: Work as a Pilgrimage of Identity.* Riverhead Books, 2002.

2. Carelli, Francesco. "The Book of Death: Weighing Your Heart." *London Journal of Primary Care* (July 1, 2011). https://www.ncbi.nlm.nih.gov/pmc/articles/PMC3960665/.

3. Santoro, Giuseppe E., Mark A. Wood, Lucia Merlo, et al. "The Anatomic Location of the Soul from the Heart, Through the Brain, to the Whole Body, and Beyond." *Neurosurgery* 65, no. 4 (October 1, 2009): 633–43. https://doi.org/10.1227/01.neu.0000349750.22332.6a; Reynolds, Stephen W. A. "The Historical Struggle for Dominance Between the Heart, Liver, and Brain." *The Proceedings of the 16th Annual History of Medicine Days*, March 30th and 31st, 2007, Health Sciences Centre, Calgary, AB. http://hdl.handle.net/1880/47541.

4. René Descartes. *The Passions of the Soul*. Translated by Stephen Voss. Hackett Publishing Company, 1989, 25–27.

5. Alshami, Ali M. "Pain: Is It All in the Brain or the Heart?" *Current Pain and Headache Reports*, November 14, 2019. https://doi.org/10.1007/s11916-019-0827-4.

6. Liester, Mitchell B. "Personality Changes Following Heart Transplantation: The Role of Cellular Memory." *Medical Hypotheses* 135 (February 1, 2020): 109468. https://doi.org/10.1016/j.mehy.2019.109468.

7. Pearsall, Paul, Gary E. Schwartz, and Linda G. Russek. "Changes in Heart Transplant Recipients That Parallel the Personalities of Their Donors." *Integrative Medicine* 2, no. 2–3 (March 1, 2000): 65–72. https://doi.org/10.1016/s1096-2190(00)00013-5.

8. Sylvia, Claire, and William Novak. A Change of Heart: *A Memoir*. Grand Central Publishing, 1998.

9. Pham, Tam N., Zen J. Lau, Annabel A. Chen, and Dominique Makowski. "Heart Rate Variability in Psychology: A Review of HRV Indices and an Analysis Tutorial." *Sensors* 21, no. 12 (June 9, 2021): 3998. https://doi.org/10.3390/s21123998.

10. Shaffer, Fred, Rollin McCraty, and Christopher L. Zerr. "A Healthy Heart Is Not a Metronome: An Integrative Review of the Heart's Anatomy and Heart Rate Variability." *Frontiers in Psychology* 5 (September 30, 2014). https://doi.org/10.3389/fpsyg.2014.01040.

11. Gillespie, Steven M., Artur Brzozowski, and Ian M. Mitchell. "Self-Regulation and Aggressive Antisocial Behaviour: Insights from Amygdala-Prefrontal and Heart-Brain Interactions." *Psychology Crime & Law* 24, no. 3 (December 11, 2017): 243–57. https://doi.org/10.1080/1068316x.2017.1414816.

12. Thayer, Julian F., Fredrik Åhs, Mats Fredrikson, et al. "A Meta-Analysis of Heart Rate Variability and Neuroimaging Studies: Implications for Heart Rate Variability as a Marker of Stress and Health." *Neuroscience & Biobehavioral Reviews* 36, no. 2 (February 1, 2012): 747–56. https://doi.org/10.1016/j.neubiorev.2011.11.009.

13. Lennartsson, Anna-Karin, Ingibjörg S. Jónsdóttir, and Anna Sjörs. "Low Heart Rate Variability in Patients with Clinical Burnout." *International Journal of Psychophysiology* 110 (December 1, 2016): 171–78. https://doi.org/10.1016/j.ijpsycho.2016.08.005.

14. Mealer, Meredith, Marc Moss, Vicki S. Good, et al. "What Is Burnout Syndrome (BOS)?" *American Journal of Respiratory and Critical Care Medicine* 194, no. 1 (July 1, 2016): P1–P2. https://doi.org/10.1164/rccm.1941p1.

15. Zhang, Min, Ling Liu, Yunke Shi, et al. "Longitudinal Associations of Burnout with Heart Rate Variability in Patients Following Acute Coronary Syndrome: A One-Year Follow-up Study." *General Hospital Psychiatry* 53 (July 1, 2018): 59–64. https://doi.org/10.1016/j.genhosppsych.2018.05.008.

16. Cleveland HeartLab, Inc. "How Burnout Harms Your Heart—Cleveland HeartLab, Inc.," February 7, 2020. https://www.clevelandheartlab.com/blog/how-burnout-harms-your-heart/.

17. Nummenmaa, Lauri, Enrico Glerean, Riitta Hari, and Jari K. Hietanen. "Bodily Maps of Emotions." *Proceedings of the National Academy of Sciences of the United States of America* 111, no. 2 (January 14, 2014): 646–51. https://doi.org/10.1073/pnas.1321664111.

18. Brown, Brené. *Daring Greatly: How the Courage to Be Vulnerable Transforms the Way We Live, Love, Parent, and Lead.* Avery, 2012, 33

19. Watkins, Calvert. *The American Heritage Dictionary of Indo-European Roots.* Houghton Mifflin Harcourt, 2000.

20. Feldman, Christina, and Willem Kuyken. "Compassion in the Landscape of Suffering." *Contemporary Buddhism* 12, no. 1 (June 14, 2011): 143–55. https://doi.org/10.1080/14639947.2011.564831.

21. Hanh, Thich Nhat. *Teachings on Love.* Parallax Press, 2002.

22. Trungpa, Chögyam. *Shambhala: The Sacred Path of the Warrior.* Shambhala Publications, 2015.

23. *Magnolia*, 1999. https://www.imdb.com/title/tt0175880/.

24. *Hidden Figures*, 2016. https://www.imdb.com/title/tt4846340/.

25. Warren, Wini. *Black Women Scientists in the United States.* Indiana University Press, 1999, 143.

26. Whyte, David. *The Heart Aroused: Poetry and the Preservation of the Soul in Corporate America.* Currency, 1996.

27. Brown, Byron. *Soul Without Shame: A Guide to Liberating Yourself from the Judge Within.* Shambhala Publications, 1998.

28. Verhaeghe, Paul. *What About Me?: The Struggle for Identity in a Market-Based Society.* Scribe Publications, 2014.

29. Arneson, Krystin. "Why Doesn't the US Have Mandated Paid Maternity Leave?" BBC.com, June 28, 2021. https://www.bbc.com/worklife/article/20210624-why-doesnt-the-us-have-mandated-paid-maternity-leave.

30. MacMillan, Douglas, Jonathan O'Connell, Peter Whoriskey, and Chris Alcantara. "The Biggest American Companies Have Turned Profits, Laid off Workers During the Pandemic." *Washington Post*, December 16, 2020. https://www.washingtonpost.com/graphics/2020/business/50-biggest-companies-coronavirus-layoffs/.

31. Lupkin, Sydney. "A Decade Marked by Outrage Over Drug Prices." NPR, December 31, 2019. https://www.npr.org/sections/health-shots/2019/12/31/792617538/a-decade-marked-by-outrage-over-drug-prices.

32. Sandler, Rachel. "Cambridge Analytica's Data May Be Sold to the Highest Bidder During Bankruptcy." *Business Insider*, May 5, 2018. https://www.businessinsider.com/cambridge-analyticas-data-may-be-sold-to-the-highest-bidder-in-bankruptcy-2018-5.

33. Cook-Greuter, Susanne. "Ego Development: A Full-Spectrum Theory Of Vertical Growth And Meaning Making." ResearchGate, November 18, 2021. https://www.researchgate.net/publication/356357233_Ego_Development_A_Full-Spectrum_Theory_Of_Vertical_Growth_And_Meaning_Making.

34. Chödrön, Pema. *Welcoming the Unwelcome: Wholehearted Living in a Brokenhearted World*. Shambhala Publications, 2020.

35. Heifetz, Ronald, Alexander Grashow, and Martin Linsky. *The Practice of Adaptive Leadership: Tools and Tactics for Changing Your Organization and the World*. Harvard Business Press, 2009.

36. Brown, Lerita Coleman. *What Makes You Come Alive: A Spiritual Walk with Howard Thurman*. Broadleaf Books, 2023.

Chapter 8: Lost and Liberated

1. "Inferno 1—Digital Dante," n.d. https://digitaldante.columbia.edu/dante/divine-comedy/inferno/inferno-1/.

2. Ellwood, Mark. "Poor, Busy Millennials Are Doing the Midlife Crisis Differently." Bloomberg.Com, February 15, 2023. https://www.bloomberg.com/news/articles/2023-02-15/millennials-are-doing-the-midlife-crisis-differently-making-less-doing-more#xj4y7vzkg.

3. Robbins, Alexandra, and Abby Wilner. *Quarterlife Crisis: The Unique Challenges of Life in Your Twenties*. Penguin, 2001.

4. Hassler, Christine. *20 Something, 20 Everything: A Quarter-Life Woman's Guide to Balance and Direction*. New World Library, 2005.

5. Almaas, A. H. *Spacecruiser Inquiry: True Guidance for the Inner Journey*. Shambhala Publications, 2002, 94–95.

6. Suzuki, Shunryū. *Zen Mind, Beginner's Mind*. Weatherhill, 1973.

7. Trungpa, Chögyam. *Shambhala: The Sacred Path of the Warrior*. Shambhala Publications, 1984, 91, 102–03.

8. Johnston, William. *The Cloud of Unknowing: And The Book of Privy Counseling*. Image, 1996.

9. Kwong, Jack M. C. "Open-Mindedness as a Critical Virtue." *Topoi-an International Review of Philosophy* (October 1, 2016). https://doi.org/10.1007/s11245-015-9317-4.

10. Siegel, Harvey. "Open-Mindedness, Critical Thinking, and Indoctrination: Homage to William Hare." *Paideusis* 18, no. 1 (October 16, 2020): 26–34. https://doi.org/10.7202/1072336ar.

11. Hillen, Marij A., Caitlin Gutheil, Tania D. Strout, et al. "Tolerance of Uncertainty: Conceptual Analysis, Integrative Model, and Implications

for Healthcare." *Social Science & Medicine* 180 (May 1, 2017): 62–75. https://doi.org/10.1016/j.socscimed.2017.03.024.

12. Hancock, Jason, and Karen Mattick. "Tolerance of Ambiguity and Psychological Well-being in Medical Training: A Systematic Review." *Medical Education* 54, no. 2 (February 1, 2020): 125–37. https://doi .org/10.1111/medu.14031.

13. Rettie, Hannah C., and Jo Daniels. "Coping and Tolerance of Uncertainty: Predictors and Mediators of Mental Health during the COVID-19 Pandemic." *American Psychologist* 76, no. 3 (April 1, 2021): 427–37. https://doi.org/10.1037/amp0000710.

14. Zenasni, Franck, Maud Besançon, and Todd Lubart. "Creativity and Tolerance of Ambiguity: An Empirical Study." *Journal of Creative Behavior* 42, no. 1 (March 1, 2008): 61–73. https://doi.org/10.1002/j.2162-6057.2008 .tb01080.x.

15. Mahmoud, Naiera Ebrahim, Shaimaa Kamel, and Tamer A. Hamza. "The Relationship Between Tolerance of Ambiguity and Creativity in Architectural Design Studio." *Creativity Studies* 13, no. 1 (March 23, 2020): 179–98. https://doi.org/10.3846/cs.2020.9628.

16. Kim, Kyung-Hee. "The Creativity Crisis: The Decrease in Creative Thinking Scores on the Torrance Tests of Creative Thinking." *Creativity Research Journal* 23, no. 4 (November 9, 2011): 285–95. https://doi.org /10.1080/10400419.2011.627805.

17. Park, Nansook, Christopher Peterson, and Martin E. P. Seligman. "Strengths of Character and Well-Being." *Journal of Social and Clinical Psychology* 23, no. 5 (October 1, 2004): 603–19. https://doi.org/10.1521 /jscp.23.5.603.50748.

18. Richman, Laura Smart, Laura D. Kubzansky, Joanna Maselko, et al. "Positive Emotion and Health: Going Beyond the Negative." *Health Psychology* 24, no. 4 (July 1, 2005): 422–29. https://doi.org/10.1037 /0278-6133.24.4.422.

19. Caska, Catherine M., and Keith D. Renshaw. "Personality Traits as Moderators of the Associations Between Deployment Experiences and PTSD Symptoms in OEF/OIF Service Members." *Anxiety Stress and Coping*

26, no. 1 (January 1, 2013): 36–51. https://doi.org/10.1080/10615806 .2011.638053.

20. Swan, Gary E., and Dorit Carmelli. "Curiosity and Mortality in Aging Adults: A 5-Year Follow-up of the Western Collaborative Group Study." *Psychology and Aging* 11, no. 3 (January 1, 1996): 449–53. https://doi .org/10.1037/0882-7974.11.3.449.

21. Kashdan, Todd. *Curious? Discover the Missing Ingredient to a Fulfilling Life*. Harper Perennial, 2010.

22. Kounios, John, and Mark Beeman. *The Eureka Factor: Aha Moments, Creative Insight, and the Brain*. Random House, 2015.

23. Bowden, Edward M., Mark Jung-Beeman, Jessica I. Fleck, and John Kounios. "New Approaches to Demystifying Insight." *Trends in Cognitive Sciences* 9, no. 7 (July 1, 2005): 322–28. https://doi.org/10.1016/j .tics.2005.05.012.

24. Headway—the brain injury association. "Prosopagnosia: Face Blindness after Brain Injury." Headway.org.uk, 2013. https://www.headway .org.uk/media/2816/prosopagnosia-face-blindness-after-brain-injury-factsheet.pdf.

25. Taylor, Jill Bolte. *My Stroke of Insight: A Brain Scientist's Personal Journey*. Plume Books, 2009.

26. Van Elk, Michiel, and André Aleman. "Brain Mechanisms in Religion and Spirituality: An Integrative Predictive Processing Framework." *Neuroscience & Biobehavioral Reviews* 73 (February 1, 2017): 359–78. https:// doi.org/10.1016/j.neubiorev.2016.12.031.

27. Clarke, Tainya C., Patricia M. Barnes, Lindsey I. Black, et al. "Use of Yoga, Meditation, and Chiropractors Among U.S. Adults Aged 18 and Over." *NCHS Data Brief* 325 (November 2018): 1–8. PMID: 30475686.

28. Black, Lindsey I., Patricia M. Barnes, Tainya C. Clarke, Barbara J. Stussman, and Richard L. Nahin. "Use of Yoga, Meditation, and Chiropractors Among U.S. Children Aged 4–17 Years." *NCHS Data Brief* 324 (November 2018): 1–8. PMID: 30475687.

29. Alda, Marta, Marta Puebla-Guedea, Baltasar Rodero, et al. "Zen Meditation, Length of Telomeres, and the Role of Experiential Avoidance and

Compassion." *Mindfulness* 7, no. 3 (February 22, 2016): 651–59. https://doi.org/10.1007/s12671-016-0500-5.

30. Hölzel, Britta K., James Carmody, Mark Vangel, Christina Congleton, et al. "Mindfulness Practice Leads to Increases in Regional Brain Gray Matter Density." *Psychiatry Research: Neuroimaging* 191, no. 1 (January 30, 2011): 36–43. https://doi.org/10.1016/j.pscychresns.2010.08.006.

31. Davidson, Richard J., and Bruce S. McEwen. "Social Influences on Neuroplasticity: Stress and Interventions to Promote Well-Being." *Nature Neuroscience* 15, no. 5 (May 1, 2012): 689–95. https://doi.org/10.1038/nn.3093.

32. Kolassa, Iris-Tatjana, and Thomas Elbert. "Structural and Functional Neuroplasticity in Relation to Traumatic Stress." *Current Directions in Psychological Science* 16, no. 6 (December 1, 2007): 321–25. https://doi.org/10.1111/j.1467-8721.2007.00529.x.

33. Eriksson, Per, Ekaterina Perfilieva, Thomas Björk-Eriksson, et al. "Neurogenesis in the Adult Human Hippocampus." *Nature Medicine* 4, no. 11 (November 1, 1998): 1313–17. https://doi.org/10.1038/3305.

34. Erickson, Kirk I., Michelle W. Voss, Ruchika Shaurya Prakash, et al. "Exercise Training Increases Size of Hippocampus and Improves Memory." *Proceedings of the National Academy of Sciences of the United States of America* 108, no. 7 (February 15, 2011): 3017–22. https://doi.org/10.1073/pnas.1015950108.

35. Curlik, Daniel M., and Tracey J. Shors. "Training Your Brain: Do Mental and Physical (MAP) Training Enhance Cognition through the Process of Neurogenesis in the Hippocampus?" *Neuropharmacology* (January 1, 2013). https://doi.org/10.1016/j.neuropharm.2012.07.027.

36. Rahrig, Hadley, David R. Vago, Matthew Passarelli, et al. "Meta-Analytic Evidence That Mindfulness Training Alters Resting State Default Mode Network Connectivity." *Scientific Reports* 12, no. 1 (July 18, 2022). https://doi.org/10.1038/s41598-022-15195-6.

37. Brewer, Judson A., Patrick D. Worhunsky, Jeremy Gray, et al. "Meditation Experience Is Associated with Differences in Default Mode Network Activity and Connectivity." *Proceedings of the National Academy*

of Sciences of the United States of America 108, no. 50 (December 13, 2011): 20254–59. https://doi.org/10.1073/pnas.1112029108.

38. Berkovich-Ohana, Aviva, Joseph Glicksohn, Tal Dotan Ben-Soussan, and Abraham Goldstein. "Creativity Is Enhanced by Long-Term Mindfulness Training and Is Negatively Correlated with Trait Default-Mode-Related Low-Gamma Inter-Hemispheric Connectivity." *Mindfulness* 8, no. 3 (June 1, 2017): 717–27. https://doi.org/10.1007/s12671-016-0649-y.

39. Ren, Jun, Zhihui Huang, Jing Luo, et al. "Meditation Promotes Insightful Problem-Solving by Keeping People in a Mindful and Alert Conscious State." *Science China-Life Sciences* 54, no. 10 (October 1, 2011): 961–65. https://doi.org/10.1007/s11427-011-4233-3.

40. Purser, Ronald. *McMindfulness: How Mindfulness Became the New Capitalist Spirituality*. Watkins Media Limited, 2019.

41. Cook-Greuter, Susanne. "Ego Development: A Full-Spectrum Theory Of Vertical Growth And Meaning Making." ResearchGate, November 18, 2021, p. 76. https://www.researchgate.net/publication/356357233_Ego _Development_A_Full-Spectrum_Theory_Of_Vertical_Growth_And _Meaning_Making.

42. Scharmer, Otto. "Theory U—Learning from the Future as It Emerges," TEDx Talks, October 26, 2016. https://www.youtube.com/watch?v= GMJefS7s3lc.

Chapter 9: Friends Between Worlds

1. Speth, James Gustave. *The Bridge at the Edge of the World: Capitalism, the Environment, and Crossing from Crisis to Sustainability*. Yale University Press, 2008, 199–200.

2. "Is America Broken?" The Gray Area. *Vox,* February 2, 2023. https://www .vox.com/the-gray-area.

3. The Nutrition Source. "Almonds," Harvard.edu, March 2, 2022. https://www. hsph.harvard.edu/nutritionsource/food-features/almonds/#:~:text=It%20 is%20a%20calorie%2Ddense,carbohydrate%2C%20and%203%20 grams%20fiber.

4. C-Win. "California Almond Water Usage—California Water Impact Network." California Water Impact Network, July 13, 2022. https://www.c-win.org/cwin-water-blog/2022/7/11/california-almond-water-usage.

5. McGivney, Annette. "'Like Sending Bees to War': The Deadly Truth Behind Your Almond Milk Obsession." *The Guardian*, October 29, 2021. https://www.theguardian.com/environment/2020/jan/07/honeybees-deaths-almonds-hives-aoe.

6. Johnson, Stefanie K. "If There's Only One Woman in Your Candidate Pool, There's Statistically No Chance She'll Be Hired." *Harvard Business Review*, February 7, 2019. https://hbr.org/2016/04/if-theres-only-one-woman-in-your-candidate-pool-theres-statistically-no-chance-shell-be-hired.

7. Brennan, Micheal. "US Employees Are 93.6% More Likely to Have a Male CEO." AllSorter, April 27, 2023. https://allsorter.com/ceo-names-study/.

8. Merton, Thomas. *Conjectures of a Guilty Bystander*. Image, 1968.

9. Brown, Adrienne M. *Emergent Strategy: Shaping Change, Changing Worlds*, AK Press, 2017.

10. Yaden, David B., J. Mark Iwry, Kelley J. Slack, et al. "The Overview Effect: Awe and Self-Transcendent Experience in Space Flight." *Psychology of Consciousness* 3, no. 1 (March 1, 2016): 1–11. https://doi.org/10.1037/cns0000086.

11. Paul, Annie Murphy. *The Extended Mind: The Power of Thinking Outside the Brain*. Mariner Books, 2021, 113.

12. Wellcome Collection. "Homesick for Planet Earth," October 29, 2020. https://wellcomecollection.org/articles/X41xTxIAAB0AgqvT.

13. Drummond, Scott. *3 Reasons Why It's Time to Move Beyond the Hero In Storytelling*. Be Inspired Films, May 22, 2020. https://www.beinspiredfilms.co.uk/ideas/3-reasons-why-its-time-to-move-beyond-the-hero-in-storytelling.

14. Monbiot, George. *Out of the Wreckage: A New Politics for an Age of Crisis*. Verso Books, 2017.

15. Bly, Robert. *The Winged Energy of Delight: Selected Translations*. Harper Perennial, 2005.

Recommended Reading

The following books provide opportunities to stretch your thinking in a time between worlds:

Akomolafe, Bayo. *These Wilds Beyond Our Fences: Letters to My Daughter on Humanity's Search for Home*. North Atlantic Books, 2017.

brown, adrienne m. *Emergent Strategy: Shaping Change, Changing Worlds*, AK Press, 2017.

De Oliveira, Vanessa Machado. *Hospicing Modernity: Facing Humanity's Wrongs and the Implications for Social Activism*. North Atlantic Books, 2021.

Haraway, Donna J. *Staying with the Trouble: Making Kin in the Chthulucene*. Duke University Press, 2016.

Ladha, Alnoor, and Lynn Murphy. *Post Capitalist Philanthropy*. Transition Resource Circle, 2022.

Speth, James Gustave. *The Bridge at the Edge of the World: Capitalism, the Environment, and Crossing from Crisis to Sustainability*. Yale University Press, 2008.

Stein, Zachary. *Education in a Time Between Worlds: Essays on the Future of Schools, Technology, and Society*. Bright Alliance, 2017.

Strand, Sophie. *The Flowering Wand: Rewilding the Sacred Masculine*. Inner Traditions, 2022.

Tsing, Anna Lowenhaupt. *The Mushroom at the End of the World: On the Possibility of Life in Capitalist Ruins*. Princeton University Press, 2021.

Yunkaporta, Tyson. *Sand Talk: How Indigenous Thinking Can Save the World*. HarperOne, 2021.

About the Author

Christina Congleton, EdM, PCC, is a professional coach committed to helping leaders bring out the best in themselves, others, and systems. She coaches through her own practice, Axon Leadership LLC, and also partners with premier consultancies to deliver learning and development programs to high-potential managers and C-suite executives.

Christina's written work on topics including emotional intelligence, the inner critic, and the millennial generation has appeared on *Fast Company* and *Entrepreneur* online, and her coauthored *Harvard Business Review* articles including "Emotional Agility" and "Mindfulness Can Literally Change Your Brain" have been printed in multiple books and magazine issues. She also coauthored chapters in *Beyond Goals: Effective Strategies for Coaching and Mentoring*. Christina has worked in several neuroscience laboratories and was on the team of scientists from Massachusetts General Hospital/Harvard Medical School that published initial research showing mindfulness practice can change the brain.

Christina holds an EdM in human development and psychology from Harvard University and a BA in biopsychology and creative writing from Oberlin College. She is a Certified Integral Coach through New Ventures West and a Professional Certified Coach through the International Coaching Federation.

Index

Artyukhin, Yuri, 193
Authority
  existence, 81
  questioning, 166
  source, 67–68
  structures, flattening, 81–82
Autonomy, slogan, 86
Avelar Santos, Fernanda, 119
Awe (Keltner), 179
Awe of God, The (Bevere), 179
Awestruck (Paquette), 178

Baby boomers, loneliness
    (feeling), 38
Banksy, 195
Basic knowledge, 164–165
Beeman, Mark, 169–170
Beginner's mind, concept, 165
Being-consciousness, 172
Belonging, heroes, 196–198
Ben-Shahar, Tal, 45–46
Berger, Jennifer Garvey,
    63, 66
Between-brain synchrony, 130–131
Between Us (Mesquita), 131
Biography of Loneliness, A
    (Alberti), 40
Biological super-system,
    existence, 143
Blair, Tony, 20
Blow, Charles M. (op-ed), 32, 34–35
Blue Cross Blue Shield, "millennial
    health shock," 39
Bodiless dream (Ovid), 96
Body
  emotional maps, 144f
  emotions, mapping,
    143–144

Body Is Not an Apology, The
    (Taylor), 113
Book of Hours, The (Rilke), 3
Bowman, Danny, 36, 95–96
Brain
  blink, 170
  blood flow, increase, 170
  change, experience (impact), 62
  default mode network, 101f
  development, understanding,
    127–128
  function, default mode,
    100–102
  gray matter concentration,
    increase, 174
  gut, crosstalk (enabling), 125
  mindful brain, 173–176
  resonance, 125–132
  self-centered chatter,
    reduction, 175
  structure, differences, 127–128
  synchrony, 125, 129–130
Brain-to-brain synchrony, 129
Bridge at the End of the World, The
    (Speth), 185
Brinkmann, Svend, 46
Britain ("Winter of Discontent"),
    19
Broca's area (language
    expression), 171
Brokenism
  discussion, 187
  flatness, comparison, 84–85
brown, adrienne maree, 191, 195
Brown, Brené, 147, 149, 153, 163
Brown, Byron, 154
Bryan, Kobe (winning
    philosophy), 24

245

Index

249

Index

255

Index

257